ON OLIGARCHY:
ANCIENT LESSONS FOR GLOBAL POLITICS

Economic power is becoming increasingly concentrated in the hands of the few, even as democratic movements worldwide allow for political power to be dispersed among the many. With their access to influence, the wealthy can shape and constrain the political power of the rest of the world. As the economic dominance of an elite minority coincides with the forces of globalization, is oligarchy becoming the dominant political regime?

This collection explores the renewed relevance of oligarchy to contemporary global politics. By drawing out lessons from classic texts, contributors illustrate how the character of oligarchical regimes informs contemporary political life. Topics include the relationship between the American government and corporations, the tension between republican and oligarchical regimes, and the potential conflicts that have opened up between economic management and political life. *On Oligarchy* deftly illuminates the significance of this regime in the context of pressing global economic and political issues.

DAVID EDWARD TABACHNICK is an associate professor in and Chair of the Department of Political Science, Philosophy, and Economics at Nipissing University.

TOIVO KOIVUKOSKI is an associate professor in the Department of Political Science, Philosophy, and Economics at Nipissing University.

EDITED BY DAVID EDWARD TABACHNICK
AND TOIVO KOIVUKOSKI

On Oligarchy

Ancient Lessons for Global Politics

UNIVERSITY OF TORONTO PRESS
Toronto Buffalo London

© University of Toronto Press 2011
Toronto Buffalo London
www.utppublishing.com
Printed in Canada

ISBN 978-1-4426-4011-5 (cloth)
ISBN 978-1-4426-0986-0 (paper)

Printed on acid-free, 100% post-consumer recycled paper with vegetable-based inks.

Library and Archives Canada Cataloguing in Publication

On oligarchy : ancient lessons for global politics / edited by David Edward
Tabachnick and Toivo Koivukoski.

Includes bibliographical references and index.
ISBN 978-1-4426-4011-5 (bound). – ISBN 978-1-4426-0986-0 (pbk.)

1. Oligarchy.   2. Wealth – Political aspects.   I. Tabachnick, David
II. Koivukoski, Toivo

JC419.O56 2011   321'.5   C2011-905604-6

This book has been published with the help of a grant from the Canadian
Federation for the Humanities and Social Sciences, through the Aid to
Scholarly Publications Program, using funds provided by the Social Sciences
and Humanities Research Council of Canada.

University of Toronto Press acknowledges the financial assistance to its
publishing program of the Canada Council for the Arts and the Ontario Arts
Council.

University of Toronto Press acknowledges the financial support of the
Government of Canada through the Canada Book Fund for its publishing
activities.

Contents

Acknowledgments

With many heartfelt thanks to our valued research assistant, Monica Do Coutto Monni, whose attention to detail and inspiring care for perfection have made this project a true pleasure.

Preface: Understanding Oligarchy

DAVID EDWARD TABACHNICK AND TOIVO KOIVUKOSKI

> SOCRATES: Surely, when wealth and the wealthy are honoured in the city, virtue and the good men are less honourable.
> ADEIMANTUS: Plainly.
> SOCRATES: Surely, what happens to be honoured is practiced, and what is without honour is neglected.
>
> – Plato, *Republic*, 551a

In the twenty-first century, economics and politics seem to have gone in opposite directions. The spread of free markets has seen a concentration of wealth in the hands of the few, while the growing reach of democracy has seen political power dispersed among the many. While people are able to choose those who govern them, they appear willing to tolerate, if not celebrate, the rise of the super rich. But in a world where wealth is the pre-eminent virtue and conspicuous consumption is the ultimate measure of achievement, there is a danger the citizenry will concede their democratic rights and hand over political power to those who seem the most virtuous and successful.

What the ancient political philosophers called oligarchy (from the Greek *oligos* 'few' + *arkhein* 'to rule') has gained a new currency in today's global politics. The rise and fall of the Russian oligarchs, China's commitment to capitalism under authoritarianism, the close relationship between corporate executives and American government, and, on a larger scale, the formation of a global network of cosmopolitan, technocratic managers all illustrate the problems and possibilities that arise when the economic power of the few coincides with political power. In each case, these contemporary oligarchies have created considerable domestic and international tensions: the degradation of democratic institutions, growing hostility between haves and have-nots, widespread perceptions of government corruption and favouritism, as well as the development of a planetary protest movement fighting against the intermingling of corporate and political elites.

Notably, there has been a recent abundance of books on the contemporary relevance of oligarchy.[1] But, despite attention and awareness of this new age of oligarchy, we have very little understanding of the make-up and function of the regime itself. While we might think to turn to political philosophers, classicists, and historians for some answers, there has been surprisingly little attention paid to this topic. And yet, for Aristotle, the tension between oligarchy and democracy occupies a central and extensive place in his *Politics*.[2] Likewise, while Plato's discussion of tyranny is the subject of intensive scrutiny, the subject of oligarchy has been given far less attention. Oligarchy plays a central role in Thucydides' account of the Peloponnesian War, and, later, Cicero presented oligarchy as a sign of the decline of the greatness of Rome. By our readings, these accounts of oligarchy are critical for our better understanding of global politics today.

This book seeks to draw lessons for today's global politics by returning to the thoughtful and articulate descriptions of oligarchy found in these ancient texts. Through a collection of essays from today's leading political scientists, historians, and classicists, this volume considers how influence over global economics has arguably been consolidated into control over governments, and how the values and structures that are embedded in oligarchical regimes inform contemporary political life.

Our contributors ask: What comparisons can be made between the place of oligarchy within early political thought and its workings in the world today? What safeguards do the ancients offer against the replacement of political autonomy by freedom for the few and the ascendancy of the economic imperative in public life? And, more generally, what is the relevance of ancient classifications of regimes to today's global politics?

On this last question, we know that the classical Greek political thinkers recognized an important interrelationship between constitutions and political culture and that these two characteristics of a regime were key to understanding politics. For example, while a democratic regime would have a constitution that viewed political legitimacy as deriving from the people, it would also possess a democratic culture infused into the daily lives of its citizens. Similarly, an oligarchic regime would not only be structured by the rule of the wealthy, but would also be characterized by a culture that valued wealth as the chief virtue.

In turn, the structure and function of a regime not only said quite a bit about the politics of a country but also about its people. In his *Politics*, Aristotle went so far as to classify constitutions or *politeiai* under the broad categories of good and bad, right and wrong, or natural and unnatural. *Generally, he decided that a good constitution will create a political community that benefits the ruled whereas a bad constitution will do the opposite, benefiting only the rulers. People living under a bad constitution would then tend to turn out to be bad people.*

It is through the lens of this organic conception of a regime, encompassing both political culture and constitution, that we can not only come to know oligarchies for what they are, but also gain a better understanding of various regimes in their relations with one another. This comparative regimes approach offers the distinctive insight that different regimes behave differently both because they are uniquely constituted and because their members can be said to 'think' differently, depending on what they hold to be their regime's purpose: whether it be freedom, as in democracies, or moneymaking, as in oligarchies, or absolute security for a solitary ruler, as in tyrannies.

Applying this very old method of analysis to today's politics might at first seem ill-advised or perhaps nothing more than an academic exercise. After all, contemporary regimes, and more generally contemporary politics, are quite different in scope and content than anything that might have occurred in the Greek polis. And yet, despite these differences, there remain lessons to be drawn from the ancients by comparing their articulations, ideas, and warnings about the character of regimes to contemporary manifestations with the hope of informing twenty-first-century global politics.

This method of reading lessons for global politics out of ancient political philosophy and history has already been demonstrated in two earlier volumes on regimes: first in *Confronting Tyranny: Ancient Lessons for Global Politics* (Rowman and Littlefield, 2006) and more recently in *Enduring Empire: Ancient Lessons for Global Politics* (University of Toronto Press, 2009). These volumes have also tapped into a largely ignored intersection of political theory and international relations, where the latter gains a broader perspective of 2,500 years and the former acquires a greater relevance to political life in the present. *On Oligarchy* continues this same approach, this time directed towards understanding rule by the rich.

We begin with five essays that provide some answers to these questions. Newell, Neill, and Sikkenga agree that while modern liberal democracies face the risk of falling into oligarchy, we have for the most part successfully insulated our politics from this possibility. Peter Simpson and Steven Skultety, however, see modern politics as both explicitly and implicitly oligarchical.

To begin, Waller Newell traces out the divisions between the arts of household management and political deliberation in Aristotle's *Politics*. He puts forward the intriguing elaboration that the divide between *oikos* and *polis* may not be as stark as thinkers such as Hannah Arendt have made it out to be. If reason is indeed architectonic for the order of a political community, then in the author's words, 'There is thus a very real sense in which the political community's shared deliberations must, if left untrammeled, transcend themselves in the direction of a rational *oikonomia* and the rule of "one or a few" statesmen of superlative prudence.' For Newell, what saves the political from such a rationalization of affairs is the limited perfection of human nature. A perfect politics could not be properly called political, and a perfect person would have no place in an ordinary polis. So we are left with the messy business of moderating between classes of rich and poor towards a mixed regime, informed by the signal classical virtue – moderation. Newell sees such a practical and virtuous option reflected in some of the characteristics of modern liberal democracies, with their robust middle classes sustained by property rights and the measure of wealth needed for civic participation. The apparent current challenges to this model consist largely of illiberal regimes that have generated wealth through the application of the coercive arts of economic management 'to create enormous centralized and repressive security regimes "owned" by dictatorial and oligopolistic elites,' a situation that speaks both to the tendency toward the rationalization of the political as well as to the fragile possibility of public virtues.

A similar point is offered by Jeremy Neill. He sees that a clear comparison can be made between Aristotle's preference for some kind of mixed regime, which includes both aristocratic and democratic elements, and the intentions of America's founding fathers. As it turns out, though, the United States never embraced the reciprocal relationship between citizen and state that is at the core of the best Aristotelian polis. For Aristotle, the best regime would be characterized by an overarching sense of a common and public good, whereas today's America is oriented toward self-interest embodied in property and material possession. Critically, this difference does not stem from Aristotle's aversion to wealth but rather from the distinctly modern idea that greed is at the core of human nature. In the modern account, appetitiveness is naturalized, along the lines of Machiavelli's casual remark that 'it is perfectly natural that men should want things.' So, even if self-interest does come to the fore as the most essential element of politics in the Aristotelian regime, it does so because the nature of the regime allows and encourages such selfish behaviour, not because greed is a reflex of human nature.

Jeff Sikkenga observes that while it may be customary to believe that democracy is ascendant in modern politics, the political science of Aristotle and the political philosophy of Plato both remind us that oligarchic rule remains a perennial possibility. Understanding this enduring element of political reality and setting aside any triumphalist nonchalance are important measures for those who care about democracy. According to this author, it was just such a care and cognizance that inspired the founders of America's liberal democracy. In this sense, the *Federalist Papers* can be read in part as a reply to the classical concern with the dangerous tension between rich and poor that is likely to arise if oligarchical machinations go unchecked. A key difference between ancients and moderns on this matter is that whereas for the ancients acquisitiveness was to be sublimated into aristocratic virtues, for the American founders it would be maintained *qua* acquisition as a strictly economic motive with links to a natural right to property ownership. Thus potential oligarchs are to be made relatively content as captains of industry, with politics kept safe from injustices that way. If there is a basis for comparison of this allowance for material accumulation with the classical position on oligarchy, it consists in the channeling of acquisitive desire in such a way as to retain both broad participation in public life along with a sense of distinction, thus ensuring equality in some respects and difference in others.

In his contribution, Peter Simpson decides that modern politics is almost wholly oligarchical in its character and that we suffer under the rule of a '*globalization* of oligarchs.' Focusing on a relatively unexplored passage of *Politics* that lists the features of 'popular rule,' the author notes that Aristotle viewed oligarchy as a contrary or opposite regime. In the style of Aristotle, Simpson provides an adapted and parallel list of the features of oligarchical rule. He then compares this list to the United States Constitution in relation to the earlier Articles of Confederation. Whereas the Articles were designed to exclude the possibility for anyone to make a career as a national politician, the Constitution sets up a permanent national government run by a 'Congress of individual oligarchs.' And while this may seem a provocative conclusion, it appears warranted taking into account the Aristotelian definition of oligarchy. Looking at the way candidates get on the ballot and elected today, it is more and more the case that only the wealthy, the privileged, and those with powerful friends can be successful career politicians. As Simpson puts it, 'How does a candidate get to be known and approved by the electorate, especially by an electorate numbering in the millions (as is invariably the case today)? The answer is to be or become an oligarch.' Through a further analysis of Britain and France, we are also warned that this answer is 'now true of virtually every nation on earth.'

In an effort to gather together Aristotle's accounts of oligarchy into a precise definition, Steven Skultety offers that it is not so much a matter of number or of wealth as such that distinguish oligarchical regimes, as much as it is a belief that merit to rule consists in wealth. So by this definition, an oligarch is one who believes that the rich ought to rule, regardless of whether the one who holds that view happens to be rich or poor, or one of the few or of the many themselves. In turn, while there are oligarchical influences in contemporary life (the author uses the example of a university in which money-generating programs have more say in academic governance), they are not explicit in contemporary American politics. And yet there is a pervasive and surprisingly popular agreement that a life of privilege also includes the right to rule. What is pressing about Aristotle's definition of oligarchy for the present is the warning that it contains concerning the character and self-understandings of political leadership. If oligarchy is essentially a matter of belief in the rightness of rule by the rich, it can come into effect even when democratic institutions seem to be in force.

In her chapter, Laurie Bagby weighs Thucydides' account of ideology in the context of the competition between the two dominant political systems of the day: democracy and oligarchy. Rather than the typical description of the *History of the Peloponnesian War* as an archetypal document of realism that highlights the common, selfish nature of human beings and the corresponding behaviour of all states, Bagby attempts to provide a more nuanced or 'multi-layered' approach to Thucydides' account. In fact, from the very start of his book, we do not get a universal definition of the state but instead a stark contrast between the character of a democratic Athens and an oligarchical Sparta. For one, Bagby argues that the Spartans' insularity and cautiousness stem from the nature of their regime. On the same note, she similarly locates the source of Athenian aggressiveness in their democracy. Where Sparta is divided among elites and thus unable to act decisively, Athens is unified and patriotic and thus able to act quickly and with great force. Bagby then asks 'How did the Greek world move from expressions of national differences and what we might call national pride to the hardened ideological positions of democracy versus oligarchy that characterized the latter part of the war?' Now, rather than warring Athens and Sparta, we see a more insidious and even more violent clash between these two ideologies that begins to tear Greece apart from the inside out.

Leah Bradshaw begins her paper with the provocative claim that John Locke 'elevates' oligarchy to the best regime. So, unlike the negative assessments of the rule of the wealthy provide by Plato and Aristotle, Locke's endorsement of property and limited government vaults oligarchy to the most worthwhile form of government. However, Bradshaw decides that the Lockean liberal democratic state does not escape the critiques of the ancient thinkers. Ultimately, the tendencies toward maximizing private profit and enlarging private estates take away from energies put into civic honour and the public good. Bradshaw decides 'the oligarch is really *anti-political*, using the city for the enhancement of private ends.' The heart of the problem, however, is the immoderation that characterizes oligarchical regimes.

Moving from Greece to Rome, Geoffrey Kellow considers Cicero's observation that the growing obsession among the youth with wealth eroded the very Roman virtues that had made it so great and that, more and more, the Roman aristocracy was transformed into an oligarchy so much so that the Roman student was 'unable to distinguish between wealth and virtue.' In large part, this shift stemmed from the generational failures of the Roman education system to instill a sense of honour and patriotism in its young citizens. In Cicero's time, these ill-educated youth were taking up positions of leadership and, in turn, transforming Roman institutions and culture away from traditional civic virtues. The way to rebuild or reinforce the eroding foundation of Rome was to move the education system away from the teaching of rhetoric, sophistry, and wealth-seeking back to its original mandate. Without this correction toward teaching boys to act like men, Cicero warned, Rome would collapse.

Toivo Koivukoski suggests that oligarchy is a reflection of the breakdown between the discrete realms of the public and private. At basis, when the necessities of household life come to dominate political

decision making, concern for individual material acquisition and accumulation obscure any notion of the common good. Notably, the infil-
tration of private goods into the political stems from the traditional
association between honour and courage and how these virtues were
symbolically represented by the erection of battle victory monuments,
trophies, and the spoils of war. But when this wealth is disconnected
from public virtue and taken as valuable in and of itself, the wealthy
rather than the courageous are viewed as the most capable to lead.
Wealth, as freedom from necessity, takes primacy over courage as
freedom from foreign domination. The oligarch then becomes the
most respected figure in the political community.

Craig Cooper begins his piece by asking, 'Does the rule of law exist
only in democracies and never under oligarchies, which by their very
nature entrench systems of inequality?' This is an important question
because, according to Cooper, the best government is not to be judged
on its form but on whether it is founded upon the rule of law: 'Oligarchy and democracy are acceptable forms of government provided the
laws are sovereign.' As he goes on to show, the tyrannical nature of
fifth-century Athenian democracy, 'dominated by demagogues like
Pericles and Cleon,' was essentially apolitical and devoid of the rule
of law. And yet it is also true that oligarchies are based in the notion
that inequality of wealth demands a proportionate inequality in justice. So, while democracies can sometimes be 'messy,' oligarchies are
always unjust. But, as we saw in Athens, democracies tend toward the
domination of the exceptional few and the retreat of the rule of law.
Cooper attempts to highlight ways to resist such oligarchic tendencies:
namely Aristotle's emphasis on local courts, knowledge, and community, and Aeschines' counsel to prosecute those 'whose speech and
styles are contrary to the laws.'

Altogether, the contributors to this volume highlight a tension
between modern democracies and their slide toward oligarchy. Some
argue that while this movement is of concern, our political institutions
and political culture are strong enough to withstand the more dangerous consequences of oligarchy. As long as the unpropertied classes
remain able to participate in and influence our politics, the rule of the
rich is of limited concern. However, others argue that this slide is a
function of our weakened and weakening institutions and culture.
Unless addressed, the rise of oligarchs represents a future of greater
disenfranchisement and a fundamental threat to democracy. Finally,
there is also the conclusion that we have long ago fallen into oligarchy

and simply have not realized it. All of our contributors, however, agree that while our oligarchs may be different in means than the oligarchs of ancient Athens, their ends remain largely unchanged.

NOTES

1 See for example David Rothkopf's *Superclass: The Global Power Elite and the World They Are Making* (Farrar, Straus and Giroux, 2008); Fareed Zakaria's *The Post-American World* (W.W. Norton 2008); Parag Khanna's *The Second World: Empires and Influence in the New Global Order* (Random House, 2008); and Robert Kagan's *The Return of History and the End of Dreams* (Knopf, 2008).

2 Here we touch on the question of the opposed values of republicanism and oligarchy, and the specific tensions between those respective constitutions and cultures. This is territory surveyed by Quentin Skinner, for whom a purely acquisitive life and the kind of licence associated with it may be answered by republican conceptions of freedom – what he calls the 'neo-Roman revival' of civic spiritedness – posed in relief against a certain void of civic spaces in the modern state. See Quentin Skinner, *Liberty before Liberalism* (Cambridge University Press, 1998).

This longing for civic life in the modernity has its bearing on the soul of the person as well as on the health of the body politic. In their account of Gershom Carmichael's dissociation of virtue from wealth, James Moore and Michael Silverthorne offer the following distinctions between republican and oligarchic values, insisting as many of our authors do that 'any man who misapplies his mind in the accumulation of wealth is engaged in a purposeless or literally endless activity alien to the nature of man. We have a duty to ourselves not to be overly concerned with our possessions, for such things may be lost or stolen or destroyed; we have a duty to avoid appropriation in excess of our immediate and foreseeable needs, for the surplus will surely spoil and thereby frustrate the end of property, which is simply to sustain life; we have, at all times, the overriding duty to maintain ourselves in a spirit of reverence for the supreme being, a mental inclination which cannot fail to direct the mind to higher concerns when we have provided by our labour for the needs of ourselves and those dependent on us.' See 'Gershom Carmichael and Natural Jurisprudence' in *Wealth and Virtue: The Shaping of Political Economy in the Scottish Enlightenment*, ed. Istvan Hont and Michael Ignatieff (Cambridge University Press, 1986), 83.

ON OLIGARCHY:
ANCIENT LESSONS FOR GLOBAL POLITICS

1 Oligarchy and *Oikonomia*: Aristotle's Ambivalent Assessment of Private Property

WALLER R. NEWELL

There is a very great pleasure in helping and doing favours to friends and strangers and associates, and this happens when people have property of their own ... The abolition of private property will mean that no man will be seen to be liberal or ever do any act of liberality.

– Aristotle

Honey, I been rich and I been poor. And rich is *better*.

– Ella Fitzgerald

Within the famous six-fold classification of regimes in Book 3 of Aristotle's *Politics*, the regime principle most closely connected with economic gain is oligarchy, the defective rule of the few based on the misidentification of virtue with wealth. However, elsewhere in the *Politics*, most notably Book 1, open-ended economic maximization tends more directly toward tyranny and, more arrestingly still, toward a certain version of rational monarchy of the kind sometimes associated with Alexander the Great but also with Xenophon's idealization of Cyrus the Great. Is this a contradiction? No, I will argue, but it does point to an interesting ambivalence in Aristotle's assessment of private property.

In this essay, accordingly, I am going to explore Aristotle's treatment of the art of household management and the proper limits and purposes of economic productivity in Books 1 and 2 of the *Politics*, including his critique of Plato's *Republic* with respect to its complete absence of property rights. Using this discussion to illuminate the evaluation of oligarchy as a regime principle in Books 3 and 4, I will conclude by suggesting that, although Aristotle is very aware of the dangers posed for a virtuous regime by open-ended economic acquisition, by the same token he believes that citizens must have an economic stake in citizenship if the pitfalls of Plato's best regime are to be avoided.

For these reasons, I hope to show, Aristotle gives a partial endorsement of oligarchy, even though it is a defective regime type, because a regime whose citizens possess private property as an incentive to their shared responsibilities in public life is preferable to the extreme of, on the one hand, a tyranny or absolute monarchy where citizenship vanishes altogether under the architectonic art of household management conducted by an all-powerful ruler, or, on the other hand, Plato's prescription for the abolition of private property which gives citizen stakeholders no material incentive to bolster their attachment to the common good. For this reason, when Aristotle attempts to blend elements of oligarchy with democracy in his discussion of 'polity,' the right to private property is retained as a sober balance to the dangers of demagogic populism and resentment of the wealthy, though that right is also tempered by an encouragement to meritocratic public service.

These issues are highly relevant to the world we now live in, where we are caught between the extremes of unfettered economic laissez-faire with its deleterious effects on liberal democracies and the rise of non-democratic regimes like those of China and Russia that appear to be able to combine economic maximization with an almost complete absence of democratic liberties. Aristotle's search for a middle ground between autocracy and collectivism is in this sense more relevant than ever.

The Conundrum: Polity Is a Blend of Two Defective Regimes

A striking feature of the classification of regimes is that the lowest-ranking of the correct regimes, 'polity,' is a combination of the lowest-ranking of the defective regimes, democracy, with the second-highest of the defective regimes, oligarchy. So an admixture of oligarchy with democracy leads to the correct form of popular sovereignty. Moreover, the name for this regime, 'polity,' is the generic term for all six regimes, *politeiai*. One among the six constitutions is simply called 'constitution.'[1]

Why? Arguably it is because, while polity is the least virtuous of the three correct regimes in contrast with monarchy and aristocracy, it is the most inclusive. Pragmatically speaking, it offers the best model for combining the largest number of citizen participants with relatively virtuous standards. Since, for Aristotle, the 'political community' is more about shared rule than the perfection of 'superlative virtue' in 'one or a few' extraordinary individuals, there is something about polity that is more broadly reflective of the everyday meaning of state-craft than the higher claims of aristocracy and monarchy.[2]

The derivation of the correct regime of polity from the two defective regimes of oligarchy and democracy confirms this interpretation. For, first of all and most of the time, politics is about the clash between these two regime principles. According to Aristotle, while people are capable of demonstrating many traits and virtues at the same time – the same people can be farmers, artisans, merchants, soldiers, labourers, and public servants – there are two types no person can be simulta-neously: rich and poor.[3] Hence, the division between haves and have-nots in politics, embodied in the contest between oligarchs and democrats, is both the most widespread and the most intractable, since its ex-tremes cannot be blended as one could blend, say, the claims of education and honour. Ameliorating the tension between haves and have-nots is therefore the indispensable precondition for establishing an environment of minimal stability and civil order, only on the basis of which could citizens find the safety and leisure to cultivate higher forms of virtuous character through shared deliberation.

The conflict between the claims of oligarchs and democrats lays bare the inherently controversial character of all political life, always in danger of escalating from verbal hostility to open insurrection and civil war. The conflict between their claims, because they are irrecon-cilable as stated, exposes with special clarity the difficulty of reconcil-ing claims to equality and inequality in politics altogether. The democrats, according to Aristotle, are correct when they claim that all men are equal – but not in all respects. The oligarchs are also correct, he observes, when they argue that human beings are unequal. But they are incorrect in claiming that superiority is identical with having more property. The task of statesmanship is to sift out the respects in which citizens are equal and unequal, both vis-à-vis one another and within the parts of their own souls, and this requires nothing less than 'political philosophy,' the first time that the study of politics is expli-citly raised to philosophical rank in the *Politics*.[4]

Moreover, there is an important difference between the claims of the democrats and the oligarchs, pointing to the need for particular reflection on property rights. The democrats are claiming that human beings are equal simply by virtue of existing. Their claim is more formal and universalistic. The oligarchs, by contrast, are making a more substantive and teleological claim. They are arguing that the character traits required for success in acquiring and preserving property bespeak a genuine moral and intellectual superiority, which is why, in practice, oligarchical regimes frequently arrogate for themselves the more honourable term 'aristocracy,' as if their success in being wealthier were tantamount to noble and good behaviour altogether.[5] As we will see, in Aristotle's view, while the oligarchs are mistaken to conflate their particular virtues with the best virtue, they are not entirely mistaken that their success in commerce does partake of some substantive claims to excellence of character.[6] To uncover the reasons why, we must turn to the detailed discussion of economics in Books 1 and 2.

The City and the Household as Regime Principles

In order to come to grips with Aristotle's assessment of the role of property rights within the political community, we must avoid imposing on it an inappropriate set of modern distinctions. Aristotle is not making a rigid distinction between something like our modern, 'bourgeois' or 'nuclear' private family and a political community selflessly dedicated to the common good, with the implication that the household is an entirely negative realm of materialism, self-interest, and apathy in contrast with an entirely communitarian realm of idealistic civic dialogue. The reality is a good deal more complicated.

It is true that the first discussion of the household reduces it to the level of necessity, thereby denying it entry to the realm of ethical choice, because it is restricted to the drives of material survival and physical reproduction.[7] However, this is the family only in its most primitive version, isolated or part of loose and scattered settlements. When the household is incorporated within a developed city, its status is also ennobled, such that, in Aristotle's second discussion of its virtues, the household and its members dwell within the properly ethical realm of deliberative choice.[8] As such, it is the first source of the city's future citizens.

Moreover, although the city, fully evolved, is devoted to the 'good life' as opposed to the 'mere life' of material survival, it does not entirely transcend that realm of material necessity, nor, therefore, the economic realm of the household. The city 'is' for the good life, but 'becomes' for material life.[9] Its telos is deliberative communal citizenship, but that highest aim is always coeval with the economic wherewithal guaranteeing the leisure for its pursuit. Moreover, to the extent that the telos of deliberative citizenship is fulfilled, the good life is actualized not only for cities, but also 'for households.'[10] Again, its proper integration within the political community ennobles household life as well as the civic life whose participants the household provides.

More than this: For Aristotle, the household is not primarily a private sub-political association at all. Allowed to unfold to its fullest degree, it is a regime-level principle of monarchical rule, the most widespread and in some ways compelling alternative to republican self-government altogether. The *Politics* opens with the crucial distinction between the political community properly speaking and the rule of a single statesman, such as a king, manager of a household, or master.[11] Although these latter three differ, they have more in common with one another than do any of them with the political community, for none of them is embodied in a polis at all. A political community is one in which citizens rule one another and are ruled in turn, and share in deliberation about the common good.[12] By contrast, all forms of rule by a single statesman involve an architectonic division of labour in which subordinate members are assigned their proper place, and the 'despotic' authority to make such decisions without consultation. Plato, Aristotle implies, was mistaken to believe that the 'political' authority of a self-governing community could be assimilated to the royal authority of a single king or household manager, as in the *Republic* or *Statesman*.[13]

The main theme of Book 1, accordingly, is the contrast between these two fundamental variants of authority, the political community and some form of '*oikonomia*,' the art of household management. Therefore, when we turn to the discussion of the latter, we must always bear in mind that Aristotle, in discussing the art of household management and the proper limits of acquisition, is always simultaneously discussing both a regime-level pattern of authority *and* a pattern of authority within private households belonging to a polis. The household manager can mean the citizen of a polis in his capacity as head of a family and its economic concerns, or the chief overseer and steward for that family head. But it can also mean the single monarchical ruler of an entire society organized according to the household paradigm. The four main themes in the rest of Book 1 are components of this overarching paradigm: 1) the authority of masters over slaves; 2) the proper art of household management; 3) how much the natural environment will provide for man's material needs; 4) the virtues that subordinate members of the household, when it is properly ordered within a city, might contribute to the family, and thereby to the political community at large.

The discussion of 'mastery' over slaves and servants introduces the fundamental criterion by which Aristotle will assess all forms of economic acquisition and production as either proper or improper – the distinction between making (*poiesis*) and doing (*praxis*). Whereas a shuttle is an instrument for making because it produces an artificial commodity other than itself, a bed is an instrument for doing because it accommodates a natural human purpose. To the extent that pure untrammelled making is the goal of household management, the best slave would be like a machine (the legendary dancing automata of Daedalus) programmed for ceaseless fabrication within the architectonic division of labour required for maximized productivity.[14] But the proper use of slaves and servants is to provide masters and household heads in their roles as citizens with the wherewithal for 'politics or philosophy.'[15] Public life is the end, moneymaking only the means. The proper purpose of economics is to furnish the *chremata*, the equipment, for actualizing the virtues. For example, you cannot be liberal toward the deserving if you do not possess an adequate income beyond what is needed for your own self-preservation.[16] Intending to reward the meritorious without the means to do so is not fully virtuous, since virtue is above all a deed, not merely a leaning or temperament.[17] Hence, while someone born into a position of wealth may have done nothing to earn it, while someone born into straitened circumstances will be compelled to labour for a living regardless of his potential merit, only the wealthier man can practise the virtue of liberality, however good may be the intentions of the poorer man.[18]

As to whether slavery or servitude is ever just, Aristotle argues that nature as a whole is characterized by the pairing of ruling over ruled, such as the soul over the body and the intellect over the appetites. In order to be just by nature, the master's rule over a slave would have to be as beneficial to the slave as the rule of the soul over the body or the intellect over the appetites.[19] By implication, this natural standard, whereby the slave is the chief beneficiary of the arrangement, since he could no more take care of himself than a body without a mind, rarely if ever coincides with the conventional institution of slavery, as evidenced by the fact that those who are masters by convention feel compelled to seek a natural justification for what is almost inevitably their arbitrary and meretricious power over other human beings.[20]

In order to maintain the distinction between the proper use of the art of household management in the service of doing and its improper use in the service of making, Aristotle argues that there are limitations on the degree to which acquisition is natural to human beings and necessary for meeting their natural needs. We need only acquire what is sufficient for life, not luxury. Wealth should primarily be based on agriculture and livestock, not commercial exchange and liquid assets. Commercial exchange, when unavoidable, should be limited to procuring the basic needs of life, not for the sake of luxury or surplus income.[21] Of course, these parameters are imprecise, meant only as general guidelines, since some level of surplus between the means for self-preservation and superfluous luxury will be required to practise virtues such as liberality that are impossible to practise without extra wealth.

If, to argue the contrary, household management *were* synonymous with open-ended acquisition, then all the virtues – Aristotle mentions courage and generalship as examples – would have to be viewed as means to moneymaking and material pleasures.[22] These examples remind us again that the art of household management can be employed at the regime level, and not only by the private family within the city. Courage and generalship are public virtues properly employed by citizens in defence of the political community's internal way of life from external aggression. If, however, the political community is swallowed up by a project for limitless economic acquisition, then these virtues could be perverted into means for pursuing imperialistic exploitation abroad. The improper use of household management, in other words, is coeval with tyranny, whether of a ruler tyrannizing over his own city or of a city tyrannizing over other peoples as a conqueror. The tyrant is in many ways like the personal owner of an enormous household made up of his subjects.[23] As we recall from the discussion of the proper end of the polis, the good life and mere life are co-present in the city. The good life outranks mere life, just as 'being' (the mode in which the good life is) outranks 'becoming' (the mode in which mere life is).[24] The household, as the sphere of mere life, must be limited and circumscribed by the city, by the good life that can only be actualized in the public deliberations of the citizenry. Otherwise, it is possible that the economic aims of the household pattern of authority may slip its boundaries and absorb the city itself, so that the polis becomes a monarchical household or even empire.

The tenability of Aristotle's distinction between the proper and improper employment of *oikonomia* hinges, at bottom, on the ontological relationship between human nature and nature as a whole. For what if, as Machiavelli will argue, nature is in truth unremittingly hostile to human efforts to survive and prosper? In order to maintain the distinction between proper and improper *oikonomia*, according to Aristotle, we need to envision nature as providing for our basic needs without an excessive emphasis on transforming nature through human productive techniques. Only in this way can we stress *praxis* over *poiesis* and circumscribe the latter by the former, which is tantamount to circumscribing the household by the polis. If, on the contrary, nature were inherently too poor, sterile, or hostile, we would be driven to remake nature and force it to yield the material for our survival – to 'master Fortuna,' as Machiavelli will put it, or as Bacon, following upon this fundamental shift, will argue, to convert science into the power for the relief of man's estate.

In an especially arresting passage, Aristotle makes a direct connection between the proper stance toward nature as the source of the wherewithal for economic sufficiency and the proper relationship between technical fabrication and the political community.[25] For, just as there should be no project for the conquest of nature, there should be no project for the conquest of human nature. We do not have to intervene radically in nature with our powers of fabrication because nature provides a sufficiency of wealth on hand through the cycles of agriculture and herdsmanship. Because a sufficiency of wealth is on hand from the start, we can stress the good life over mere life and need not be preoccupied with scarcity and survival.

Similarly, we do not need to recreate or radically recraft human nature to achieve political order. Nature provides a sufficiency of sound human material from the start, a widespread parity among human beings in their receptivity to an education in or habituation to virtue. This allows us to stress the actualization of our potential for moral and intellectual virtue through the political community – to stress the good life for citizens over a project for sheer political coercion. The parallel is clear and compelling. If nature at large is too poor, we will have to stress economic productivity over purposeful use. If human nature is too vicious from the outset, if its material is too poor or intractable, statecraft will have to stress compulsion based

on fear over relying on people to be capable of virtue if properly educated in an environment where the laws support virtue.

Aristotle is not unaware of the need for coercion in political life –
for base natures, or for noble natures who occasionally lapse into base-
ness, education may require the supplement of punishment and the
dread it instils.[26] But if politics is assimilated into a project for the
rational reconstruction of human nature to coerce it to behave in an
orderly way, then the very prospect of a virtuous political community
vanishes into the Gulag and the re-education camp. *Poiesis* would
entirely displace *praxis*. We would be brought to the Hobbesian model
of sovereignty, where both of Aristotle's criteria are reversed: Nature
is inherently hostile to human hopes for survival and must therefore
be remade in order to yield material wealth. Human nature inherently
lacks a sufficiency of excellence for the capacity for a voluntary accep-
tance of virtue, and must therefore be reconstructed by a Sovereign
who employs terror openly as the only alternative to disobedience
leading to anarchy.[27]

To return to Aristotle's own terms, the danger posed by the household paradigm of rule is not merely the danger that the polis might be
usurped by a tyrant or a tyrant city. While every decent person would
surely agree that the political community should not be swallowed up
by the improper use of the art of household management, what about
the possibility that it might be assimilated by the *proper* use of that art?
The deeper difficulty is that there is something inherently rational
about the division of labour itself. Human nature is fulfilled, Aristotle
has told us, by citizens employing *logos* to debate what is just, noble,
and advantageous.[28] But here he tells us that '*logos* is an *architechton*' –
reason itself is a master craftsman, the architectonic art.[29] In other words,
the search for reasoned clarity about the meaning of justice, nobility and
the advantageous may lead ineluctably away from shared deliberation
toward the hierarchical distinctions uncovered by unhindered reason,
since, as we recall, the cosmos is constituted by hierarchy. There is thus a
very real sense in which the political community's shared deliberations
must, if left untrammelled, transcend themselves in the direction of a
rational *oikonomia* and the rule of 'one or a few' statesmen of superlative
prudence.[30] This is why Aristotle will eventually tell us that 'the whole
of justice' must occasionally be sacrificed to preserve the 'political justice'
of the city (as in the ostracism of the best men),[31] and why the best regime
per se may not be a self-governing aristocracy so much as a rational
monarch who exercises prudence and rules over 'cities and peoples'

according to the paradigm of the art of household management.[32] The fullest employment of reason in politics may threaten the existence of politics.

Oligarchical Virtue

Having reached this region of rather thin air, let us take off our oxygen masks and return to our more foursquare consideration of the place of property rights in a political community. Having devoted the bulk of Book 1 to exploring and keeping at bay the claim of *oikonomia* to swallow up the city, in Book 2 Aristotle treats the issue of property as one that is already wholly circumscribed by the political community. We are now dealing not with a regime-level claim of monarchical *oikonomia*, but with the status of citizens who are also property holders within a polis. This is done through a critical review of plans for reforming the city offered by Plato, Phaleas, and Hippodamus. We will leave the most famous one for last and begin with Phaleas.

Phaleas, inaugurating a never-vanishing delusion, proposes that all people be given an equal amount of property, either through founding a new city or legislating that the rich must give dowries but not receive them, while the poor must receive but not give them, thus equalizing wealth over time. But what, says Aristotle, if families vary in size? Then equal plots will not be sufficient. More importantly, what size is appropriate? Estates could be equal, but so small as to lead to constant penury, or so large as to promote luxury. Size is relative to need, and education is required to moderate need. One cannot impose simple, rationalistic solutions based on arithmetical equality while paying no attention to human psychology.

Phaleas provides for everyone receiving an education, but pays no attention to its content, in particular failing to address the ambition for excessive wealth and honour. The love of honour is as much a motive for political discord as unequal property, so a more complex understanding of human nature is required. Moreover, Phaleas assumes that pleasure is reducible to the desire for self-preservation: if the means for survival are given to everyone equally, everyone will be satisfied. But, Aristotle observes, people also commit crimes for excessive pleasures far beyond the level of mere self-preservation. ('Men do not become tyrants in order to get in out of the cold.')[33] Phaleas's scheme works only for petty crime and discontent, not such grand aberrant passions. After a modicum of material wealth has been secured for everyone to ensure self-preservation, Aristotle argues, education must specifically instil habits of moderation and encourage the potentially large-scale criminals and usurpers to study philosophy in order to experience the purest of pleasures and one that does not depend on exploiting others.[34] Desires must be limited in order for the polis to be stable and happy. The only alternative to shaping moral character through education is fear.

Phaleas's simplistic equalization of property also ignores the crucial matter of national security – his plan makes no mention of the military. The city's collective wealth, Aristotle observes, must be large enough to support a military capability, but small enough to avoid envy from potential aggressors.[35] Finally, quite apart from the danger posed to the city by men attracted to tyranny through excessive ambition or passion, unequal property is not the main cause of ordinary social strife. The upper classes resent the levelling of honour implied by equalizing property. They are as much bothered by the implication that they are not superior in status and character to the poor as they are by the actual equalization of material possessions. The lower orders, on the other hand, want *more* than what they currently possess, not just the same amount as everyone else. Why shouldn't they be able to strike it rich?[36] The wealthy must therefore be educated not to identify their prestige wholly with their superior wealth, while the poor must be restrained from acting on their envy of the better-off.

The second scheme discussed by Aristotle, that of Hippodamus, would simply proclaim workers, farmers, and soldiers to be equal. But how, Aristotle asks, do you restrain the soldiers from taking over? How, moreover, do the three classes interrelate? Do the farmers provide the soldiers' food? Do the soldiers farm on their own? Or is a fourth, unmentioned class needed to farm for them? The scheme, including its fondness for triads, is too abstract and simplistic.[37]

Hippodamus would also award public honours for new inventions to spur the economy.[38] Here we encounter a crucial tension between *oikonomia* and the political community. Economically driven progress in the technical arts can foment major changes in the laws and even the regime (think of the effect of the invention of the cotton gin on the politics and society of the United States). But stable laws are the element of any regime hoping to promote virtue. Yet, Aristotle concedes, many laws and conventions are silly or outmoded, while improvements in the arts, such as medicine, have tangibly improved the human condition. People naturally want the good, and prefer it to convention if the two conflict. Mankind has evolved since its most primitive beginnings, in large part because of technical progress. In earliest times, Aristotle observes, the entire human race was like the most foolish individuals are today. Laws have to change, and statesmanship must admit the possibility of progress. No set of laws can anticipate everything – room must be left for modification. However, not implementing a reform, especially if it is not momentous and clearly needed (the 'if it ain't broke, don't fix it' rule), may well be preferable to encouraging people to habitually question the law in their addiction to innovation.[39] Lawfulness requires habit, so there is no easy harmony between law and technique, or between political community and *oikonomia*. It must wait for modern thinkers like Hegel to argue that human community and technique progress harmoniously together.

Now we turn to the most famous communist utopia of them all, Plato's *Republic*. According to Aristotle, Socrates' demand for the total unity of the city turns it into an *oikos*, a household, ruled by its owner, the philosopher-king. The polis is entirely swallowed up by the economy. Perfect unity, Aristotle maintains, is not appropriate for the plural, composite nature of the city. The more the city tends toward complete unity, the more it moves in the direction of *oikonomia* and royal rule with its architectonic division of labour.[40] Human nature is a composite of intellect and appetite. These can be well arranged, but not made unitary, nor can classes be sorted out on the basis of only one trait or the other (as Plato does with the Guardians and Auxiliaries). The division of labour is not practicable in political communities, where freezing the ruling element permanently in place will cause outrage, especially among the spirited men whom the *Republic* is meant to assuage.[41] The division of labour is natural to the arts. No rotation is needed because each artisan and expert is assigned his most efficient place. But in cities, offices must rotate because citizens are equal, or if not entirely equal, sufficiently on a level with one another so as to not need to be ruled permanently[42] (because, as we recall from Book 1, nature will provide sufficiently sound human material for statesmanship from the outset). If you want to promote civic virtue, you must mute the claims of the architectonic art, which leads to monarchy.

Based on that general premise, Aristotle then critiques the *Republic*'s specific proposals for the communism of property and the family. The two are intimately connected because, as the etymology of the word for household suggests, the household with its concomitants of family ties and private property is at the heart of the love of one's own.[43] Aristotle's main points are as follows: 1) People will take more care over their own property than over public property (think of the carefully mowed suburban lawn versus the subway blighted with graffiti). 2) If everyone is your son, as in the *Republic*, you won't care about any one of them. Humans learn to care for others first through their blood ties. 3) People are first habituated into not harming or slandering their parents and siblings. Only on that basis can they extend decent treatment to their fellow citizens. If people had no blood ties, they would commit these outrages more frequently. 4) It is private family affections, the bonds between fathers, sons, and brothers, that wed us to the political community. The family is an incubator for wider civic affection. 'There are two impulses,' Aristotle observes, 'which more than all others cause human beings to cherish and feel affection for each other – "this is my own" and "this is a delight." '[44]

Ranging beyond the *Republic*, Aristotle then asks more generally whether land should be held in common. Once more, his main points are as follows: 1) Land could be held and worked communally, but with goods distributed according to individual needs. In practice, however, this will lead to disputes about who does the most work and to resentment if the hardest-working feel they are not being adequately rewarded. 2) The opportunity to own property and make money is a spur to productivity: 'with every man busy with his own, there will be increased effort all around.'[45] (Or, a rising tide will raise all boats – Milton Friedman, meet Aristotle.) The individual opportunity to acquire more will dispel recrimination, whereas communal property will lead the hardest-working to resent others as freeloaders. Some compromise is possible, however, between public and private ownership – for example, Sparta's common meals. 3) Social strife does not come from the existence of private property, but from vice and depravity. In fact, there is more social strife when property is held in common, since, for the reasons just cited, resentment is rife. In cities with private property, by contrast, disputes among parties to contracts are few in comparison with the overall very large number of owners. 4) Returning specifically to the *Republic*, Aristotle asks: If both the Guardians and the Artisans have communism, why is one entitled to rule over the other? Aren't they morally equal? On the other hand, if only the Guardians have communism, while the Artisans have ordinary market economies with private property, how are they a single city at all? Are they not two separate cities existing side by side?[46] (Or, as a student of mine once put it, isn't the rule of the Guardians over the Artisans like sending the Pope to rule over Las Vegas?)

All these points converge in Aristotle's central argument: There is nothing wrong with self-interest, only with *excessive* self-interest. (Hence my pairing at the beginning of this essay of the philosopher and the songstress.) It is worth quoting the entire passage:

> It is surely no accident that every man has affection for himself; this is according to nature. Selfishness is condemned, and justly, but selfishness is not simply to be fond of oneself, but to be *excessively* fond. So excessive fondness for money is condemned, though nearly every man is fond of everything of that kind. And a further point is that there is very great pleasure in helping and doing favours to friends and strangers and associates; and this happens when people have property of their own. None of these advantages is secured by those who [like Plato] seek excessive unification of the state, And, what is more, they are openly throwing away the practice of two virtues – self-restraint ... and liberality with regard to property. The abolition of private property will mean that no man will be seen to be liberal and no man will ever do any act of liberality; for it is in the use of articles of property that liberality is practised.[47]

In sum, abolishing private property amounts to 'throwing away' extra virtues like liberality. And why would anyone want to make do with fewer virtues when more are available?

The Ennoblement of Oligarchy through Polity

Let us consider whether the foregoing reflections on property rights help illuminate the conundrum with which we began – that, unique among the six-fold classification of regimes, a correct regime, 'polity,' is comprised by combining two defective regimes, oligarchy and democracy. As we saw in discussing Book 1, an excessive emphasis on economic acquisition can lead to tyranny and to the assimilation of *praxis* and of all civic life by *poiesis*. The restrictions Aristotle places on acquisition are therefore meant not only to curb tyranny, but to moderate the oligarchs' own pursuit of wealth within their particular regime. This involves appealing to their prejudice as gentlemen not to conflate their wealth with their self-esteem, but instead to view their pursuit of virtue as the basis for their honour and their economic wherewithal as equipment for that pursuit.[48]

But if an excessive concern with wealth is bad, so is its complete elimination. Wealth does help you practise more virtues. Moreover, the oligarchical regime, while defective, can be viewed in the best case as open to embracing the limitations placed on excessive productivity in Book 1. It is, after all, a communal regime, and cannot fully embrace the untrammelled individualism of the art of household management, which would lead either to tyranny or to rational monarchy. Indeed, if the oligarchs were to advance their wealth as their sole claim to merit to the furthest degree, their own regime principle would self-destruct, since either one or a few among their number, or the democratic 'many' collectively, might well possess wealth far exceeding their own, thereby deserving, on the oligarchs' own identification of the justice of their authority with wealth, to rule over them.[49]

The potential within the oligarchical outlook for moderating the pursuit of wealth is especially encouraged by 'polity,' the mixed regime, where private property both stabilizes the regime against excessive egalitarianism and populist envy while being shaped further in the direction of being employed as a means to the cultivation of moral character – a transformation already implied in the limitations placed on acquisition in Book 1, where *oikonomia* is circumscribed by the political community, where wealth is mainly landed and commercial exchange limited, and where the primary purpose of household management is to give citizen-householders the leisure for pursuing man's two chief ends, 'politics and philosophy.'[50]

The possibility that 'polity' might further deflect the oligarchical outlook from a tendency toward excessive materialism to a more moderate view of wealth as providing the wherewithal for the cultivation of virtue is evidenced by Aristotle's examples of how the principles of democracy and oligarchy could be 'blended' in that correct version of popular sovereignty. Statesmen in a polity, he argues, can do this in three ways: 1) Adopt features from both oligarchy and democracy. Oligarchies sometimes fine the rich for not serving on juries to punish them for abusing their privileges and not defending the interests of their class. Democracies, by contrast, pay the poor to serve and do not fine the rich, promoting the democratic class interest while encouraging the wealthy to opt out. Instead, in a polity, you should both pay the poor *and* fine the rich over jury duty, encouraging the poor to participate in public life and punishing the rich for being apathetic.

2) Take a middle course between the two principles. Democracies tend to have no property qualification for being a voting member of the assembly, while oligarchies have a huge one to keep the privilege to themselves. Instead, set a medium property qualification, so as to make sure the assembly excludes men who are so poor that they are tempted to seek office out of desperation and solely in order to profit for themselves, and to give the moderately well-off a direct role in promoting political stability. 3) Finally, you can mix the two principles. Democracies award office by lot (since, everyone being equal, no one can claim office on the basis of superior virtue) with no property qualification. Oligarchies have elective office and a property qualification, keeping political influence to themselves while implying that winning office is a competition among the meritorious, which they conflate with being prosperous. In a polity, however, you could have elective office *without* a property qualification, thereby upholding both meritocracy and widespread participation. This is the only example Aristotle calls 'aristocratic.' It transcends the earlier conflict between the principles of democracy and oligarchy, between the denial of all rank and a specious claim to merit. Polity can combine democracy's equality of opportunity with standards for recognizing unequal merit, thereby incorporating the sense in which citizens are equal in some respects and unequal in others, the primary task of 'political philosophy.'[51]

Polity at its best can lead to a diluted version of true aristocracy through the redirection of wealth and freedom toward pursuing a degree of pure virtue. It tempers oligarchical narrowness with democratic inclusiveness, and democratic volatility with the stability that comes from the oligarchical preservation of private property. While meant primarily to encourage social peace between the two most widespread and lethally hostile of factions, it can provide a platform for a more aristocratic political culture to evolve. It is essential for the success of this mixed regime that a new 'middle class' emerge from the co-optation of both democrats and oligarchs, a self-governing citizenry that will comprise a political majority of the poorest of the rich and the better-off among the poor.[52] The wretchedly poor have too little at stake to support a stable regime and social order, while the super-rich tend to be too arrogant to submit to any authority. By contrast, the moderately rich want protection from the big shots, while the better-off among the poor want social peace and an absence of political violence or factional strife so they can hold on to what they possess and enjoy it in peace. The super-rich at their worst tend to be criminals, will not obey the authorities, are unruly, contemptuous of others, and the objects of plotting. The most wretched of the poor also tend to be criminals, as well as mean-spirited, slavish, envious, open to bribery, and constantly plotting to despoil their betters. Polity must find a way of excluding these combustible extremes so that the middle class can coalesce as a moderate majority.

Oligarchy and *Oikonomia* Today

Do Aristotle's reflections on the proper limits of economics speak to our contemporary dilemmas? The world's earliest liberal democracy, America, has often been called a 'middle-class' regime, recalling Aristotle's prescription for polity. To be sure, there are crucial differences, owing both to history and to the Enlightenment political philosophy informing the American founding. Whereas Aristotle's polity is a collective coalescing of the moderate elements of two classes, liberal democracy is based on universal suffrage and representation. Its aim is not primarily to promote civic virtue, but to enable the will of the majority to be expressed in different ways through the three branches of government, out of a concern that if the majority could coalesce and exercise its authority collectively and directly, it would overwhelm the minority. Moreover, although, as we have seen, Aristotle does recognize that property rights and commerce do encourage self-advancement, his prescription for polity makes no explicit provision for the equality of opportunity for the earned economic inequality of result, as does James Madison, echoing John Locke, in *Federalist* 10. Aristotle's polity may be the largest and most inclusive of the six regimes, but it is still, by modern standards, a relatively small city-state. To foment, as do Madison and the other founders, the limitless expansion of commerce over a limitless geographical extent would, for Aristotle, reduce politics to economics, with the common good diluted and distended into something akin to a trade alliance.[53] For all that, however, the middle class in modern liberal democracy does share in some of the stabilizing and meritocratic features attributed by Aristotle to his equivalent of it, and represents one of the more successful attempts to adapt a simulacrum of classical virtue to modern liberalism. In particular, the success of the middle class in advancing itself economically has been viewed as a bellwether for the health of the liberal democratic regime altogether, giving the average person a stake in its stability and success.

By the same token, the competition between *oikonomia* and the political community first explored by Aristotle has never vanished from human affairs and lives on today. The thinkers and statesmen of liberal democracy at its inception – Locke, Montesquieu, the American founders – tried to follow Aristotle's prescription for a mixed regime steering a middle way between the extremes of tyranny and mob rule. At the same time, however, the age-old pattern of patrimonial authority has remained vibrant in many regions of the world. Its power has been compounded by the non-liberal version of modernization launched by Hobbes, which harnesses Machiavelli's call for the conquest of nature to an authoritarian and rationalistic monarchy that gives its subjects the right to acquire property and prosper through commerce in exchange for yielding all political authority to the Sovereign, in effect a modernizing version of what Aristotle meant by the art of household management.

While frequently endangered by war, civil strife, and economic reversals, the Enlightenment's best child, liberal democracy, inaugurated by America and spreading throughout North America, the Old World, and outposts beyond, has endured with impressive success. While it did not, strictly speaking, endorse Aristotle's contention that economic wealth should be wholly for the pursuit of the highest human excellences ('politics and philosophy'), it did at least agree that a virtuous character was required both for economic success and sound democratic politics. In its noblest version, liberal democracy never viewed the purpose of individual rights as the exclusive and limitless pursuit of prosperity. Instead, our natural freedom as individuals was viewed as the basis for a number of rights and opportunities including religious tolerance, liberal education, political participation, family life, aesthetic cultivation, and freedom of speech. Property rights were but one tangible dividend of this underlying emphasis on our natural liberties as citizens of free, self-governing communities.

In the post-communist and globalizing age through which we are now living, however, the household pattern of authority appears to have made a roaring comeback at the regime level. Large-scale multinational and geographical empires like China and Russia appear to be employing the art of household management to create enormous centralized and repressive security regimes 'owned' by dictatorial and oligopolistic elites which at the same time generate open-ended economic maximization that in some cases rivals the West. These emerging world powers are surrounded by a constellation of more or less illiberal, authoritarian oligarchies whose 'sovereign wealth funds' arguably comprise the largest source of capital in the global economy. The disturbing implication, its final outcome still too distant to forecast, is that it is possible to combine economic maximization with an illiberal regime, or, what is saying the same thing, that the connection between economic prosperity and the civic virtue of free self-governing peoples may be tenuous, historically fragile, and only one possible combination among others. Perhaps now more than ever, therefore, Aristotle's warning that *oikonomia* and its hierarchical structure of despotic technical management might swallow up the political community should engage our most sober reflection.

NOTES

1 I use the following translations, occasionally amended from the Greek: Aristotle, *The Politics*, trans. T.A. Saunders (New York: Penguin, 1981; Aristotle, *The Nicomachean Ethics*, trans. H. Rackham (London: Loeb Classical Library, 1975); Aristotle, *The Politics of Aristotle*, ed. W.L. Newman, with an introduction, two prefatory essays, notes critical and explanatory, 4 volumes (Oxford: Clarendon Press, 2000). References to the *Nicomachean Ethics* are designated *NE*. All other references to Aristotle are to the *Politics*.
2 1284a1–10; 1275b15–25; 1277a12–25; 1277b25–32.
3 1291a40–1291b14.
4 1280a5–15, 20–30; 1282b20–5.
5 1280a25–35; 1281b15–35; 1249a9–29.
6 At 1281b15–20, Aristotle appears to enter vicariously into the oligarchs' indignation over the democratic claim that the pooled virtues of 'the many' collectively outweigh those of the 'serious few' by swearing an oath: 'That is far from clear, by God!' This dramatic detail is buried in most translations. It amounts to Aristotle's recognition that, in the oligarchs' own self-understanding, their wealth may not be their sole claim to virtue, but a consequence of their overall excellence of character (the term *spoudaios* means a 'serious man,' one of moral gravity, mature experience, and sober judgment, particularly in public affairs, a quality that, to the oligarchical mind, cannot possibly be possessed by the common run of people – hence the tendency noted by Aristotle of most oligarchies in practice to designate themselves as aristocracies). By briefly taking on their role in the debate by swearing an oath, Aristotle concedes that the oligarchs might plausibly regard the

democratic view as impugning their honour and debasing the meaning of
public life. This is a motive he can value precisely because he wants to
solidify the oligarchs' belief that their wealth and status proceed from
their honour, and not the other way around, and that their wealth should
be viewed as a means to the pursuit of honour, not as being synonymous
with it.

7 1252a24–1252b27.
8 1259a37–1260b20.
9 1252b25–1253a30.
10 Literally, 'community in those things makes a household and a city.'
11 1252a1–24.
12 1261a38–1261b6; 1275a22–b22.
13 Consider Waller Newell, 'Superlative Virtue and the Problem of Monarchy
in Aristotle's *Politics*,' *The Western Political Quarterly* 40, no. 1 (1987):
159–78.
14 1253b23–1254a8.
15 1255b30–1256a1.
16 1263a40–1263b7.
17 *NE* 1098b30–1099a5; 1176b1–5.
18 *NE* 1120a4–15.
19 1254a17–1254b32.
20 1254b32–1255a3; 1255a20–1255b16.
21 1256a1–1256a18; 1256a40–1256b7; 1257a5–1257b40.
22 1257b40–1258a14.
23 1259a25–1259a37.
24 1252b28–30.
25 1258a19–27.
26 *NE* 1179b1–30.
27 Consider Waller Newell's 'Is There an Ontology of Tyranny?' in *Confronting Tyranny: Ancient Lessons for Global Politics*, ed. Toivo Koivukoski and
David Tabachnick (Lanham, MD: Rowman and Littlefield, 2005), 141–60.
28 1253a10–20.
29 1260a13–18; *NE* 1094a25–30.
30 1277a15–25; 1277b25–32; 1278a40–b6.
31 1284b1–30.
32 1285b20–35.
33 1267a2–1267a17.
34 1266b24–1267a20.
35 1267a17–30.
36 1267a37–1267b13.

37 1268a14–1268b4.
38 1286a6–10.
39 1268b22–1269a29.
40 1268b22–1269a29.
41 1264b6–26.
42 1261b5–1261b16.
43 The noun for household, *oikos*, is cognate with the adjective *oikeon*, which means belonging to or akin to one's own.
44 1261b32–1262b24.
45 1263a25–30.
46 1262b37–1264b15.
47 1263a40–1263b15.
48 Consider *NE* 1095b20–1096a5.
49 1283b5–35.
50 1255b35–40.
51 1294a35–1294b13.
52 1295b1–13.
53 1280a34–1281a2.

2 Aristotle and American Oligarchy: A Study in Political Influence

JEREMY S. NEILL

What would the Greeks have thought of modern innovations like nation-states and liberal-democratic freedoms? What would they have thought of representation, citizenship, and mass elections? In this article I shall explicate an Aristotelian approach to the American political system, or at least to some of its major elements. America is formally a representative democracy, and in large part it acts as such. But when the American system is approached from the standpoint of the *Politics*, it becomes evident that there are entrenched elements of oligarchy in American politics that are damaging the public sphere and preventing the government from meeting the needs of the people. To support this thesis, I shall in the first and second sections of this article recapitulate the accounts of democracy and oligarchy that Aristotle develops in the *Politics*. In the third section I shall use this explication to identify the oligarchic elements in American politics. I shall conclude in section four with an international expansion of my understanding of oligarchy. My goal throughout the article will be to employ the Aristotelian taxonomy for descriptive purposes, rather than to use it to propose alternatives to oligarchy in American politics. Identification is half of the battle if one intends to undertake reforms in an age and political climate in which publicity is an all-important virtue.

Aristotle on Democracies and Political Constitutions

The taxonomy that Aristotle develops in the *Politics* is divided into six different political constitutions. Aristotle identifies three of these constitutions (monarchy, aristocracy, and polity) as acceptable and three of them (tyranny, oligarchy, and democracy) as deviant.[1] For Aristotle a democracy is a political regime in which a majority of the citizens, by which he means the free, poor, and underprivileged classes, are dominant over the political process.[2] An oligarchy, by contrast, is a political regime in which the wealthiest classes are disproportionately powerful and rule for the sake of their private interests.[3] In the first two sections of this article I shall explicate Aristotle's accounts of democracy and oligarchy, discussing in particular the reasons why he sees oligarchies as deviant political regimes.

Unlike his great predecessor Plato, Aristotle is not as much an idealist as he is a realist interested in the actual operation of the governments of Greek city-states. His view is strikingly similar to the realism of the great classical historian Thucydides, whose rejection of the idealist histories of his predecessors is skilfully chronicled by Laurie Bagby in this same volume. The Aristotelian account is an analysis of Greek city-states that were demographically small and intellectually homogeneous by contemporary standards. In this focus his starting point is the same as that of Thucydides – Bagby correctly notes that Thucydides, as a historical realist, was aware that Greek city-states like Sparta and Athens were much more than just systems of government. In fact he acknowledged their 'national character,' by which Bagby means that they were comprehensive approaches to life whose policies constituted an integrated understanding of the good and of human flourishing.[4] Like Thucydides, Aristotle thinks of political constitutions as ways of life that permeate the institutions and customs of entire city-states (though Aristotle himself could hardly have imagined it, the Greek city-states of his day were far more intellectually and practically homogeneous than are our modern nation-states, in which it is common for a variety of world views to flourish alongside each other under the same system of government).[5] Finally, Aristotle's political realism leads him repeatedly to make the claim that there are inherent limitations on the success of constitutions.[6] Rather than speaking of universally valid political constitutions, he considers it more accurate to speak of some political constitutions as being better than others in a general sense because they operate more effectively in a variety of times and places.

Democracy is in the Aristotelian taxonomy the best of the three deviant political regimes. In a nutshell it is a political system in which a majority of the citizens is dominant. Peter Simpson rightly points out in an essay for this volume that democracy for Aristotle is a system of government in which the people are direct participants in the proceedings. There is no representation system like we currently experience today. In Book 4 of the *Politics* Aristotle identifies five different democratic constitutions and uses at least two criteria to distinguish these constitutions from each other.[7] The first criterion is the property and class qualifications which citizens must meet before they are allowed to participate in the political process. The second criterion is a distinction that Aristotle makes between the rule of law and the rule of men. By the rule of law Aristotle means a manner of governance in which the political leaders are constrained beforehand by principles which are known to the citizen body.[8] A political regime that defers to the rule of law is in his opinion superior to a regime in which the present generation alone is dominant.

In all but one of his five democracies Aristotle envisions the rule of law as taking precedence over the rule of men. The first of his democratic constitutions, for example, is dominated by the rule of law and is distinguished by the financial parity of its citizens. In it there is a financial redistribution that equalizes the resources of the wealthy and the poor.[9] The second democracy is unlike the first in that it grounds the right of political participation in a set of material qualifications. Its citizens must reach a threshold of property ownership before they can be elected as magistrates. Aristotle sets the property requirements of the second regime at a low level, probably out of a fear that the regime will slide into oligarchy. The third of Aristotle's democracies is distinguishable by its threshold of political disqualification: it excludes misbehaving citizens from civic participation. The fourth Aristotelian democracy is like our modern democracies in that it uses citizenship to regulate political participation: everyone who is a citizen is entitled to a place at the political table. The fourth democracy defers to the rule of law and is merit-based. It seeks only to promote the most capable persons to positions of social prominence.

The fifth Aristotelian democracy is a regime in which there are dangerous populist elements. It repudiates the legal tradition and favours the whims of the existing generation.[10] This populist turn leads to the rise of the social demagogue. Over time the demagogue preys on the desires of the multitude and urges them to reject the established political norms. Aristotle is critical of the final kind of democracy on the basis of his distinction between the rule of law and the rule of men. Democracies in which the rule of men is dominant are dangerous and unstable political regimes. Their opposition to the legal tradition ensures that desire (and not wisdom) will dominate their political proceedings.

Throughout his explication, Aristotle voices his preference for the moderate democracies of Solon and Athens rather than the more populist regimes of the non-Athenian city-states. Moderate regimes reward excellence and involve a variety of people in the political process. Aristotle prefers moderation because he is sceptical of democracies in which there are suffrage rights for the morally and intellectually inferior. His worry is that the involvement of inferior elements in politics will introduce negative influences into the political process. Several times in the *Politics* Aristotle reflects with horror on the eagerness with which the poor and the uneducated seek to gratify their desires. The moral and financial short-sightedness of a desire-driven population is massively chaotic and is a threat to stable governance. Instead of populist regimes Aristotle favours democracies in which there are limited participation rights. Among the groups that Aristotle does *not* envision as participating in democratic politics are children, slaves, resident aliens, women, and workers who do ignoble things like mechanical labour and financial exchange.[11]

Thus even in his treatment of properly functioning democracies Aristotle is careful to emphasize the advantages of aristocracy. His grounds for doing so are his conviction that the economic elite, as a class, are in general more virtuous than their underprivileged counterparts. They are usually better educated and are brought up more responsibly; and they are usually more inclined than the poor to act in ways that are magnanimous.[12] Indeed, so virtuous are the wealthy in Aristotle's mind that as long as they are willing to devote themselves to the public welfare, he is eager to champion their dominance in democracies. One way in which Aristotle would probably have introduced aristocratic elements into a democratic constitution is formally in institutional construction – perhaps as a financial threshold that must first be attained by citizens before they are allowed to participate in public life. Another way is informally in public life – perhaps through civic forums which honour the wealthy and promote the aristocratic virtues. The point is that Aristotle is a proponent of a prominent place for the wealthy and would have considered a mixture of democratic and aristocratic elements to be a practical ideal.

Aristotle's preference for a mixed constitution is similar to the political ideals of the American founders. And his emphasis on the virtues of the wealthy is a lot like the reasoning of the American founders when they set up a bicameral representation system – one in which there is an aristocratic chamber that embodies the virtues of the wealthy, and also a populist chamber that embodies the virtues of the people. Similarly, the financial threshold that Aristotle invoked to limit political participation is a lot like the financial limitations that in practice in America end up being preconditions for political influence. Thus the Aristotelian understanding of democracy is a relevant perspective from which to approach the American system. In structure and content it is similar to the *original* and eighteenth-century establishment of the American system. But it is sufficiently different from the contemporary operation of that system to offer us a critical perspective.

Aristotle intended for his taxonomy to be a scientific analysis of democratic political regimes. He knew, though, that democracies in practice are capable of functioning differently than their formal construction.[13] As mentioned, he certainly would not have considered this difference between theory and practice to be pernicious if it meant a turn in an aristocratic direction.[14] However, in spite of the fact that Aristotle would have embraced certain kinds of mixtures of wealth and politics, he would *not* have favoured democracies in which the wealthy are concentrating on their own self-interest. For Aristotle there are right and wrong ways of mixing wealth and politics, and only the right ways are acceptable in his taxonomic classification.

Deviant Political Regimes: Aristotle on Oligarchies

Aristotle defines oligarchies, which are the *wrong* way to mix wealth and politics, as regimes in which the wealthy are dominant and rule for the sake of their own interests.[15] Oligarchies as Aristotle imagined them, and as Simpson notes in his essay for this volume, were systems of direct involvement in which wealthy persons participated directly in the governmental proceedings. The rough-and-ready difference between oligarchies and democracies is financial: 'Wherever men rule by reason of their wealth, whether they be few or many, that is an oligarchy, and where the poor rule, that is a democracy.'[16] The leaders of oligarchies, being economic elites with little commitment to the common good, are distinguishable from aristocrats. In aristocracies the economic elites are acting out of virtue and for the sake of the general welfare. In oligarchies, by contrast, they are ruling out of self-interest and in a way that is ignoble.

Aristotle's taxonomy of oligarchies is less detailed than his taxonomy of democracies, and it would probably be considered underdeveloped by contemporary standards. Nevertheless, in book four of the *Politics*

Aristotle does construct a four-part account of oligarchies. His grounds for his four-part division are considerations of heredity and wealth stratification. The rulers of Aristotle's oligarchies are all in control of large fortunes and are all seeking to govern for private interests. The first of the four Aristotelian oligarchies is a regime that imposes property qualifications upon its participants. Citizens must meet this threshold of property ownership before they are allowed to participate in the governing process (presumably the property qualification is higher here than in the first democracy, so as to exclude the poor from political governance). In the second oligarchy the vacancies in the government are 'filled by co-optation,' by which is meant that the members of the upper classes are selected to fill them. Heredity is the basis of the third and fourth kinds of oligarchy. The third regime is a government of the elites in which there is a hereditary succession for the sake of private interest. The fourth is hereditary but is a regime in which the rule of men is dominant and not the rule of law (in this sense the fourth regime is similar to the final democratic regime in which the rule of men is also dominant).

Aristotle identifies oligarchies as deviant forms of government. He does so because of the pernicious motives which inspire their wealthy classes to participate in the political process. Oligarchies are not driven by excellence and are not mixed with other political elements in a way that would promote the common good. Rather, they are regimes in which the welfare of the elite is favoured over the interests of the general population: 'The true forms of government, therefore, are those in which the one, or the few, or the many, govern with a view to the common interest; but governments which rule with a view to the private interest, whether of the one, or of the few, or of the many, are perversions.'[17] To describe oligarchs in the sense that Aristotle intended it is convenient to use Peter Simpson's collective noun a 'sophistry of oligarchs,' used so wittily in an essay in this volume. For that is truly what oligarchs are – elite engaged in political enterprises that are obstructing clear and truthful forms of reasoning. In oligarchies as Aristotle describes them the wealthy are dominant, the processes of governance are aimed at private interests, and the needs of the many are not being met.

The Aristotelian political taxonomy was developed out of an analysis of small and pre-industrial city-states. The liberal democracies of the twenty-first century are vast, powerful, and heterogeneous. No single system of religion or ethics is dominant over the rest. Aristotle could hardly have imagined the size and diversity of nation-states, theories of the state that are divorced from the comprehensive good, or understandings of governance that are constrained by the rights of citizens. Contemporary philosophers have developed views of the state in which there is room for a variety of different belief systems. But the regimes that are listed in the Aristotelian taxonomy were all constructed around a particular understanding of the good.

Nevertheless, in spite of these differences between Aristotle and our modern theories of governance, the *Politics* is a valuable perspective from which to approach the American political system. Its worth stems from the fact that it was developed more than two thousand years before the revolutions of the eighteenth century.[18] Aristotle is a classical thinker who does not conceive of democracy as merely a system of government. He rather thinks of it as a way of life, an entire approach to the world, that pervades the minds and customs of citizens. As such, Aristotle would not have considered a modern concept like the political conception of justice – which is advertised by political liberals as a domain that is independent from the general society and regulated by its own cooperative norms – as a practical possibility. It would have seemed dubious to his classical mind to talk of a specialized and distinctly political domain. For Aristotle the state is more organic and less atomistic than it is for twenty-first-century liberals. Today, for example, we would not think of self-interest as a particularly vicious form of political participation. Rather, we would think of it as a justifiable attitude that is capable, if properly ordered, of contributing to the welfare of society. In *Federalist* 51, for example, Hamilton said that an effective way to mitigate private agendas is to divide citizens into groups and to pit their private agendas against each other: 'The defect must be supplied, by so contriving the interior structure of the government as that its several constituent parts may, by their mutual relations, be the means of keeping each other in their proper places.'[19] Aristotle would have disagreed with Hamilton and would have approached the general welfare in a much more organic way – one which would have straightforwardly condemned such exercises of self-interest. Political self-interest would have seemed to him to be a threat to stability and a menace to the capacity of the state to promote the flourishing of its members. This classical perspective is valuable because it is different enough from our own to offer some critical bite.

An Aristotelian perspective is also advantageous because, as a classical thinker, Aristotle was capable of understanding the weaknesses of democracy in ways that those of us who have grown up in the modern era cannot. For example, Aristotle considered the greatest weakness of democracy to be its reliance upon the multitude. People who are driven by desire are a threat to the functional success of the government. Regimes that jump from policy to policy in accordance with the whims of the people are weak and vacillating. This concentration of Aristotle's on the weaknesses of democracy is a way of thinking that is foreign to our modern temperament. As such, it provides us with a convenient starting point from which to discuss the problems with the oligarchic and self-interested elements in American politics.

A Modernization of the Aristotelian Taxonomy: Formal Oligarchy

Aristotle's critique of oligarchies in book four of the *Politics* is a productive standpoint from which to evaluate the oligarchic elements in American politics. In its past the American system has been far more oligarchic than we might like to imagine. The wealthy classes have typically exerted a disproportionate amount of influence upon the American political system. Whenever they have used this influence for the sake of their private interests they have caused that system to be oligarchic in a way that Aristotle would have considered to be pernicious.

The most visible way in which oligarchy has been manifested in American history is formally in the institutional framework. By this I mean the system of interlocking and mutually supporting associations that John Rawls has identified as the basic structure. Rawls includes in the basic structure institutions like 'the legal protection of freedom of thought and liberty of conscience, competitive markets, private property in the means of production, and the monogamous family.'[20] Sometimes institutions have been formally oligarchic by determining that certain classes of people are worthy of fewer privileges than the rest. This manifestation of oligarchy as discrimination has occasionally appeared in America as a formal disenfranchisement of certain persons and classes.[21]

It might be wondered whether Aristotle's *Politics* is a good place to turn for resources to evaluate oligarchy-as-discrimination. After all, as I have mentioned, Aristotle did advocate the disenfranchisement of women, slaves, and non-propertied classes. But Aristotle's endorsement of disenfranchisement does not diminish the moral authority of his critique. The Aristotelian understanding of disenfranchisement, while unacceptable by our modern standards, is different in a variety of ways from the instances of disenfranchisement in American political history. Aristotle advocated a policy of disenfranchisement because he believed that excellence is an optimal basis for politics and that it is more abundant in the wealthy classes. American disenfranchisement has rarely been justified by a narrative of excellence. Rather, it has much more commonly been justified by a narrative of inferiority: certain classes of persons are inherently inferior and are less capable of governance than the rest of the population.

Consider as an example of this narrative the Jim Crow laws of the postwar American South, which denied the basic rights of political participation to a large and disadvantaged African-American population. Today the Jim Crow laws are viewed as racially motivated. This assessment is correct, but it can hardly be disputed that the economic inequalities that existed at the time contributed greatly to the culture of discrimination in which the Jim Crow laws were developed. Fortunately these historical injustices have been corrected by the twentieth-century civil rights movement. Disenfranchisement on the basis of inferior wealth or class status is no longer a threat to American political life.

More common in American history than formal disenfranchisement has been the idea that special *privileges* ought to be accorded to a particular class of people, on the basis of their wealth, that are out of proportion to the privileges that are accorded to everyone else. Aristotle discusses oligarchy-as-privilege in his accounts of the two hereditary oligarchies. It is pernicious, on his view, for governments to offer the wealthy classes a special set of advantages that are not offered to the poor. It has in fact been common in America for particular kinds of people – usually the upper classes in general or sometimes just the financial titans – to be accorded these special kinds of privileges.

In recent years it has become commonplace in America for the tax code to privilege the wealthy. The trend toward oligarchic taxation has been more or less continuous since the 1980s and has occurred under the leadership of both parties. A prominent manifestation of this trend has been the diminishment of capital gains taxes. Today in America the capital gains taxes are markedly lower than those of the other capitalist democracies.[22] They are inordinately advantageous to the wealthy because the wealthy are the ones who are equipped to make the capital gains, whereas the poor are unable to achieve similar capital gains because of their more limited income. In America it is routine for stock options and other corporate perks to be almost wholly protected from conventional modes of taxation.[23] Recent years

have also seen an explosion of trusts, hedge funds, and other investment vehicles which are exempted from mainstream capital gains
taxes (and which are using minimal investment thresholds to prevent
the poorer classes from participating). Today the tax code permits off-
shore accounts, living trusts, and numerous other vehicles of financial
concealment. The development of these investment devices has come
about through extensive lobbying efforts and formal legal changes.
Most of the legal changes have been out of proportion to the conventional norms of taxation in the twentieth century. The inordinate tax
advantages for the wealthy are interpretable as an attack upon the
poor and the working classes. By stacking the conditions of the market
against the common people, whose greater ignorance about the economic process already places them at a competitive disadvantage, the
tax advantages are destabilizing and oligarchic.

Informal Oligarchy in American Politics

In spite of its increasingly oligarchic tax code, the basic structure in
America is still remarkably non-oligarchic in comparison to many of
the other regimes of the world. The long-standing American insistence
on the equal treatment of its citizens has tended to minimize its formal
development of oligarchic elements. It has been much more common in
America in recent years for oligarchy to be manifested *informally* in the
give and take of everyday politics. By this I mean a political arrangement in which the wealthy attempt to get away with what they can
short of changing the legal order. For the economic elite it is easier to
obtain political favours in back rooms than through visible changes to
the legal code. When their actions are secret they are not viewed by the
people as being permanent or as a threat to public morality.

Again it might be wondered whether it is appropriate to approach
American oligarchy from an Aristotelian standpoint. This time the
problem is a difference between the Aristotelian understanding of oligarchy and our own. The Aristotelian critique is directed at city-states
which were intellectually homogeneous and oligarchic in a formal
and institutional sense. By institutional oligarchy I mean an official
system in which the constitution of the city-state is explicitly built
around the interests of the wealthy. Aristotle does not appear to have
been thinking of informal and secretive kinds of oligarchy when he
condemned it as a pernicious form of government. This raises doubts
about the relevance of his account for the American experience. Most

of the oligarchy that takes place in America is unofficial and concealed from the public eye. The problem with invoking Aristotle is that he is not usually talking about the kind of oligarchy that we are familiar with in America.

Nevertheless, in spite of the gap that separates the formal and informal manifestations of oligarchy, the Aristotelian critique is applicable to political regimes in which oligarchy is taking place unofficially. Aristotle aimed his critique at the *motives* of oligarchs rather than at their actions. He condemns oligarchies as forms of government because he views their elites as obstructing the general welfare.[24] This point is significant, because the informal oligarchs in America are driven by motives that are essentially the same as those of the classical oligarchs of Aristotle's day. Even though they act differently in public in the different regimes, the reality is that in formal and informal oligarchies alike the elites are influencing politics from a self-interested perspective. Thus since Aristotle is targeting the motives and not the actions of oligarchs, and since the motives of American oligarchs are in essence the same as those of classical oligarchs, it is reasonable to view Aristotle's critique as applying to the American situation. If in practice the American system favours the wealthy, then, regardless of the public form that is taken by this favouritism, the system is operating as a kind of political regime that Aristotle would have condemned.

There are a variety of ways in which oligarchic elements have arisen informally in recent years in American politics. I shall divide these informal manifestations of oligarchy into two kinds – a direct kind that occurs when wealthy persons attempt through monetary pressure explicitly to influence elections, and an indirect kind that occurs when the wealthy attempt to shape the opinions of the public more generally.

One of the most prominent ways in which oligarchy is manifested in the American system is directly in political campaigning. As an example one needs only to think of the elite caste of fifteen to twenty families who are vastly over-represented in the American system (Kennedy, Gore, Bush, Blunt, Carnahan, Gonzales, and so forth). The political success of these dynasties is indicative of the importance of financial and personal connections in America, and the relative insignificance of leadership skills and professional competence.

An even greater symptom of oligarchy in America is the campaign finance system. In 1976 in *Buckley v. Valeo*, the Supreme Court was willing to place limits on the campaign contributions that are made by individual citizens, but it failed to place restrictions on soft money (i.e., money that is contributed to mediating organizations and committees, rather than directly to candidate campaigns and political parties), unlimited self-funding by political candidates, and the funding of candidates by national parties.[25] Today in America the campaign finance system is a labyrinth of contradictory rules and regulations.

One of the chief problems in American campaign finance is that candidates are allowed to fund themselves as much as they wish. Economic elites like Ross Perot, Jon Corzine, and Michael Bloomberg have made explicit attempts in recent years to translate their money into political power. It is relatively easy for the wealthy to depict themselves as legitimate candidates in an age in which money buys practical exposure, television time, and countless advertising trinkets. But the rules of the campaign finance system do not provide a comparable amount of public financing for the opponents of these wealthy candidates.

Even more common than personal advancement in American elections is the outpouring of wealth that is contributed to the campaigns of others – a phenomenon that Peter Simpson keenly chronicles in this same volume in his account of the oligarchic elements in American politics. Simpson is absolutely right, for to gain elected office in contemporary America it is necessary for the candidates to transform themselves into thoroughgoing oligarchs in the sense that Aristotle intended – courting the wealthy, manifesting their own wealth, gaining office by promising a dispersal of wealth, and so forth. The questions and abuses have reached the highest levels of government. One famous example is President Clinton's attempt to sell a night at the White House in return for high-level campaign contributions.[26] Also symptomatic of the confusion is the prevalence of soft-money organizations like political action committees (PACs). The purpose of these committees is to influence election-related activities through the unlimited and unregulated contributions of corporations, unions, and even individuals. Through PACs a *lot* of special-interest money is reaching the candidates and is influencing the highest levels of political decision making. It should come as no surprise that for every member of the United States Congress there are 125 congressional lobbyists who are working on behalf of PACs and other interest groups.[27]

In spite of the numerous attempts in recent years to reform the campaign finance system, the electoral process in America continues to be inordinately dominated by the wealthy. As evidence one needs only to think of the extraordinary expense of political campaigning. Way back in 1996, when Ronald Dworkin wrote an essay on campaign finance entitled 'The Curse of American Politics,' campaigns for the Senate cost from US $5 million to $30 million, and for House campaigns the average cost was $2 million.[28] Members of Congress at that time were spending a greater percentage of their time raising campaign funding than in proposing and reviewing legislation. The cost of a presidential campaign at that time was an astonishing $600 million to $1 billion. Undoubtedly these costs have only increased in this last decade.

Not all of the contributions that are made to politicians are taking place in elections. Today the wealthy are using their money to buy favours from all sorts of political figures. Consider the ignoble pardon of Marc Rich in January of 2000 by President Clinton.[29] Rich had for many years failed to report his multi-million-dollar income to the IRS. He had also assumed a large amount of corporate tax liability. At the time he was avoiding prosecution by hiding in Switzerland. In 1999 his wife Denise made a significant contribution to the Clinton presidential library. Shortly thereafter President Clinton cleared Rich of all charges of fraud and corporate malfeasance. In recent years there have been sales of a variety of other favours as well. I don't mean to pick on President Clinton, but Clinton's more recent ties to contributors were not disclosed in their totality until the Senate confirmation of his wife as Secretary of State in the Obama administration. As of the end of 2008, Bill Clinton has raised $492 million for his charitable organization in the time since he has left the White House. His donors are global elites, some from countries that are hostile to America, who are attempting to curry favour with a man who is still a major force in the Democratic party.[30]

There is a second, more indirect way in which oligarchic influence has come to be manifested in American politics. This second way is as an effort to exert a general-purpose influence upon the public conversation – things like everyday deliberation and the conduct of legislative business. The wealthy in America spend a lot of money in efforts to influence the political conversation. Sometimes the conversation retains the air of objectivity. But usually it is being shaped from behind the scenes by elites.

There has in fact arisen a stereotype in America of an economically advantaged class which advertises its private agenda as the public welfare. Examples of this stereotype are abundant in the corporate world. Rex Tillerson, CEO of ExxonMobil, has for a long time sought to influence American environmental policy from the perspective of his corporation's economic interests. Tillerson and his lobbyists have repeatedly appealed to 'scientific' treatises to cast doubt on the role of fossil fuels in global warming.[31] Their efforts to downplay the pernicious role of these fuels have obscured the real science on the matter, which seems to indicate the opposite result.

The Aristotelian taxonomy offers us a powerful and morally robust platform for evaluating the elements of informal oligarchy in American politics. In America the elements of informal oligarchy are pernicious because they are causing the system to fail to function as the democracy that it purports to be. If transparent politics is understood as a brand of politics that is accountable to the people and that embodies the ideals of popular sovereignty, then in America the government frequently cannot be understood as acting in a transparent manner. Rather, it all too often is acting as a quasi-democracy that is preventing the rights of speech and participation from being realized by the majority of its citizens. Its pernicious effect on society is that it is not involving the majority of its citizens in the processes of political decision making. In doing so it violates our understanding of liberal-democratic principles.

Aristotle would not have criticized just the oligarchic elements in America for principled and a priori reasons. He would also have targeted their negative *consequences*. In general in modern times the political regimes in which there have been elements of oligarchy have been less stable than regimes in which there have been no such elements. The economic elites who push their private interests in such regimes are almost always doing so at the expense of the rest of the population – their society as a whole is certainly not benefiting from their political efforts. Oligarchies are unstable because it is relatively easy for their rich to oppress their poor and also for their poor to be filled with jealousy and to agitate for overly rapid social change. If this instability has yet to be realized in America it is either because it has been masked by the many other more virtuous elements in the American system, or because it has yet to advance to its pernicious maturity.

Transnational Oligarchy and the American Political System

Since the end of the Cold War there has developed a third form of oligarchy that now reaches across the borders of nation-states. The globalization process that has spread around the world in the last several decades has increased the power of markets and money in countless ways. Back in the Cold War the superpowers intervened in the affairs of other states for the sake of their geopolitical strategies. But the development of oligarchy since the collapse of communism has been in directions that are independent of the policies of states. Today oligarchy is manifested internationally as a form of political intervention in which businesspersons and their corporations act independently of governments and seek on their own to influence the politics of other states. In this way wealthy persons who are not citizens and who do not have a formal political status in a particular state are often more influential than the persons who do have such status. The difference between domestic and international oligarchy is that the economic elites who are driving the latter are not themselves subjected to the laws of the states that they are attempting to influence. Rather, they are making their political deals from afar in an effort to avoid the duties of citizenship and the oversight of the legal code.

Americans have become particularly comfortable acting as international oligarchs in recent decades. In part this is because American business is such an extraordinary force in the world, and because it is not often that the economic elites of other countries are capable of interfering in American domestic politics. When they attempt to do so, as the Chinese did during the Al Gore campaign finance fiasco in the late 1990s, the public outcry is immediate and overwhelming. It is much more typical for the power of wealth to flow away from America rather than toward it. Examples of American influence abroad are not hard to come by. While it may be hard to believe, today American-based multinational corporations like Nike, McDonald's, and Wal-Mart are economically more powerful than developing nations like Bolivia and Congo. Their power makes it relatively easy for them to negotiate advantageous business deals. The effect of these deals is to compel the developing nations to act in ways that are damaging to their native populations. Sometimes the perks that are sought by the American corporations are relatively innocuous things like land grants and tax breaks. But sometimes they are more damaging things like export processing zones. The ideal for the American corporations is to obtain from the developing nations the right to set up shop in processing zones in which the working conditions are substandard and where there is an absence of organized labour and of political oversight.

Nike is a classic example. Its typical overseas practice is to obtain from developing nations the right to hire labourers at wages that are far less than acceptable in the developed world. A case in point is when Nike first outsourced its footwear lines to China. Very quickly it muscled the local authorities into providing it with advantageous labour conditions. In the words of Nike company vice-president David Chang, 'one of the first things we told the Chinese was that their prices had to be more competitive with our other Far East sources because the cost of doing business in Chinas was so enormous.'[32] The exploitative labour policies which Nike has practised for so long are very widely disliked by the native populations from which its workforce is drawn. The dislike is significant enough that it sometimes explodes into outright worker opposition – grass-roots movements in which the labourers themselves are agitating for changes in Nike's hiring practices. Nike faces down these worker movements by bullying the local governments into corporate-friendly labour settlements. In the 1990s, for example, there was a strike at a Nike factory in Indonesia (one which directly resulted from mediocre working conditions). Anton Supit, who was chairman of the Indonesian Footwear Association at the time (an organization which represents contractors for Nike, Reebok, and Adidas), lashed out at the local political authorities for failing to provide Nike with greater police support: 'If the authorities don't handle strikes, especially ones leading to violence and brutality, we will lose our foreign buyers. The government's income from exports will decrease and unemployment will worsen.'[33] Supit's attitude is commonplace among American-based multinational corporations which are outsourcing their production lines to developing nations. Around the world these corporate oligarchs are holding whole nations hostage in the name of favourable economic conditions.

At other times wealthy Americans are acting in an individual capacity as international oligarchs. One of the most stereotypical instances of this is their influence on the domestic politics of Israel. The stereotype, although perhaps overdrawn, is of the wealthy Jew from Long Island whose donations to political parties in Israel are of greater and more lasting significance than the lobbying efforts of ordinary Israelis. While it would be wrong to say that Israeli industry and commerce are wholly dominated by Americans, certainly in Israel the opinions of wealthy Americans are a powerful force that shapes the trajectory of commercial and political activities. Thomas Friedman has quoted a senior Israeli official as saying that 'Israelis are certain that America is a country that spends all its time being either for or against Israel.'[34] Friedman has also documented the dependence of Israel upon

American economic support. Even now, at a time when diplomatic relations between the United States and Israel are strained, the commercial relations between the two countries are thriving. Israeli politicians are familiar with the integrated economic relationship between the two countries, and on this basis they often feel the need to spin their policies in ways that will satisfy their American supporters.

Today the economic interests of Americans are spread around the world. As such, some readers might be inclined to construct a narrative on which it is reasonable for Americans to dominate the politics of other countries. For example, if one were to accept Robert Dahl's principle of affected interests, which asserts roughly that it is reasonable to expect political representation in situations in which one's interests are touched, it might seem justifiable for Americans to intervene in the affairs of foreign states.[35] They are not citizens of those states in anything like a formal sense, but their lives and possessions are undoubtedly affected by the political development of those states.

The problem with this just-so narrative, at least from an Aristotelian perspective, is that it does not deny the principled perniciousness of international oligarchy. Since international oligarchs do not possess a formal status as citizens of the states which they are seeking to influence, their efforts to influence the politics of those states are undermining the rights and privileges of the persons who *are* formal citizens. Aristotle, whose opinion on the matter is underdetermined but can be elicited from textual evidence in the *Politics*, would almost certainly have been opposed to oligarchic arrangements which undermine local sovereignty. The Aristotelian conception of the polis is that of a self-sufficient cooperative arrangement that is centred on a particular understanding of the good. The interference of foreigners for reasons of self-interest is almost always an arrangement that undermines the ability of a regime to achieve this good. When the elites in America are attempting to influence the internal affairs of other states they are setting up a dubious situation in which wealthy non-citizens are influencing the governments of foreign countries for reasons that have very little to do with those countries' long-term goals and welfare.

Apart from these principled problems with international oligarchy, it is uncommon in practice for international oligarchs to improve the operation of foreign governments. Americans are rarely as knowledgeable about the domestic politics of other countries as the native inhabitants of those countries. Even when they *are* as knowledgeable as the native inhabitants, their primary interest as economic oligarchs is in the promotion of their own interests. Only rarely are their interests aligned with the policies and procedures that are in the best interests of the foreign states. Thus even when wealthy Americans do happen to be knowledgeable about the internal affairs of foreign states, it is not often that they are inclined to use their information to promote the genuine welfare of those states.

Given the differences between their own interests and the interests of foreign states, it is little wonder that the actions of international oligarchs are destabilizing to foreign regimes. In political situations that are dominated by international oligarchs it is typical for the native inhabitants to observe the disparity between their numbers and their actual political influence and to agitate for populist changes. Consider the reaction in the 1990s in Nigeria to the Shell Oil Company, an American affiliate of the Royal Dutch Shell Company. By that time Shell had for forty years reaped handsome profits from oil that it had extracted from the homelands of the Ogoni people. Unfortunately the Ogoni people had been systematically excluded from the drilling profits through the duration of their association with Shell. Over the course of several years in the early 1990s there developed among them a non-violent campaign against Shell's drilling practices and environmental damage. The leader of the campaign was Ken Saro-Wiwa, the president of the Movement for the Survival of the Ogoni People. Saro-Wiwa and his allies pleaded with their Nigerian government to pressure Shell to cease its environmentally destructive practices and to compensate the Ogoni for the extracted oil. Shell reacted to the populist uprising by withdrawing in 1993 from the homelands of the Ogoni. But this placed an even greater amount of pressure on the Nigerian military regime of General Sani Abacha, which was by that time deeply dependent upon Shell oil profits. The regime, desperate to keep Shell happy, responded to the populist agitation by targeting the Ogoni for military retribution. Saro-Wiwa and his allies were speedily arrested and tried by a Nigerian military tribunal in 1995. The charges which were brought against them were recognized across the international community as unfounded and politically motivated. The leaders of the Ogoni (including Saro-Wiwa) were immediately executed upon the conclusion of the trial. The Ogoni, many thousands of whom were killed in the ensuing crackdown, knew exactly what was being done to them but were unable to do anything about it. They 'not only blamed Abacha for the attacks, they also accused Shell of treating the Nigerian military as a private police force, paying it to quash peaceful protest on Ogoni land, in addition to giving financial support and legitimacy to the Abacha regime.'[36] The actions of Shell Nigeria are unfortunately all too common and are an indication of the threat of international oligarchy to the stability of developing political regimes.

International oligarchy is dubious for both principled and practical reasons. Yet in spite of its problems, it is relatively difficult for the governments of foreign countries to control it or to place it under legal oversight. International oligarchs pump a lot of money into needy and industrializing economies, and foreign governments that would seek to diminish the influence of oligarchs are cutting their countries off from valuable economic stimuli. Moreover, since international oligarchs are outside of the legal superstructure, their efforts at political influence are often logistically difficult to regulate as well. Thus it is not usually very reasonable to expect foreign governments to subject international oligarchs to legal regulation.

Conclusion: Some Positive Results of Oligarchy

In this chapter I have spent a lot of time attacking the excesses and corruption of oligarchy. But I want to end this article on a note of hope. The twenty-first-century marketplace, which is the breeding ground for oligarchs, is a ubiquitous presence in our daily lives. On the whole it is a successful system and is not likely to go away anytime soon. As such it is reasonable to conclude that oligarchic influence is a permanent feature of American political life. As long as the market continues to dominate the exchange of wealth in America, a certain percentage of Americans will continue to grow wealthier and more influential than the rest, and the American government will continue to allow those who are wealthier to exercise a disproportionate amount of public power. In light of this reality I shall conclude by highlighting some ways in which wealth might be productive for American politics. If it were to be recognized as such, even in a narrow and restricted capacity, then perhaps it could be directed toward the general welfare.

As I have mentioned, one way in which Aristotle sees value in wealth is in the political contributions of a virtuous elite. For Aristotle governments are ideal when they are 'mixed' and combine the excellence of the elite with the motivation of the masses – the elite are generally more virtuous than the people, but the people are not usually as tempted by the acquisition of power. Regimes in which the wealthy are virtuous are well adjusted and capable of balancing out the popu-lism of democracies. For Aristotle a class of virtuous elites would be a welcome political element in the American public sphere.

But even apart from a class of virtuous elites, it might sometimes be profitable in American politics for the wealthy to act out of their own interests. For example, in the age of the mass media it is relatively easy for large groups of citizens to be swayed by charismatic leaders. The opinions of economic elites are based on more established inter-ests and are not as likely to be influenced by rhetoric and persuasive leadership. The acumen and relational skills by which the elites have climbed to their position of influence often also provide them with resources for resisting the appeal of charisma. Self-interested elites are sometimes capable of rejecting rhetoric and behaving more pru-dently than the population as a whole – they can, for example, sniff out and oppose economic reforms that try to do too much too fast. They are also capable of mitigating idealism that has become unteth-ered from the political reality. As such, perhaps there *is* occasionally a productive role for oligarchic elements in American and interna-tional politics.

NOTES

I am grateful to Eric Silverman for his critical comments on this article.

1 The taxonomy of political constitutions is introduced in the *Nicomachean Ethics* at 1160a31–1161b23. In this article I am using Aristotle, *The Nicoma-chean Ethics of Aristotle*, trans. and ed. Terence Irwin (Indianapolis, IN: Hackett, 1985); the taxonomy is also listed in the *Politics* at 1279a21–b19. My translation of this work is Aristotle, *Aristotle's Politics*, trans. C.D.C. Reeve (Indianapolis, IN: Hackett, 1998). My interpretations of these works are guided by Mary Nichols, *Citizens and Statesmen: A Study of Aristotle's* Politics (Savage, MD: Rowman and Littlefield, 1992); Fred Miller Jr, *Nature, Justice, and Rights in Aristotle's* Politics (New York: Oxford University Press, 1995); and also Richard Kraut, *Aristotle: Political Philosophy* (New York: Oxford University Press, 2002).
2 Here 'majority' is *plethos*. See *Politics* 1291b34–7.
3 See *Politics* 1279a28–32 and 1290b1–2; in the modern era the term 'plutoc-racy' is more often used than the term 'oligarchy' to describe regimes in which the wealthy rule for the sake of their private interests.

4 'These are conditions without which a state cannot exist ... which is a community of families and aggregations of families in well-being, for the sake
of a perfect and self-sufficing life ... the end of the state is the good life,
and these are the means towards it.' *Politics* 1280b33–5 and 1280b39–40.
5 'A constitution is the organization of offices in a state, and determines
what is to be the governing body, and what is the end of each community.'
Politics 1289a15–17; later in his account Aristotle says that 'the constitution
is in a figure the life of the city.' *Politics* 1295a40–1295b1.
6 See *Politics* 1289b28–9 and also 1290a5–6.
7 Aristotle's five-fold division of democracies occurs in *Politics* 4.4 1291b30–
1292a39. The first of the five forms, which levelled the economic distinctions between rich and poor, appears to be subsumed under the second in
Aristotle's four-fold division of democracies in *Politics* 4.6 1292b28–
1293a10. The third division of democracies appears in *Politics* 6.2 1318b6ff.
I am following contemporary scholarship and taking the taxonomy of *Politics* 4.4 to be the canonical one. See Andrew Lintott, 'Aristotle and Democracy,',*The Classical Quarterly*, n.s., 42, no. 1 (1992): 114–28. See also
Mortimer Chambers, 'Aristotle's "Forms of Democracy,"' *Transactions and
Proceedings of the American Philological Association* 92 (1961): 20–1; also see
C.I. Papageorgiou, 'Four or Five Types of Democracy in Aristotle?' *History
of Political Thought* 11, no. 1 (1990): 1–8; for an equivalent modern taxonomy, see David Held, *Models of Democracy* (Stanford, CA: Stanford University Press, 1987).
8 The mere existence of a legal code does not guarantee the rule of law. Upright
behaviour also plays an important part as well: 'We must remember that
good laws, if they are not obeyed, do not constitute good government. Hence
there are two parts of good government; one is the actual obedience of citizens to the laws, the other part is the goodness of the laws which they obey;
they may obey bad laws as well as good.' *Politics* 1294a1–8.
9 'Of forms of democracy first comes that which is said to be based strictly
on equality. In such a democracy the law says that it is just for the poor to
have no more advantage than the rich; and that neither should be masters,
but both equal.' *Politics* 1291b30–4. The rest of Aristotle's account of
democracies continues through 1292a38.
10 My account of the final kind of democracy is drawn from Aristotle's first
two taxonomies, both of which are referring to the same kind of regime.
See *Politics* 1292a7–37 and *Politics* 1292b41–1293a9.
11 See *Politics* 1275a7–16 and *Politics* 1328b33–1329a26; J.T. Bookman, 'The
Wisdom of the Many: An Analysis of the Arguments of Books III and IV of
Aristotle's Politics,' *History of Political Thought* 13, no. 1 (1992): 1–12,

especially at page 1ff., where Bookman references the exclusion of women, children, and slaves.

12 *Politics* 1281a3–8; See Bookman, 'Wisdom of the Many,' 2–3.

13 'It should however be remembered that in many states the constitution which is established by law, although not democratic, owing to the education and habits of the people may be administered democratically, and conversely in other states the established constitution may incline to democracy, but may be administered in an oligarchical spirit.' From *Politics* 1292b11–17.

14 Thanassis Samaras, 'Aristotle's *Politics*: The City of Book Seven and the Question of Ideology,' *The Classical Quarterly* 57 (2007): 79.

15 See *Politics* 1279a28–32 and 1279b40–1280a2. 'But the form of government is a democracy when the free, who are also poor and the majority, govern, and an oligarchy when the rich and the noble govern, they being at the same time few in number.' *Politics* 1290b16–20.

16 See *Politics* 1280a1–3; see *Politics* 1292a39–1292b11.

17 See *Politics* 1279d28–32. Polity, which is an 'attempt to unite the freedom of the poor and the wealth of the rich,' is a political constitution that incorporates elements of both oligarchies and democracies. In polities the finances of the wealthy and poor are equalized as much as possible, and the political regime relies for its stability and success upon the middle class. *Politics* 1294a16–17; see also *Politics* 1293b33–4. For a contemporary treatment, see Papageorgiou, 1990, p. 6.

18 For a resourceful application of Aristotle to modern democracy, see Martha Nussbaum, 'Aristotelian Social Democracy,' in *Liberalism and the Good*, ed. Gerald M. Mara, Henry S. Richardson, and Bruce Douglass (New York: Routledge, 1990), 203–52.

19 Alexander Hamilton, James Madison, and John Jay (1788), *The Federalist* (New York: Random House, 1963), 336–7.

20 John Rawls, *Theory of Justice*, rev. ed. (Cambridge, MA: Harvard University Press, 1999), 6.

21 See Carrie-Ann Biondi, 'Aristotle on the Mixed Constitution and Its Relevance for American Political Thought,' *Social Philosophy and Policy* 24, no. 2 (2007), especially 190–6.

22 Edmund L. Andrews, 'Report Finds Tax Cuts Heavily Favor the Wealthy,' *New York Times*, 13 August 2004, http://www.nytimes.com/2004/08/13/politics/campaign/13tax.html (accessed 9 June 2009).

23 Paul Krugman, 'The Tax-Cut Con,' *New York Times*, 14 September 2003, http://www.nytimes.com/2003/09/14/magazine/14TAXES.html (accessed 5 June 2009).

24 See *Politics* 1279a28–32.

25 *Buckley vs Valeo*, 481 U.S. 1, 20 (1976).

26 'Strange Bedfellows,' *Newsweek*, 10 March 1997, 28.

27 For a listing of lobbyists, see J. Valerie Steel et al., eds., *Washington Representatives* (Washington, DC: Columbia Books, 1996).

28 Ronald Dworkin, 'The Curse of American Politics,' *New York Review of Books*, 17 October 1996, 1, 19.

29 Clinton himself has attempted to justify his pardons. Bill Clinton, 'My Reasons for the Pardons,' *New York Times*, 18 February 2001, http://www.nytimes.com/2001/02/18/opinion/18CLIN.html (accessed 6 June 2009).

30 Chuck Bennet, 'Bill Clinton Releases Donor List,' *New York Post*, 18 December 2008, http://www.nypost.com/p/news/national/item_sRZwpFwFkyWj Snbp5ovpmKjsessionid=70A0B7D9B41EE3A8FE614E8992CCD189 (accessed 4 June 2009).

31 David Rothkopf, *Superclass: The Global Power Elite and the World They Are Making* (New York: Farrar, Straus and Giroux, 2008), 141–2.

32 Naomi Klein, *No Logo: Taking Aim at the Brand Bullies*, 2nd ed. (New York: Picador, 2002), 227.

33 Ibid.

34 Thomas Friedman, *From Beirut to Jerusalem* (New York: Anchor, 1989), 440.

35 Robert Dahl, *Democracy and Its Critics* (New Haven, CT: Yale University Press, 1989), 93–5, 119–31.

36 Klein, *No Logo*, 103ff. Later the Shell Oil Company was brought to trial in New York on the accusation of collaboration with the military executions. It settled out of court in June 2009 for US $15 million.

3 Overcoming Oligarchy: Republicanism and the Right to Property in *The Federalist*

JEFFREY SIKKENGA

It seems fair to say that oligarchy has been eclipsed by democracy as a force in the hearts and minds of human beings. Political parties or leaders openly devoted to oligarchic principles do not exist, and no one calls for a return to oligarchy. Democracy finally seems to have triumphed over its old enemy.

But is democracy's victory complete? Some countries are still described as having oligarchic political structures, and many political scientists think that oligarchic forces exist even in democratic regimes. Indeed, some argue that modern democracy is just a disguised form of oligarchy – that liberal democracy has overcome the problem of oligarchy only by capitulating to an impoverished view of democracy that preseves many oligarchic features, especially its commitment to property.[1] According to this argument, liberalism and its protection of the rights of property has thwarted democracy. While liberal democracies like America may not be oligarchies in the old-fashioned sense, they are nevertheless oligarchic systems set up to ensure that the rich hold a disproportionate share of power.

Plato and Aristotle would not be surprised by claims that oligarchy persists. In their view, oligarchy is a permanent political problem that can be ameliorated but never completely left behind. Oligarchy is part of humanity's political condition. This chapter will examine their claim in light of one of the most important works defending American liberal democracy, *The Federalist*. In responding to criticism that the new Constitution created an oligarchic system subverting true republicanism, *The Federalist* lays out the argument for how liberalism, rather than subverting democracy, actually makes possible a democratic republic that can overcome the problem of oligarchy. To

understand the argument of *The Federalist*, this chapter will first outline the argument of the ancients, starting with Plato's understanding
of the oligarchic soul and moving to Aristotle's analysis of the types of
oligarchic regimes and the ways in which legislators can deal with the
problem of oligarchy. We will then present the reply of *The Federalist*.

The Permanent Problem of Oligarchy According to Plato and Aristotle

Plato's most systematic analysis of oligarchic regimes is found in Book
8 of the *Republic*.[2] In the beginning of Book 8, the conversation returns
to a discussion interrupted at the end of Book 4 about the relative justice of five regimes: aristocracy (the rule of philosopher-kings), timocracy, oligarchy, democracy, and tyranny. The ensuing conversation
between Socrates and his interlocutors Glaucon and Adeimantus
focuses on the oligarchic soul because, according to Socrates, regimes
acquire their character from the *psyche* of those who establish and
hold the ruling offices. As he asks Glaucon at the beginning of the
Book: 'Do you suppose that the regimes arise "from an oak or rocks"
and not from the dispositions of the men in the cities, which, tipping
the scale as it were, draw the rest along with them'?[3]

According to Socrates, the oligarch starts as a moneymaker. Socrates
tells the story of a son of an honour-loving warrior (a 'timocrat') who
was a general or 'held some other great ruling office.' In the beginning,
the son too has a timocratic soul 'and at first emulates his father and follows in his footsteps.' But the father 'then got entangled with the court –
suffering at the hands of sycophants – and underwent death, exile, or
dishonor and lost his whole substance.' 'The son seeing and suffering
this and having lost his substance is frightened' and 'thrusts love of
honor and spiritedness headlong out of the throne of his soul; and
humbled by poverty, he turns greedily to money-making; and bit by bit
saving and working, he collects money.' The trauma of experiencing the
ruin of his father changes the son's soul so that 'such a man now puts the
desiring and money-loving part on the throne, and makes it the great
king within himself, girding it with tiaras, collars, and Persian swords.'
Indeed, the young man goes so far as to make 'the calculating and spirited parts sit by it on the ground on either side and be slaves' to his desire
to acquire money.[4]

The son retreats into a life of moneymaking because he experiences
a 'fear' so powerful that it dissolves timocratic visions of military

honour and shows him that the reputation gained from victory cannot prevent him from losing his 'substance' or from suffering 'death' at the hands of enemies. In short, fear sobers him up to the reality that he cannot take self-preservation for granted; he must worry first and foremost about securing the means not of glory but simply of life. Fear of physical privation is a fundamental part of the moneymaker's psychology. Without this experience of pressing necessity, the desire to acquire money cannot be born.

At the same time, this fear by itself does not spark powerful acquisitiveness: there must also be a desire for honour or distinction. The son turns to moneymaking not only because of fear but also because he is 'humbled' by poverty, indicating that fear does not destroy the desire for honour he inherited from his timocratic father. Rather, it changes what he believes will bring him respect, from military accomplishment to money, which provides a more durable (if less spectacular) kind of honour. Money gives the son a solid means to stay above privation and to recover the reputation lost by his father. Thus Socrates portrays the moneymaker's soul as 'in a sense two-fold,' born from a combination of the desire to acquire security and the desire to acquire honour. For the moneymaker, wealth satisfies both desires.

But moneymakers are not oligarchs – that is, human beings moved by distinctly oligarchic political principles. Moneymakers are politically happy if the city allows unlimited acquisition and the laws 'diligently hold down by force' crimes against property. But oligarchs demand that the city honour wealth by imposing a property qualification for holding office that excludes the vast majority of inhabitants. According to Socrates, the oligarchic soul comes into being when the rich face a democratic revolution that insists on equality. Full-fledged oligarchs are born when 'rich men ... whose property' is threatened or 'taken away' in a democratic revolution 'are compelled to defend themselves by speaking before the people and by doing whatever they can ... For this they are charged ... with plotting against the people and being oligarchs ... And, therefore, when they see that the people are trying to do them an *injustice* ... they at last end up, whether they want to or not, by becoming *truly oligarchs*.'5 Unlike moneymakers who gather up their property and flee when threatened, these wealthy people have become willing to risk 'impeachments, judgments, and contests' in order to defend the dignity and justice of the moneymaking way of life, which resides not so much in the simple accumulation of wealth as in the nobler fact that such a person rules himself through the dominance of the orderly (moneymaking) desires over the disorderly (spendthrift) desires. In their view, the justice of oligarchy is that it recognizes the moral excellence of the acquisitive person's orderly soul and publicly distinguishes it from lower ones that lack these virtues. For such people, oligarchy must be fought for because it is the only regime that gives the city's highest authority and honour to the best human beings, the people who deserve these distinctions. What makes some moneymakers 'truly oligarchs' is their moral attachment to a specific notion of justice that opposes the democratic idea of equality. Thus, while acquisitive desire for wealth is born from fear and shame, Socrates suggests that it becomes a bold demand for political honour fuelled by a growing attachment to what the rich see as the nobility and justice of oligarchic distinction.

Given the relative weight that an oligarchy could give to material security or political authority and honour, we can also recognize in Socrates' presentation the possibility of a wide range of oligarchic regimes. As Socrates makes clear in the beginning of Book VIII, however, a comprehensive outline is not the purpose of his discussion with Glaucon and Adeimantus. In the *Politics*, Aristotle takes up where Socrates leaves off and presents such a comprehensive examination of the variety of oligarchic regimes. Like Plato, Aristotle contends that there is an oligarchic soul that is distinguished as such by its attachment to the justice of oligarchy, and that such an attachment presents a permanent problem for democracy. Aristotle extends and qualifies Socrates' presentation, however, by showing how a legislator can reform oligarchy to make it a better regime.

According to Aristotle, the city or political community is a partnership of citizens in a regime or arrangement of political offices (*politeia*).[6] In every city, there are the rich and the poor; in some cities, there is also a middle class. The question for a legislator is whether the rich and poor (and middle class) will share in a common regime, and if so, how. According to Aristotle, oligarchy denies any sharing: it is a regime 'in which those who are well off and few in number have the offices' and rule with a view to their own advantage.[7] As Steven Skultety notes in this volume, one can 'open Aristotle's *Politics*, and find people called "oligarchs" who, far from relaxing in the lap of luxury, are taking the oath: "I will be hostile to the people and shall plan whatever evil [*kakon*] I can against them," and forming constitutions whose very mission is, in part, "to ill-treat the multitude, drive them out of the town, and disperse them." '[8]

Aristotle notes, however, that there are a variety of oligarchic arrangements, ranging from the rule of newly rich moneymakers to dynasties of a very few old, wealthy families who are not permitted to engage in moneymaking. What unites these oligarchs – indeed, what *makes* them oligarchs – is that all of them believe that only the rich deserve to rule, and they enforce this idea by having a high property qualification for voting and office holding. The variety of oligarchies shows, however, that oligarchs disagree over why wealth is worthy of honour. Oligarchic regimes devoted to the endless accumulation of wealth believe that the life of acquisition is the good life. For them, what makes human beings noble is the act of overcoming material privation and freeing oneself from necessity. But the other types of oligarchies show that the passion fuelling oligarchs cannot be reduced to the desire to acquire money. For these oligarchs, wealth is honourable because it is the only means to a higher end; hence, Aristotle says, these oligarchs 'are held to occupy the place of gentlemen' by the many and 'in most places' even mistake themselves for aristocrats.[9] These gentlemanly oligarchs believe that both wealthy moneymakers and the poor should be excluded from office because both groups are 'vulgar' (*apeirokalia*): that is, inexperienced in the nobler matters that are necessary to elevate the mind in preparation for political rule. There seem, then, to be several kinds of oligarchies rooted in different notions of what type of human being is truly good and deserves to rule. Yet within these differences lies the common idea of all oligarchy: an unbreakable link between wealth and political merit. To be an oligarch is to believe that the rich (at least certain rich people) deserve mastery over the city.

Given the despotic character of oligarchy, the legislator faces a difficult task in guiding it toward becoming a better regime such as aristocracy or polity. The oligarchs not only must be forced to rule more justly but also must become concerned with pursuing and encouraging virtue for its own sake.

According to Aristotle, the first step is to make oligarchy less politically exclusive through limited democratization – for example, by letting the respectable among the *demos* hold minor offices and audit high officials. This is a small step, but it forces oligarchs to become more concerned with justice identified as the common advantage, since they must, by institutional arrangement, give some hearing to the wishes and interests of the 'better part of the people' who are involved in the regime.[10] If the oligarchs begin to consider the interests of the many, their rule will move toward political rule and away from mastery, since the characteristic of political rule is that the rulers look to the good of the ruled in conditions of at least rough political equality. And while what the many consider to be their interest may not be particularly noble, the act of such consideration forces oligarchs to think of themselves more and more as rulers of free human beings. According to Aristotle, this change is important because 'rule over free persons is nobler and accompanied to a greater extent by virtue than ruling in the spirit of mastery.'[11] As oligarchs move more toward political rule, they necessarily begin to look away from themselves toward the *demos*, which they previously had considered no better than a multitude of 'beasts.' This looking away from one's own immediate interest is a critical part of the most important of the moral virtues, justice.[12] By becoming more like polity in its institutions, oligarchy can become more aristocratic in its spirit as the rulers become more habituated to the practice of a fuller, truer version of justice.

Another necessary part of the oligarchs' moral improvement is changing their attachment to property. As oligarchs, they view the possession of wealth as honourable and a sign of noble character. But in a mixed oligarchy, they would be required to give heed to the democratic desire for a more equitable distribution of property, which would force them to change the way they use their own property. For example, in order to support popular inclusion in the lower offices, oligarchs would pay taxes. In addition, Aristotle implies that reforms could make the oligarchs fund 'magnificent sacrifices and festivities' and have them pay for adorning the city 'with votive statues and buildings.'[13] Indeed, he goes so far as to say that a reformed oligarchy should make it the duty of wealthy families to give poor families land or jobs, and even to follow the example of the Tarentines in requiring the rich to make their excess possessions common in use with the poor.

Aristotle stresses this sort of reform because the virtuous use of property is critical for an education in nobility. Nearly all people believe that acquiring or having wealth is the good life or is at least a vital part of the good life. Aristotle argues, however, that attachment to property actually lowers the mind by directing it to 'bodily gratifications' rather than to the nobler goods associated with the higher activities of the soul. An education in noble virtue therefore must begin for most people by freeing them from the lure of private wealth, with its ensnarement of the mind in merely necessary and self-regarding goods.

Such reform is particularly important in oligarchies because they are the only regimes that publicly honour wealth above all. To persuade the oligarchs to use their property moderately and to some extent for the sake of their old enemy, the poor, is to begin to change their most deeply held opinions as to what is most honourable or virtuous. If the legislator simply concentrates on giving the many a 'minimum of property and work' without changing the oligarchs' opinion, the *demos* may be content to possess a small amount of property and to be left alone, but the *oligoi* will continue to try to acquire ever more money or political authority because they are more spirited, have greater desires, and are more likely to think that they merit great things than most of the multitude.[14] If their opinion of the honourable use of property can be changed, however, their souls will begin to shed one of the greatest impediments to improvement. But if their minds are not changed about the honourable use of property, they will resist further reform.

While a well-mixed oligarchy would still maintain that the good life is associated with wealth and the things provided by wealth, its institutions and law would embody the notion that property is not the sole honourable end and that the acquisition and use of wealth for self-aggrandizement is base. In this scenario, the wealthy would begin to see their riches as a means to larger political ends rather than simply viewing the city as a means to enriching or honouring themselves alone. By institutionalizing the factions' clash of opinions on justice in a mixed regime, the legislator can make some progress in addressing the oligarchs' partial view of justice, which Aristotle sees as the fundamental political and moral problem of this regime. Broadening the oligarchs' view of justice might help to foster a sense of common endeavour or even partnership between the rich and the poor. This is the best that can be hoped for in most cities because the oligarchs will not go away. As long as people's political nature is not suppressed and politics therefore maintains its high dignity, political office will be seen as a place (perhaps *the* place) for the noblest or most honourable people. In such a situation, the desire for honour driving the acquisitive opens them to becoming real oligarchs. For Plato and Aristotle, this is especially true in a democratic city built on principles of equality opposed to the oligarchs' notion of what constitutes human excellence. As we will see now, however, *The Federalist* argues that a republicanism built on a proper kind of equality – equality of natural rights – can overcome the supposedly permanent problem of oligarchy.

Overcoming Oligarchy: The Solution of *The Federalist*

Almost from its first publication in 1787–8, *The Federalist* has been considered one of the most authoritative expositions of the principles of
American republicanism.[15] Under the pen name of 'Publius,' Alexander Hamilton, James Madison, and John Jay argue for a republican
government 'derived from the great body of the society, not from an
inconsiderable proportion, or a favored class of it.'[16] According to
Publius, oligarchies are an entirely different kind of political order
from a republic: 'otherwise a handful of tyrannical nobles, exercising
their oppressions by a delegation of their powers, might aspire to the
rank of republicans, and claim for their government the honorable
title of republic.'[17]

To understand the difference, we should start with Publius's use of
the word 'oligarchy.' The first and most important use occurs in *The Federalist* no. 57, which is titled: 'The supposed tendency of the plan of the
convention to elevate the few above the many.' According to Publius,
the opponents of the Constitution argue that representatives 'will be
taken from that class of citizen which will have the least sympathy with
the mass of people, and be most likely to aim at an ambitious sacrifice of
the many to the aggrandizement of the few.' He contends that 'of all the
objections which have been framed against the federal Constitution, this
is perhaps the most extraordinary' because by arguing that voting districts will be too large to elect anyone except 'the rich,' 'the learned,' and
'the haughty heirs of distinguished names,' the Anti-Federalist opponents of the Constitution are actually denying the ability of the people to
select the best possible representatives to govern themselves. Hence
'whilst the objection itself is leveled against a pretended oligarchy, the
principle of it strikes at the very root of republican government.'[18]

Publius's use of 'oligarchy' suggests that he understands it very
much like Plato and Aristotle: as a system of government based on
'the elevation of the few on the ruins of the many,' which gives exclusive political power in one of two ways: either 'some unreasonable
qualification of property' is 'annexed to the right of suffrage,' or 'the
right of eligibility' is 'limited to persons of particular families or fortunes.'[19] In either case, the purpose of such an arrangement of offices
is to ensure the political domination of the 'the wealthy and well-
born' few over the rest of the political society.[20]

According to Publius, the spirit of oligarchy can be seen in a political society that many previous writers mistook for a republic – Venice.

The 'political writers' mis-characterized Venice not because they mis-understood oligarchy but because they did not understand true republicanism.[21] Not only does Venice fail to select its rulers by vote of the great body of the society, but it also subordinates the proper end of government – the protection of the people's natural rights – to the self-aggrandizement of the noble families. In contrast, American republicanism is marked by a 'noble enthusiasm of liberty' and hostility to the accumulation of power in the hands of a few. This spirit of liberty flows Americans' conviction that government exists to secure the 'the happiness of the people' through 'protection to their liberty and property.'[22]

From Publius's point of view, previous writers such as Montesquieu have inaccurately called oligarchy a type of republic because they do not fully draw out the link between the legitimate purpose of politics (the liberty or security of the person) and the popular republican institutions necessitated by that purpose. They did not see that true republicanism is democratic in form because it is liberal in spirit (i.e., its purpose is to secure natural rights). As the purpose of government, protection of individual rights presumes that government need not direct individuals to a certain way of life or even tell them how best to live beyond living as a free person. In short, liberal government's 'honorable determination' is that individuals are capable of governing themselves. And if individuals are capable of self-government, then 'the people' (i.e., the collection of individuals) is also capable of participating in governing (given the right circumstances and institutions). Hence true republicanism is liberal *and* democratic ('popular') because both rest on the fundamental principle that characterizes 'all our political experiments': belief in 'the capacity of mankind for self-government.'[23] Therefore the happiness of the people requires more than laws moderating the conduct of oligarchs (as the ancients suggest); it entails the wholescale rejection of oligarchic 'republicanism' in favour of a constitutional order that establishes a democratic republic in which the spirit of self-government flourishes. But given the ancients' claim that oligarchy is a permanent political problem, how can Publius be so confident that such a republic can be established and sustained, especially given the fact that oligarchy in one form or another has been a much more widespread and resilient form of government than the kind of republic sought by Publius?

Publius's confidence in overcoming oligarchy is rooted in his view that there are no permanent 'oligarchic' forces in human nature or political society. The most politically important element of human nature is the faculty of reason, the greatest power of which is its ability to lead to 'the discovery of truth.'[24] Reason leads to political truths in two ways: first, it can establish axioms of logical necessity that govern all discourse, including political arguments; second, it can reflect upon experience and sift out general truths about human nature and the legitimate ends of government.

With regard to establishing useful axioms of logic, reason has unrivalled power. According to Publius, 'in disquisitions of every kind there are certain primary truths, or first principles, upon which all subsequent reasonings must depend.' These principles, which are 'antecedent to all reflection or combination,' contain 'an internal evidence which ... commands the assent of the mind' because they are entailed by the principles of reason itself. According to Publius, some fundamental 'maxims in geometry' have this status as well as certain 'maxims in ethics and politics.' These principles are: 'that there cannot be an effect without a cause'; 'that the means ought to be proportioned to the end'; 'that every power ought to be commensurate with its object'; and 'that there ought to be no limitation of a power destined to effect a purpose which is itself incapable of limitation.' These are self-evident truths 'in the class of axioms,' which the mind will fail to accept only under 'the influence of some strong interest, or passion, or prejudice.'[25]

The second task of reason is to show that the self-evident axioms in geometry, ethics, and politics are actually discoveries of reality, not merely reflections of one's own passions. According to Publius, it is possible for 'the dictates of reason' to illuminate a true standard of 'justice' because by nature reason searches for 'enlarged and permanent' truths above the individual's own mind.[26] Hence the mind has the inclination or impulse to transcend the self and try to find all kinds of truth (including moral truth) untainted by 'prejudice, passion, or interest.' While 'it cannot be pretended that the principles of moral and political knowledge have, in general, the same degree of certainty with those of the mathematics,' 'they have much better claims in this respect than to judge from the conduct of men in particular situations we should be disposed to allow them. The obscurity is much oftener in the passions and prejudices of the reasoner than in the subject. Men, upon too many occasions, do not give their own understanding fair play.'[27] Reason has the capacity to ascertain moral and political reality and articulate a way of life ordered according to those natural principles of justice.

According to Publius, the foundational political insight given by reason is the recognition of 'that original right of self-defense which is paramount to all positive forms of government.'[28] This 'original right' of self-defence comes from the primary right to self-preservation, which is the most fundamental right given by the 'transcendent law of nature and of nature's God.' Publius maintains that the right to self-preservation comes from the very nature of the self, which is compelled by nature to seek its preservation. Along with a desire for happiness, the self's desire for preservation is the strongest and most ubiquitous desire from which human beings cannot escape as long as they are alive. Publius reasons that the desires for self-preservation and happiness become rights to self-preservation and the pursuit of happiness because if nature gives human beings these irresistible impulses, then 'the rules of just reasoning and theoretic propriety' require that nature sanction all means necessary for achieving that end, since 'whenever the end is required, the means are authorized; whenever a general power to do a thing is given, every particular power necessary for doing it is included.'[29] In short, Publius argues that if nature gives individuals the irresistible impulse to preserve themselves and pursue their happiness, it must give them the right to do so as long as they do not attempt to go beyond the laws of nature. This first principle of rational justice both sanctions and limits human actions to the reasonable purpose of effecting 'their safety and happiness' (as the Declaration of Independence puts it).

While reason has the desire and ability to discover natural principles of justice, people do not live according to the dictates of reason because 'human selfishness' is too strong.[30] According to Publius, this selfishness is driven by the passions rooted in self-love. He observes that there is in each person a 'connection which subsists between his reason and his self-love' such that a person becomes attached to his opinions not only because he believes them to be right but also because they are his own.[31] It is no surprise, therefore, that 'there is nothing so apt to agitate the passions of mankind as personal considerations.'[32]

This passionate attachment of every person to himself is at the heart of the most powerful types of political and economic acquisitiveness. Publius portrays the desire to acquire as taking three forms: industry, avarice, or ambition. For most people, 'those passions which have the strongest influence upon the human heart' are connected to 'the hopes and fears ... immediately' linked to their 'lives, liberties, and properties.'[33] Hence much ordinary acquisitiveness is the industrious desire to acquire the material goods necessary for economic security and comfort. At the same time, there are those – like 'the assiduous merchant, the laborious husbandsman, the active mechanic' – whose acquisitiveness takes the form of 'avarice,' which is a powerful type of acquisitiveness. This passion 'serves to vivify and invigorate all the channels of industry and to make them flow with greater activity and copiousness.'[34] Avarice can be 'as domineering and enterprising a passion as that of power or glory,' and it transforms the acquisition of property into part of building an economic empire that gives a person significant power or pre-eminence.[35] In this respect, avarice contains an element of ambition, which is the 'love of power.' But such avarice is not intrinsically a political desire: that is, it does not inherently long for the 'dignity,' 'importance,' and 'splendor' attached to the great concerns of government such as 'commerce, finance, negotiation, and war.'[36]

Finally, the desire to acquire can take the specifically political form of 'ambition,' which finds its satisfaction in acquiring political power. According to Publius, ambitious people want political power because they believe it will allow them to aggrandize themselves over others, giving them 'pre-eminence' and even 'exalted eminence' in society. In 'the noblest' of these people, 'personal aggrandizement' takes the form of a longing to be 'exalted' at 'the summit of [their] country's highest honors.' This desire for 'fame' spurs them to seek the highest political offices so that they can 'plan and undertake arduous enterprises for the public benefit' and in turn receive enduring glory from the whole community. Only with such glorious exultation of themselves is their ambitious 'passion' satisfied.[37]

If both reason and desire orient human actions to 'the more powerful sentiment of self-preservation,' why would anyone ever be so ambitious, especially since ambition makes people risk their comfortable preservation?[38] Publius suggests that the answer lies in the character of self-love. Self-love originates in the desire for self-preservation – in other words, people love themselves because they desire to preserve themselves. But self-preservation is not the only human impulse; we also want to be happy. For some people, the 'charms' of power promise a happiness beyond comfortable preservation, which can detach self-love from its original source. At that point, self-love becomes less concerned with preservation and more concerned with self-aggrandizement and even self-glorification, which is irrational but very powerful.

The task for the modern legislator is how to take this understanding of self-love and encourage the beneficial form of acquisitiveness (industry), channel the ambiguous form (avarice) into beneficial activities, and use the potentially dangerous form (ambition) to protect republicanism. If that can be done, republics need not concede anything to oligarchy. They can be 'unmixed' republics. The problem of oligarchy can be overcome. But the legislator must know how to deal with the central oligarchic force: property.

As we have seen, Publius believes that justice requires a republican order founded on protecting the individual's fundamental rights to self-preservation and the pursuit of happiness, and the other 'natural rights' flowing from those, especially the rights 'to liberty, and to property.' Of these rights, Publius gives special emphasis to the right to property. In a well-known passage, he argues that 'the first object of government' is to protect 'the faculties of men from which the rights of property originate,' including 'the protection of different and unequal faculties of acquiring property.'[39] The acquisitive faculties must be protected because their exercise allows people to secure the goods necessary for continuing their life and for pursuing their happiness by maintaining in society their rightful independence from the arbitrary, coercive will of others. With protection for the present possession and future acquisition of property, citizens can enjoy 'that repose and confidence which are among the chief blessings of civil society.'[40]

Publius's sympathy to the possession and acquisition of property appears to make him susceptible to the Anti-Federalist charge that the new constitutional order will 'court the elevation of the "wealthy and the well-born" to the exclusion and debasement of all the rest of the society.'[41] It certainly seems plausible that if government protects and encourages the acquisitive faculties, there would be a concomitant rise of ambitious passions and the danger that those with unequal faculties of acquisition would dominate politically. How can the legislator ensure that the desire to acquire does not turn into an oligarchic ambition that eventually leads the wealthy to despise a republican order embracing the natural equality of human beings and the political equality of all citizens?

Publius certainly admits that protection of the acquisitive faculties will lead to inequality of wealth, which was the building block of oligarchy in the ancient polis. A society that protects acquisition therefore has the makings of a commercial elite, from which it is one step to an oligarchic faction.[42] How can a legislator prevent the rise of oligarchic ambition among the rich in a republic, especially when most national office holders will be drawn from 'land-holders, merchants, and men of the learned professions'?[43]

The first step is to frustrate political ambition generally. The legislator must understand that the ambitious act 'with a view to getting rid of all external control upon their designs of personal aggrandizement' because 'power controlled or abridged' is not able to fulfil the promise of 'exalted eminence.' To avoid such abridgement, power always seeks more power and has 'an impatience of control that disposes those who are invested with the exercise of it to look with an evil eye upon all external attempts to restrain or direct its operation.'[44] Those who have power will want more, and the ambitious love of power, once awakened, grows stronger and stronger if left unchecked.

The effects of ambition can be minimized, however, if the legislator establishes the right kind of republic. It may true, as Peter Simpson argues in this volume, that the Founders believed that the Constitution would create a 'Congress of oligarchs' in the sense that 'elections for office must inevitably favor the privileged few' in a large republic.[45] But the extended republic also works strongly against the rise of true oligarchs because if the size of the republic is enlarged beyond the old city-states of Plato or Aristotle, there will be such a 'great variety of interests, parties, and sects' that no one ambitious faction of the wealthy could capture the legislative and executive power of the whole country. Indeed, while 'land-holders, merchants, and men of the learned professions' will have significant political influence as representatives in such a large republic, the very possibility of a coherent political faction of the rich is greatly reduced in a country where the economic interests of the wealthy vary so much from region to region.

Yet even in an extended republic, power must be institutionally separated and checked if oligarchy is to be thwarted. The first separation comes from the federal 'composite' nature of the republic, in which powers and duties are divided between states and the central government. Even if the Anti-Federalist fears were correct and a faction of the rich captured one level of government, the powers exercised by other levels would remain free from their grasp. At the national level, Publius follows Montesquieu – 'the oracle who is always consulted and cited on this issue' – and advocates separating the legislative, executive, and judicial powers and assigning the bulk of each of them, with some mixture among the other branches for checks and balances, to a different 'department' of the central government. This institutional separation of powers, combined with checks between branches, can prevent 'the intrigues of the ambitious or the bribes of the rich' from allowing 'the wealthy and well-born' to capture one or more branches of government and gradually concentrate all political power in their hands.[46] By enlarging the size of the republic, by dividing political power between states and the national government, and by designing the constitutional system to separate power and to check all branches of government, the legislator can frustrate political ambition, including those among the wealthy who might otherwise be inclined to oligarchy.

Despite Publius's faith in the 'great improvement' in political science brought by knowledge of 'the regular distribution of power into distinct departments,' he admits that a republican order also must impede the rise of oligarchic passions in the first place. According to the ancients, checking the rise of such passion requires constant coercive intervention by the legislator. In the *Republic*, for example, Socrates suggests that *nomoi* must be established that in effect reproduce the original fearful insecurity that keeps acquisitiveness from giving way to honour seeking (oligarchy). Without such a check, the ambitious aspect of acquisitiveness may emerge and slowly turn many industrious acquirers (and especially their sons) into honour-loving oligarchs. In Aristotle's view, the intrinsic connection between acquisitiveness and political ambition is evident from the fact that the materially acquisitive become more politically ambitious as they become richer, and especially as more and more of their wealth is inherited, removing them further and further from the fear of poverty's pressing necessity. For the ancients, acquisitiveness cannot be de-politicized because acquisitiveness is a form of ambition and therefore all acquisitive desire contains some love of honour.

Publius suggests, in contrast, that acquisitiveness is more fundamental than ambition. Indeed, ambition is really one form of the desire to acquire. Ambitious acquisitiveness is therefore more flexible than the ancients believed – the most 'enterprising' human beings can be directed toward either political power or economic empire, depending on what 'charms' them. In ancient republics like Rome that devoted themselves to political or military glory and despised moneymaking, conquest was the source of pre-eminence. Hence enterprising people inevitably went into politics, not business. In such non-commercial republics, political ambition flourished because politics replaced property as the source of the 'power' and 'pre-eminence.' But if the acquisition of property is no longer publically dishonoured (indeed, even honoured), those seeking honour will pursue it. Publius believed that this was already the case in America, which is largely free of the unnatural political stimulation of the ancient republics or the European monarchies. Here 'the industrious habits of the people of the present day' are not directed toward becoming 'a nation of soldiers,' conquerors, or politicians but are 'absorbed in the pursuits of gain, and devoted to the improvement of agriculture and commerce.'[47] According to Publius, the pervasively 'commercial character' of republican America shows that acquisitiveness gives rise to an oligarchic class only when people of an 'adventurous spirit' are denied the opportunity of obtaining pre-eminence in society by economic means. In effect, ancient regimes (located in small territories) artificially politicized acquisitiveness to the point of making the most vigorous citizens look with contempt on security, comfort, and moneymaking. But since most acquisitiveness is naturally 'economic,' what is required to make it politically benign is not to artificially distort its true character.

Not surprisingly, Publius therefore devotes much time and energy to proving that the new Constitution will bring 'an unrestrained intercourse between the states themselves' that 'will advance the trade of each, by an interchange of their respective productions, not only for the supply of reciprocal wants at home, but for exportation to foreign markets.'[48] In the new republic, 'the veins of commerce in every part will be replenished, and will acquire additional motion and vigor from a free circulation of the commodities of every part. Commercial enterprise will have much greater scope.'[49] Thus sober industriousness will be excited into economic avarice while many of the more ambitious forms of acquisitiveness will be channelled away from politics into building economic empires. In both cases, republicanism will be strengthened because the right to property will be exercised with greater vigour, and the love of power will be turned into a more economically beneficial passion.

To complete the disarming of oligarchic passions, citizens also must understand *why* the acquisition of property is honourable. Specifically, both the rich and the poor need to understand that acquisition of property is an exercise of the natural right to property belonging to all individuals, and it is the possession and vigorous exercise of natural rights that confer nobility on human beings. To acquire property therefore is an act of a naturally free person engaged in 'self-government,' the belief in which 'animates every votary of freedom.'[50]

In Publius's view, such an attachment to property helps to overcome oligarchy in two important ways. First, it checks the tendency of those pursuing wealth to neglect the public sphere, which can be a particular problem in an extended republic that frustrates political ambition. If 'enterprising' people are so absorbed in the private pursuit of their own wealth that they forget the public sphere, the right to property – and indeed all rights – could be threatened by a faction hostile to property. To survive, Publius's new order needs people who are more than bourgeois moneymakers; they must be public-spirited citizens with 'sufficient virtue ... for self-government,' which means that they must be vigilant against the political intrigues of all factions.[51] If citizens understand that everyone has an equal right to acquire property, both rich and poor alike – and middle class – will see that any political attempt to restrict others' property is really a threat to the *right* to property shared by all. With such an 'enlightened' understanding, citizens of all economic conditions can become 'friends ... of public and personal liberty' who realize that when the rights to acquire, possess, or enjoy property are threatened (e.g., by irresponsible printing of paper money, legislative abolition of debt, or confiscation of land by executive decree), they must offer a spirited defence of property rights. If the people are not hostile to property, the rich have less reason to want to create oligarchic political structures to protect their wealth from unjust, factious laws.

Second, understanding that property is honourable because it is the product of the exercise of a natural right has the effect of making the rich into friends of republicanism rather than its enemies. If the true source of wealth is the exercise of a right that all people share, then the source of the honour conferred by property is something that rich and poor have in common rather than something that divides them into those who are naturally superior (and therefore deserve to rule) and inferior (and therefore deserve to be ruled). The rich can therefore admire their wealth as the product of being successful in exercising the right to acquire property rather than as a moral claim to rule despotically over those who are less successful. When enlightened in this way, the rich will defend property not because wealth implies natural superiority, but because threatening property by implication calls into question the sanctity of natural rights, which they know is the foundation of the happiness they enjoy under a republican government. If the interests of the rich do coalesce on certain issues, it will likely occur because the 'principles' of 'justice and the general good' are being threatened, as when there is a widespread assault on property rights. In such a case, however, the 'least wealthy' will also rise to defend property, or at least not look with hatred on the wealthy who do defend their property rights. Thus while divisions between rich (successful acquirers) and poor (less successful acquirers) will produce 'different sentiments and views,' the poor know that they can pursue property by exercising their rights (rather than by mob confiscations), and the rich realize that they can defend their property by protecting everyone's liberty (rather than by overthrowing republicanism). True republicanism thus democratizes the passion once thought to be an inevitable spur to oligarchy. A political order built on property as an equal natural right can defend the property of everyone (including the rich) without succumbing to oligarchy.[52]

Conclusion

Plato and Aristotle hold that while acquisitiveness is part of the human condition, the political community must educate and elevate the acquisitive desire through all kinds of written and unwritten *nomoi*, especially by legal discouragement of business activity and by the reformation of moneymaking and money-lending practices that encourage expression of acquisitive desires. In this way, the ancients seek to re-focus oligarchic passions, ultimately directing their inherently noble element away from property toward a moderate form of political rule and a leisured appreciation of political study and deliberation. In effect, they cultivate the gentlemanly aspect of oligarchic ambition while suppressing the material. In their view, to try to de-politicize the oligarchic passion would be foolish; this would only frustrate its nobler aspects and would remove the most significant source of potentially ennobling passions in most cities, thereby creating serious harm to a healthy civic order.

   In contrast, Publius denies oligarchic elements any place in his new republic. He rejects the idea that acquisitiveness necessarily contains any element of noble strivings that republican politics should accommodate in order to foster a healthy civic life, especially since such an accommodation as the ancients recommend requires a mixed regime that provides a special place in political office for the wealthy. Publius sees oligarchic ambition (the desire to rule based on wealth) as a perversion of acquisitiveness, not an inherent part of it. Thus, for him, the passion that must be frustrated, channelled, and transformed is political ambition, not the desire to acquire property. According to Publius, the same acquisitive desires that make people rich do not necessarily make them want to rule. Instead of following the ancients in restraining and educating acquisitiveness to draw out some of its nobler aspects, Publius sanctions the liberation of acquisitiveness while simultaneously creating a large federal republic that forces the ambitious over and over again to confront the limits of what politics can achieve and thus what limited glory politics can deliver, especially when compared with acquiring great wealth by building an economic empire. Since the enterprising will probably not tolerate the slow and frustrating political process, many of them will turn to business rather than to political office. And in a place that protects the acquisition of property because it is a natural right of all people, the rich will have neither the need nor the desire to seek to establish an oligarchic political order.[53]

Thus, if the wealthy have a disproportionate influence in Publius's republic, it will not be as a faction united around a passionate hostility to sharing rule with the less wealthy but as representatives of a multiplicity of factions advocating policies that advance the particular interests of 'land-holders, merchants, and men of the learned professions.' The American experiment in republicanism can finally sever the link between the desire to acquire and the passion to rule, which was supposed to make oligarchy an inevitable political problem. If Publius is right, then liberalism has not thwarted democratic republicanism – it has made it possible. If democracy dominates the world today, Publius would say that it is in no small part due to the fact that liberalism has tamed the rich and thus overcome democracy's great rival.

NOTES

1 See, for example, Jennifer Nedelsky, *Private Property and the Limits of American Constitutionalism: The Madisonian Framework and Its Legacy* (Chicago: University of Chicago Press, 1990), 1.
2 Citations of the *Republic* are taken from Plato, *Republic*, trans. Allan Bloom (New York: Basic, 1991). In the Platonic corpus, oligarchy also appears in the *Statesman* (301a, 302d), *Laws* (710c, 712c), *Apology* (32c), *Menexenus* (238e), *Epist. V* (321d), and *Epist. VII* (326, 348a).
3 Plato, *Republic*, 544d–e.
4 All citations in this paragraph are taken from Plato, *Republic*, 553b–d.
5 Plato, *Republic*, 565b–c.
6 Aristotle, *Politics*, 1252a6, 1275b16–20, 1276b9–10. Citations of the *Politics* are taken from Aristotle, *Politics*, trans. Carnes Lord (Chicago: University of Chicago Press, 1984).

7 Aristotle, *Politics*, 1279b28–36.
8 See Steven C. Skultety's 'The Threat of Misguided Elites: Aristotle on Oligarchy' in this volume. Citation from Aristotle, *Politics*, 1310a9–10, 1311a10–15.
9 Aristotle, *Politics*, 1293b40–1, 1294a18–19.
10 Aristotle, *Politics*, 1293a12, 1292b5, 1279a29–37, 1278b33–40.
11 Aristotle, *Politics*, 1333b27.
12 See Aristotle, *Nicomachean Ethics*, 1129b15–35..
13 Aristotle, *Politics*, 1321a35–40.
14 Aristotle, *Politics*, 1267a9–15.
15 Thomas Jefferson claimed, for example, that *The Federalist* was the 'greatest work yet written on the principles of government.' Despite its overall unity of thought, it was a collaborative effort between thinkers who did not always agree on the policy or even institutional implications of the principles of liberal republicanism. On the problem of differences in thought between contributors to *The Federalist*, especially James Madison and Alexander Hamilton, see David Epstein, *The Political Theory of the Federalist* (Chicago: University of Chicago Press, 1984), 2.
16 Publius, *The Federalist* no. 39, paragraph 3. Citations of *The Federalist* are taken from *The Federalist* [1787–8], ed. Jacob Cooke (Hanover, NH: University Press of New England, 1961).
17 Publius, *The Federalist* no. 39, paragraph 3.
18 All citations in the paragraph taken from *The Federalist* no. 57, paragraphs 1–2.
19 Publius, The *Federalist* no. 57, paragraphs 3, 15.
20 Publius, *The Federalist* no. 60, paragraph 11. The other explicit mention of 'oligarchy' occurs in *The Federalist* no. 77, written by Hamilton. In this paper, Hamilton criticizes the method of executive appointment practised by the numerous executive council of New York. He contends that extending New York's practice to the national government would create a system in which 'the private attachments of a dozen, or of twenty men, would occasion a monopoly of all the principal employments of the government in a few families and would lead more directly to an aristocracy or an oligarchy than any measure that could be contrived' (Publius, *The Federalist* no. 77, paragraph 7).
21 While castigating 'the extreme inaccuracy with which the term [republic] has been used in political disquisitions,' Publius (Madison) laments that 'the same title [republic] has been bestowed on Venice, where absolute power over the great body of the people is exercised in the most absolute manner by a small body of hereditary nobles' (*The Federalist* no. 39,

paragraph 3). In making this remark, Madison is chastising not only Montesquieu but also Hamilton and Jefferson, both of whom call Venice a republic. To be fair, however, Hamilton qualifies the republican appellation by calling Venice a 'haughty republic,' while Jefferson says, in a passage quoted from his *Notes on the State of Virginia*, that Venice is run by 'one hundred and seventy three despots' (*The Federalist* no. 6, paragraph 12; *The Federalist* no. 48, paragraph 8). Madison offers a more direct criticism of Montesquieu's classification of the forms of government in his 1792 essay entitled 'The Spirit of Governments.'

22 Publius, *The Federalist* no. 1, paragraph 9.

23 Publius, *The Federalist* no. 39, paragraph 1.

24 In the opening paragraph of *The Federalist* no. 1, the founding of American itself is characterized as an experiment in whether 'reflection and choice' can replace 'accident and force' as the foundation of 'political constitutions.'

25 All citations in this paragraph are taken from Publius, *The Federalist* no. 31, paragraph 1.

26 Publius, *The Federalist* no. 15, paragraph 12, *The Federalist* no. 42, paragraph 11.

27 Publius, *The Federalist* no. 31, paragraph 3.

28 Publius, *The Federalist* no. 28, paragraph 6.

29 Publius, *The Federalist* no. 73, paragraph 5, *The Federalist* no. 44, paragraph 16.

30 'In a nation of philosophers, this consideration ought to be disregarded. A reverence for the laws would be sufficiently inculcated by the voice of an enlightened reason.' But 'a nation of philosophers is as little to be expected as the philosophical race of kings wished for by Plato' (Publius, *The Federalist* no. 49, paragraph 6). Indeed, 'had every Athenian citizen been a Socrates, every Athenian assembly would still have been a mob' (Publius, *The Federalist* no. 55, paragraph 3).

31 Publius, *The Federalist* no. 10, paragraph 6.

32 Publius, *The Federalist* no. 76, paragraph 5.

33 Publius, *The Federalist* no. 16, paragraph 7; *The Federalist* no. 45, paragraph 9.

34 Publius, *The Federalist* no. 12, paragraph 2.

35 Publius, *The Federalist* no. 6, paragraph 9.

36 Publius, *The Federalist* no. 17, paragraph 1.

37 All citations in this paragraph are taken from Publius, *The Federalist* no. 72, paragraph 4. At the same time, there is a different type of political passion linked to self-love, which Publius calls 'republican jealousy.' This is a

'jealousy of power' in which people demand that no one be exalted for fear that such exaltation will destroy the 'equality and security' necessary to protect themselves (Publius, *The Federalist* no. 6, paragraph 3).

38 Publius, *The Federalist* no. 38, paragraph 2.
39 Publius, *The Federalist* no. 10, paragraph 6.
40 Publius, *The Federalist* no. 37, paragraph 6.
41 Publius, *The Federalist* no. 60, paragraph 5.
42 The danger of oligarchic intrigue is not eliminated by America's 'absolute prohibition of titles of nobility.' While nothing short of a constitutional revolution could transform America into an hereditary aristocracy, Alexis de Tocqueville points out that a prohibition on titles does not eliminate the possibility that successful commercial families over time could become an informal aristocracy. See Alexis de Tocqueville, *Democracy in America*, ed. J.P. Mayer (Garden City, NY: Doubleday, 1969), vol. 2, part 2, chapter 20.
43 Publius, *The Federalist* no. 35, paragraph 9.
44 Citations in this paragraph are taken from Publius, *The Federalist* no. 15, paragraph 13.
45 See Peter Simpson, 'A Corruption of Oligarchs,' in this volume. Simpson is correct only if his definition of an oligarch is correct: 'I mean by oligarchs what Aristotle means, those who are rich and have the privileges that naturally accompany riches, as good birth and family, education, personal accomplishment, wealthy and powerful friends, public prominence and the like.' But that definition is incomplete because Aristotle makes it clear that rich, powerful gentlemen are not necessarily oligarchs: an oligarch is someone who believes that the rich *deserve* to rule despotically over the non-rich. Not all of the rich in the ancient world had such an understanding of justice, and if Publius is right, almost none of the wealthy hold such a view in modern liberal democracies, especially in America.
46 Publius, *The Federalist* no. 58, paragraph 16.
47 Publius, *The Federalist* no. 8, paragraph 8.
48 Publius, *The Federalist* no. 11, paragraph 12.
49 Publius, *The Federalist* no. 11, paragraph 12.
50 Publius, *The Federalist* no. 39, paragraph 1.
51 Publius, *The Federalist* no. 55, paragraph 9. Writers like Montesquieu tried to attach wealth to salutary political passions by putting wealthy hereditary nobles into a separate chamber of the legislature, thus simultaneously isolating and politicizing them in defence of their property, prerogatives, and by extension the general liberty. Publius rejects this solution because he sees it as a potentially dangerous political foothold for the rich, as unsuited to the republican 'genius' of America, and as offensive to the

equality of citizens that is the political reflection of natural human equality.

52 In his chapter in this volume ('Oligarchy and the Rule of Law'), Craig Cooper makes the interesting argument that 'the way to resist oligarchic tendencies inherent in modern democracies and other forms of modern governments is through freedom of speech that allows all members of society to voice their opinion.' While preserving the right to free speech may be important for presenting and defending the democratic idea of equality, reforming the way that citizens understand the right to property seems more fundamental. If the rich can understand property as a personal right held by all people rather than an exclusive claim to rule, there will not be an oligarchic party that attacks the idea of equality, at least the liberal idea of equality that everyone possesses the same natural rights.

53 According to Lord Bryce, the most ambitious people in America tend to shun politics in favour of 'the business of developing the material resources of the country.' James Bryce, *The American Commonwealth* (1914) (Indianapolis, IN: Liberty Fund, 1995), vol. 1, chap. 8.

4 A Corruption of Oligarchs

PETER SIMPSON

Introduction: A Collective Noun for Oligarchs?

Certain languages rejoice in the phenomenon of what is called the *collective noun*, whereby particular objects are given a special name when thought of in groups, and this special name describes a distinctive feature of the objects in question. Birds in a group on the wing, for instance, can be called a flight of birds. Other and more evocative examples are a pride of lions or a school of porpoises, suggesting that these animals are expressing characteristics of pride and skilled display. The conceit is a happy one and gives colour as well as instruction to our speech. Moreover, it admits of indefinite extension, for we can, if we choose and as we please, construct collective nouns for other groups of objects that currently do not have one. Indeed, certain refined parlour games consist of such verbal invention. We might, for instance, speak of a group of well-born and well-groomed ladies as an elegance of ladies, or of an array of lighted lamps as an illumination of lamps.

What collective noun, however, should we invent for oligarchs? We might naturally focus first on their smallness of number and speak of them as a minority of oligarchs (for oligarchs are always few among many). Or we might focus on the narrowness of their rule and call them a confinement of oligarchs (for oligarchs permit only a few to share control). But since such narrowness of rule requires also a certain hiddenness of deliberation and decision, so that the many have no knowledge of what the rulers are deciding nor have influence on deliberation but must follow what is later presented to them as a settled determination, we might speak of a conspiracy of oligarchs.

Another suggestion would be to borrow a word that Aristotle uses for the devious practices of oligarchs and speak of a sophistry of oligarchs. For Aristotle calls oligarchic devices sophistries when he discusses how oligarchs give to their control the outward appearance of democracy while retaining the reality of exclusive rule. A particular instance is that attendance at the assembly is open to all but a fine is imposed on the wealthy if they do not attend and the poor are left alone.[1] The device looks democratic because the rich suffer a penalty for their wealth but the poor none for their poverty. The real effect is to ensure that the wealthy always or usually attend the assembly while the poor seldom or never do and so to ensure that the wealthy will always or usually be in the majority when it comes to voting. In the same context Aristotle notes that the contrary sophistry is practised by democratic leaders, who provide pay to the poor if they attend the assembly but impose no fine on the rich if they do not.[2] These sophistries are neat although no longer of relevance as popular assemblies have ceased to exist. Still, if the particular cases are outmoded, the general strategy of using tricks to exclude people from rule is not. Were Aristotle alive today he would note that the modern world has deployed a few tricks of its own. He would also note that these tricks are all on the side of oligarchs. But perhaps we should first get clear about what Aristotle meant by oligarchy.

Aristotle's Theory of Oligarchy

Oligarchy is spoken of in several places in the *Politics* (as well as briefly in the *Ethics*), but there is one passage of particular interest that has not been much explored or exploited by commentators. The reason is in part that Aristotle himself omits to spell out its details, leaving them to be inferred from an earlier passage. The earlier passage is about democracy, and in it Aristotle gives his most instructive account of democracy's self-understanding and structure. Since the passage is the source for inferring the omitted and contrasting details about oligarchy, it deserves to be quoted in full:

> Freedom is the supposition of the democratic regime, for it is the usual thing to say that only in this regime do people partake of freedom, since freedom, they say, is what every democracy aims at. One sort of freedom is to rule and to be ruled in turn, for popular justice is numerical equality and not equality according to merit. But if this is what justice is, then the

multitude must necessarily be in control, and whatever seems good to the majority must be what the end is and what is just (for they assert that each citizen must have equality). Consequently, in democracies the needy must have more control than the well-off, since they are the majority, and what seems good to the majority has the control. So one sign of freedom is this, and it is what the whole popular party lays down as the defining mark of the regime. Another sort of freedom is to live as one likes, for they say this is the work of freedom since to live as one does not like is characteristic of the slave. This, then, is the second defining mark of democracy. From it has come the feature of not being ruled, by anyone at all preferably, but, failing that, of being ruled only by turns; and that is how this defining mark contributes to freedom based on equality. From these suppositions and from this sort of principle come the following features of popular rule:

1 choosing all the offices from everyone
2 everyone ruling each and each ruling everyone in turn
3 having all the offices chosen by lot, or as many as do not need experience and skill
4 having no property qualification for any office or the smallest qualification possible
5 having no one occupy the same office twice or rarely or only in the case of few offices (excepting those related to war)
6 having all the offices, or as many as possible, of short duration
7 having everyone, or those chosen from everyone, decide all court cases, or most of them and those that are most important and have most control, such as those to do with the giving of accounts and with the regime and private contracts
8 having the assembly in control of everything or the most important things and no office in control of anything or as few things as possible ...
9 next, having pay provided for everyone, for the assembly, the law courts, and the offices if possible, or if not, for the offices, the law courts, the council, and those meetings of the assembly invested with most control or for those offices where common messes are a necessity
10 further, since oligarchy has the defining marks of family, wealth, and education, their opposites seem to be marks of popular rule – no family, poverty, and vulgarity
11 in the matter of offices, having none of them perpetual but if one might be left over from an ancient revolution, stripping it of its power and having it chosen by lot and not by election.[3]

I have numbered the features of democracy here for ease of comprehension, but that they follow from the idea of freedom, or from the supposition of democracy as Aristotle calls it, seems evident enough.[4] The
picture of democracy we thus get is not at all that of democracy today,
but we may readily explain the difference, as modern political theorists
have long grown accustomed to doing, by the distinction between
direct and representative democracy. Aristotle means by democracy
direct democracy where the people themselves directly make decisions
about law and policy. What we mean by democracy is representative
democracy where the people make such decisions indirectly through
those whom they elect to represent them. Direct democracies must be
small, as they were in Aristotle's day. Only representative democracies
can attain the size of our modern democracies.

As for oligarchies, on the other hand, and what their self-understanding
and structures are, Aristotle merely says the following:

> How oligarchies must be constructed is also pretty well manifest from these
> considerations. For each oligarchy must be brought together from the con-
> trary features, with the democracy opposed to it used as the analogue.[5]

An earlier passage, just before the listing of the supposition and features of democracy, runs as follows:

> Democracies are made different when the features that accompany
> democracies and that seem to be proper to this regime are put together,
> since fewer of them accompany one democracy, more another, and all of
> them a third. It is useful to be able to recognize each of these features,
> both for establishing whichever democracy one may happen to want and
> for making corrections.[6]

Aristotle intends us, therefore, to take the model of his analysis of
democracy and, by putting opposites to opposites, construct a parallel
for oligarchy. I will carry out that intention here by repeating the passage about democracy and making the necessary replacements at each
point (I put the whole into italics to indicate that it is my adaptation):

Wealth and privilege and family are the supposition of the oligarchic regime,
for it is the usual thing to say that only in this regime do the notables partake
of freedom, since the notables, they say, are what every oligarchy aims at.
One sort of being well off is to rule and not to be ruled in turn, for oligarchic

justice is proportional equality or equality according to merit. But if this is what justice is, then the wealthy must necessarily be in control, and whatever seems good to them must be what the end is and what is just (for they assert that no citizen must have equality but only according to merit). Consequently, in oligarchies the well-off must have more control than the needy, since they are the notables, and what seems good to them has the control. So one sign of being well off is this, and it is what the whole oligarchic party lays down as the defining mark of the regime. Another sort of being well off is to live a privileged life, for they say this is the work of wealth since to live a needy life is characteristic of the poor and base and slavish. This, then, is the second defining mark of oligarchy. From it has come the feature of always ruling, but, failing that, of ruling for a long time and not by turns; and that is how this defining mark contributes to notability based on wealth. From these suppositions and from this sort of principle come the following features of oligarchic rule:

1 *choosing all the offices from some*
2 *some always ruling all and all always being ruled by some*
3 *having no offices chosen by lot*
4 *having high property qualification for all offices*
5 *having the same people occupy the same office often or always*
6 *having all the offices, or as many as possible, of long duration*
7 *having some, or those chosen from some, decide all court cases, or most of them and those that are most important and have most control, such as those to do with the giving of accounts and with the regime and private contracts*
8 *having the assembly in control of little or nothing and especially not the most important things, and the offices in control of everything or as many things as possible*
9 *next, having pay provided for no one, not for the assembly, the law courts, or the offices, and especially not for the offices, the law courts, the council, and those meetings of the assembly invested with most control or for those offices where common messes are a necessity*
10 *oligarchy has the defining marks of family, wealth, and education*
11 *in the matter of offices, having all or some of them perpetual and investing traditional ones (or those attacked in democratic revolutions) with more power and having them chosen by election.*

Rephrasing Aristotle's account of democracy to produce this parallel account of oligarchy is easy and straightforward enough, and it fits what he says elsewhere about the character and features of oligarchy and oligarchs. We may, then, fairly take it as a basis for deciding which constitutional structures will, in Aristotelian terms, count as oligarchic.

We need, however, also to keep in mind the sophistic practices that such structures and those who support them may also engage in to hide the oligarchy. For this purpose it will be well to quote the passage where Aristotle lists such sophistic practices (which I again number for ease of comprehension):

> The sophistries in regimes devised by way of pretext against the populace are five in number, and concern the assembly, the offices, the law courts, bearing arms, and physical training.

> 1 As regards the assembly, the sophistry is that attendance at its meetings is open to all, but a fine for nonattendance is imposed only on the well-off, or the fine on them is much heavier.
> 2 As regards the offices, the sophistry is that those with a property qualification are not permitted to abjure but the needy are.
> 3 As regards jury courts, the sophistry is that a fine is imposed on the well-off if they do not sit on juries, but the needy are let off with impunity, or, as in Charondas' laws, the fine on the former is heavy but on the latter light. In some places, enrolling for the assembly and juries is open to all, but heavy fines are imposed on those who enroll but fail to attend the assembly or sit on juries, the aim being to get people to avoid enrolling because of the fine and, because of not enrolling, neither to sit on juries nor to attend the assembly.
> 4 Legislation is passed in the same way about acquiring arms and physical training. For the needy are allowed not to acquire arms, but a fine is imposed on the well-off if they do not.
> 5 And should they not train, no fine is imposed on the former, but one is imposed on the latter so that the latter will, because of the fine, take part while the former, having nothing to fear, will not.[7]

Aristotle's listing of sophistries has a certain comprehensiveness in covering all three parts of the regime that he also lists: the deliberative, the offices, the courts[8] (the addition about arms and training in their use reflects the obvious fact that control over who is to share in these parts must ultimately rest with those who have the wherewithal to coerce everyone else). The particular instances Aristotle mentions are doubtless not exhaustive, nor meant to be. Human inventiveness and the changes of circumstance to which it responds are never wholly predictable. Still, nothing prevents the overall patterns and general analyses from being the same, even about the very different politics of our own day.

Modern Practice: The United States

A striking case in point is the United States Constitution and its relation to the Articles of Confederation that preceded it. One should note, to begin with, that the Articles, for all their difference from the Constitution, are not a democracy according to Aristotle's description. But neither are they an oligarchy. They are a controlled delegation of powers of the several States to a central Alliance (it is called a League of Friendship). Notable features are that effective power and sovereignty rest with the States; that States send a committee of delegates to Congress (at least two and no more than seven); that these delegates are appointed annually; that they can be recalled at any time; that no one may be a delegate for more than three years in any six; that the delegates are maintained by their respective State; that delegates have no individual vote but only a single vote as the delegation of their State; that there is no army in peacetime, whether for Congress or the States; that the States maintain, equip, and command their own contingents for the general army; that the committee which sits when Congress is in recess consists of one delegate from each State and that no one can serve as its president for more than one year in any three; that the agreement of nine out of the thirteen States is required for deciding questions of major import; that Congress has no permanent supreme judiciary but convenes, by a process of delegation and lot, a panel of judges to hear and judge disputes.[9] The Articles do not set up a national government or provide the means for anyone to make a career as a national politician, but rather go out of their way to exclude the possibility of both. Everything is done to keep effective authority and power in the hands of the States.

The Constitution, by contrast, does the opposite, setting up a permanent national government where individuals, albeit individuals from the several states, have a share as individuals in rule and in the rewards of rule. These individuals are elected by the people or appointed by the states for periods of two or six years and there is no right of recall nor are these individuals maintained by their States. There is an elected president, a standing army, and a permanent judiciary. None of these things is funded or maintained by the States but instead by a national treasury that is itself funded through taxation levied directly on individuals and no longer on States. The powers of Congress, President, and Judiciary are also all greatly extended so as to be, in principle or at least in cases of emergency, unlimited within the national sphere.[10]

The Constitution, therefore, makes two different changes at the same time: from a league to a national government and from a Congress of delegates to a Congress of individual oligarchs. I say oligarchs because of the features of oligarchy from Aristotle listed above. The key is the role played in the Constitution by election. However, to understand this point some remarks of Aristotle about election need to be noted first.

Election is always of some people by some people, and, for Aristotle, everything depends on who chooses whom and how. The options are that all may choose from all or from some or from both; or some may choose from all or from some or from both; or all and some may choose from all or some or both. When all choose from all, the election is democratic; when some from some, it is oligarchic; when mixed, it is aristocratic or political depending on the mixture.[11] Under the United States Constitution as first proposed, only Representatives were chosen by all from some (by all the citizens of the respective State from proposed candidates). The election of President and Senators was by some from all or from some (by the Electoral College or by the State legislatures from whomever they might wish). The election of the President, however, quickly became in fact by all from some (by all the citizens of all the States from the proposed candidates), but it took over a hundred years before, by the 17th amendment of 1913, Senators came to be elected by all the citizens of the respective State. The same practice prevails in State and local elections, so that all elections are now by all from some, namely by all the citizens of the relevant constituency from the candidates named on the ballot.[12]

One might conclude from this analysis that the system of elections in the United States would, by Aristotle's classification, count as aristocratic or political. With respect to form it may be so. With respect to practice it is not. For an element of political sophistry here intervenes, since there is a key difference between what we mean by elections and what Aristotle means by them. We mean by elections choosing between candidates whose names are on the ballot and who have, before the election, been going about soliciting people for their votes.

Aristotle means by election choosing from among candidates who are not named on any ballot and who have not been going about soliciting votes. Aristotle opposes soliciting for votes because it encourages vice and crime. At any rate he says:

> It is also not right that anyone who is going to be judged worthy of office should himself have to ask for it. If a man is worthy of office, he should rule whether he wants to or not ... No one would ask to rule who was not in love with honor, yet men commit most of their crimes from love of honor or money.[13]

And again:

> Regimes also undergo change without faction ... as in Heraia because of vote-getting; for elections were being won by those campaigning for votes and so they had the officials chosen by lot instead.[14]

Aristotle's point is clear. Those should rule who are worthy of it, but electioneering ensures that the unworthy, the ambitious and greedy and criminal, rule instead, and it does so for two reasons: first because those who would stoop to campaign for election are mainly the ambitious and greedy, and second because, where campaigning for election is allowed, those who campaign win while those who do not lose. We might note also another remark of Aristotle's, that the ambitious and greedy will inevitably use office to make money.[15] Indeed, if we go by revelations of political money-grubbing over the years, we may well be astonished not merely by the effrontery but by the enormity of the thefts that modern politicians conceive and carry out and get away with.[16]

Nowadays election campaigns are inseparable from elections and we cannot imagine one without the other. The result is that candidates, in order to win or retain office, must first and indeed only become successful in campaigning. Success in campaigning is a function of several things but principally of what we call name recognition and image, that is to say, of the candidate being known to the electorate and of his public persona being approved by them. How does a candidate get to be known and approved by the electorate, especially by an electorate numbering in the millions (as is invariably the case today)? The answer is to be or to become an oligarch. I mean by oligarchs what Aristotle means, those who are rich and have the privileges that naturally accompany riches, as good birth and family, education, personal accomplishment, wealthy and powerful friends, public prominence, and the like.[17] Such things do not guarantee election, but without them election is well-nigh impossible. Those who do not have them must somehow acquire them, or acquire friends who have them, in order to be successful in winning office. The following facts should suffice to prove the point.

The first fact is that elections for office must inevitably favour the privileged few. Elections are won by number of votes cast in one's favour and no one can receive many votes who is not known and admired by many. The features that attract attention and give renown are wealth, high social class, prominent family, conspicuous achievement, striking physical beauty, and the like. To possess some or other of these marks brings one notice and so puts one among the notables, as they may rightly be called. The notables are, of their nature, the known, and the marks they are known by are, of their nature, among things admirable. The notables need not be the best, or the wisest, or the most just, but they cannot avoid being the most electable. A second fact is that the more numerous the voters the fewer will be the notables who are likely to win any great number of votes. Among a hundred or a thousand there are many, even of a moderate standing, who could enjoy a known reputation; among a hundred thousand likely none of them will; among a million, let alone the estimated 300 million and more who currently live in the United States, only the outstandingly extraordinary would do so. Many cast votes; an extreme minority receives them. All choose; from whom they choose are very few. A third and closely related fact is that election campaigns are expensive and require leisure from necessities so that one may spend all or most of one's time seeking votes. Only the wealthy and privileged or those supported and maintained by the wealthy and privileged can afford either the money or the time. The middle class and the mass of the poor can afford neither. A fourth fact is that elections are never just a matter of casting votes for whomever one wills, for there is also the advance selection of candidates. When it comes time for the people to choose their representatives, the existing representatives along with their friends and paid retainers (I mean the political parties and their agents) have already determined the candidates for whom alone the people may vote. Most often the existing representative is the chief of these candidates and the favourite to win again. Sometimes the people, or a limited part of them, are also given a say in this determining of candidates (as in the primary elections). But not always do they have such a say, and even when they do, they have no say in determining who will compete to be a candidate (there are no primary elections for primary elections). Those who compete to be candidates are self-chosen, if they are already among the wealthy notables, or also chosen by those who are prominent and powerful in the political parties. At no point are the people encouraged to choose whomever they wish. The eligible candidates are carefully selected for them beforehand.

Such facts have become true of politics in the United States because of the United States Constitution. They did not and could not become true of it under the Articles of Confederation. Such facts also prove the United States to be an oligarchy according to Aristotle's definition. For if we run through the features of oligarchy in his list we will see that each applies to the United States:

1 All the offices are chosen from some, namely the rich and privileged and their protégés.
2 These some are always the rulers (as a class if not as individuals) while the poor and unprivileged are always ruled.
3 No offices are chosen by lot.
4 High property qualifications are, *de facto* if not *de iure*, required for office.
5 The same individuals, by being repeatedly re-elected, occupy the same office often or always.
6 All the offices are of long duration (none last only a year).
7 The same class or their protégés also become the judges and lawyers and decide questions of law, even controlling, to a large extent, the composition of juries; certainly this class and the elected officials control the most important cases, as those to do with the giving of accounts and with the regime and private contracts.
8 There is no popular assembly and the people as such control nothing.
9 There is no need for public pay, save in the case of juries; the people are not paid to vote, or only unofficially and illegally, if they promise to vote for him who pays them (elected officials are paid, of course, with both salary and expenses, but the effect is to enhance the wealth of the wealthy, not to provide leisure for the poor to engage in politics).
10 The rulers have the defining marks of family, wealth, and education.

11 The offices of monarch and the monarch's governor, as existed in each colony under British rule but were overthrown during the American Revolution, have been restored under the Constitution in the form of the President and the State Governors, and these offices have the same or more power than before and are all chosen by election.

Not all these features were necessarily realized at once (as in particular the choosing of Senators, which, as already noted, has only been by popular election since 1913). But the chief oligarchic features were there from the beginning. Moreover, some of these features are achieved by what Aristotle calls oligarchic sophistry, as item 4, since the requirement of high property qualification for office is not a matter of law but of the nature of election campaigns. For only the wealthy could afford the expense or the time or could secure the number of supporters to win election or even, indeed, to get their name on the ballot. The case, in fact, is analogous to Aristotle's example of oligarchs permitting all to have arms but ensuring, by the imposition of fines, that none but fellow oligarchs either have them or learn to use them. So, in the United States all are permitted to run for office but only the wealthy could afford to do so or have any serious chance of winning. That one may be an oligarch, not by one's own personal wealth, but through membership in a party whose candidate for a given election one has managed to become, makes no difference. The candidate inherits, as it were, the wealth and support and time of the party for the purposes of winning the election.

Such political parties and their oligarchic character were known to Aristotle. He calls them political clubs, and thus describes their role in election campaigns:

> Oligarchies are ... changed from within, as through the rivalry of demagogues ... when those in the oligarchy are demagogues to the crowd, as the regime guardians were in Larissa, for instance, because it was the crowd that elected them. The same is true of all oligarchies where those who provide the rulers are not those who elect to office, but the offices are filled from high property qualifications or from political clubs, and those possessed of heavy arms or the populace do the electing.[18]

This passage describes almost to the letter the practice of elections to office in our own day. We call it representative democracy, as I remarked before. Indeed we pride ourselves on the discovery of representation, holding it to be something of which the ancients were ignorant.[19] But Aristotle knew of it. He refrained, however, from calling it either representation or democracy. He called it, as just indicated, demagogic oligarchy. Our term of representative democracy,[20] and our praise of it as a way to extend democracy to vastly greater numbers of people than ancient democracies ever conceived of, he would call oligarchic sophistry. It is a trick to make people believe they share rule when in fact they do not. We should, then, according to Aristotle, pride ourselves, if pride be the right word, not on discovering universal democracy but on discovering universal sophistry.

Modern Practice: Britain and France

The general oligarchic character of American politics under the Constitution is now true of virtually every nation on earth (the exceptions are tyrannies or military despotisms, which, if anything, just exaggerate the worst elements of oligarchy). In illustration I will take, but briefly, the cases of Britain and France.

Britain, or I should rather say England and Wales, had become effectively oligarchic by the revolution of Henry VIII, which had abolished the ancient religion and built on its ruins and its confiscated monastic lands a new class of very rich (new either in persons enriched or in degree of enrichment).[21] The autocratic monarchy of Henry declined under his Tudor and Stuart successors until a combination of the rising bourgeoisie and the new class of rich destroyed it entirely in the English Civil War. The subsequent Restoration of the monarchy under Charles II kept the gains of the Civil War by keeping the King weak, and these gains were cemented and further extended by the so-called Glorious Revolution of 1688 that replaced the autocratic James II with the pliant William III. The oligarchy, risen thus to power on theft and war and intrigue, dominated into the eighteenth century. The allegedly popular element in the regime, the House of Commons, was in fact under the control of the oligarchs, who both occupied the highest offices and appointed or elected many of its members, even if those they chose were sometimes men of ability (as notably Edmund Burke, the protégé in Parliament first of Lord Fermanagh and later, after an interlude as member for Bristol, of the Marquis of Rockingham). The oligarchy was perhaps more refined in outward manners because of the absence of popular election campaigns that marked and supported the oligarchy in America, but it was no less real as an oligarchy. The path was anyway opened up to Americanization by the several reform bills and other changes in electoral practice that took place during the nineteenth and early twentieth centuries. These changes were all in the direction of giving the vote to greater and greater numbers of electors from lower and lower classes until the process of winning election became, as it had long been in America, a question of the rich or those in the pay of the rich expending time and treasure on soliciting votes from the people in expensive election campaigns. The same extremes of electioneering were not reached, and have still not been reached, but the effect is no less oligarchic. The popularly elected, that is oligarchic, House of Commons has become the one seat of political power. The rest, the Monarchy and the Lords, oligarchic themselves in principle if not always crudely so, are mere appendages.

The progress in France has had the same result, for popular elections favouring oligarchs in the way described are as much the norm there as anywhere else. But the different course of events enables us to see another way in which oligarchy has achieved total dominance of the political world. The evidence is twofold, first from de Tocqueville's painstaking analysis of the Old Regime that preceded the Revolution, and second from the modern doctrine of the Rights of Man.

De Tocqueville proved that the centralization typical of France since the Revolution had already come to exist under the last years of the Old Regime. The difference was that while the outward forms of aristocracy and of feudalism still lingered on under the Old Regime they were swept away by the Revolution.[22] What was left was the pre-existing centralization. The natural consequence was that everything which had been determined by the central government of the King and his council was thereafter determined by the central governments that replaced it, whether republics or empires or restored monarchies, up to and including the current Fifth Republic.

These changes in political action were accompanied and facilitated by changes in political thought. I refer to the modern doctrine of rights begun by Hobbes but popularized in the French case by Rousseau. This doctrine is deceptively described as one of equal rights for all. Everything depends on what is meant by equality. Proportional equality, where each gets what is individually deserved, is an equality no less than is mathematical equality, where each gets what is quantitatively the same. Ancient and medieval doctrines of rights applied proportional equality to the distribution of political power and understood the divisions within society between which proportional equality held, notably the lords, the commons, the monarch, and the clergy, as relatively, but by no means absolutely, fixed. Moreover, medieval doctrines recognized, because of feudal practice, the differences of places and peoples and guaranteed to each their many separate practices and customs.[23] Rights in the medieval world were realized in a host of differences between classes and places and persons.

The modern doctrine of rights took offence at medieval difference and sought to abolish it with universal sameness. The cry of equality became, in practice, the cry of uniformity,[24] and hence became, at the same time, the cry of revolution, for uniformity could only be introduced by overthrowing the existing difference. I quote one historian's judgment:

> Two world wars and the technological and industrial revolution have accelerated a development which began with Napoleon's liquidation of the Holy Roman Empire. Deliberately uprooted, the colourful diversity of life in Europe has gradually withered away. The great drive to make countries, political institutions and men uniform and conformist, the drive so successfully promoted by Richelieu, Mazarin, Louis XIV and the great revolution, in the nineteenth century also made its impact on the German central core of Old Europe. Englishmen and continental Europeans assisted alike in the forward march of this process through which Europe developed its technical, economic and military potential and made for itself new and freely expanding labour markets, spheres of influence and battle-grounds. Much has been lost to Europe as a result ... The Holy Roman Empire had contained within it many fatherlands and motherlands, all the greater and lesser principalities and lordships which it sheltered under its roof. Goethe remained a Frankfurter all his life. Schiller was a Swabian in exile. Beethoven's 'fatherland' was Bonn.[25]

Of course the difference and proportion prevalent and celebrated in all the parts of the Holy Roman Empire were not called difference and proportion by the purveyors of the modern doctrine of rights, but rather privilege and despotism. The charge is disingenuous. The modern doctrine of rights has introduced as much if not more privilege and despotism than the older one. The French Revolution is itself the classic instance since no man in the Old Regime, not even the monarch, ever held the power and authority over others' life and property that Robespierre or Napoleon managed to secure. There were too many restraints of law and right and custom ever to grant the monarch or lord so absolute a command. Moreover, for the same reason, no monarch or lord of medieval times ever held as much power over the people as modern presidents and prime ministers do. That modern presidents and prime ministers are elected, at least for the most part, while medieval lords and kings were hereditary, makes no difference, for the modern concentrations of power at the centre, however one comes by the right to exercise it, exceed by far anything that a medieval monarch could boast of. One has to return to the tyrants of the ancient world to find parallels.

Where equality is understood, as it is in the modern doctrine of rights, to be uniformity, the result is not only revolution but also centralization. In the case of France, therefore, the doctrine just went to confirm and to find reciprocal support in the centralization already achieved by the Old Regime. Ancient and medieval rulers had not been able to control things easily from the centre, not because of absence of personnel or technology, but because of absence of uniformity. Each locality, being different in its customs and so also in its rights, had to be treated according to its customs and rights, and a law or command from the centre adapted to the peculiarities of one locale would not fit those of another, so that there had to be almost as many commands as there were locales.[26] The new doctrine of equal rights repudiated difference, so that people not only ceased to possess, but even ceased to believe, the right to be different. The force of command from the centre could thus proceed directly to all the parts without being diverted or checked or modified by either the fact or the conviction of local difference. Centralization became real in thought and in deed. When, therefore, through the process of elections and universal suffrage, the reins of centralized power fell, as they have now fallen, into the hands of the wealthy (however dependent the wealthy may be on periodic displays of electoral support), the triumph of oligarchy became complete.

Conclusion

Aristotle would recognize the oligarchy of modern rule but he would perhaps be surprised by the universality of its success. If he had an explanation, it would be found in what he says of business and the tendency of business to corrupt both thought and practice and to twist everything into versions of itself.[27] Business, at least in its form as pursuit of money and not the real wealth of natural sufficiency, has no natural limits.[28] So oligarchy too, as founded on money (whether through industry or taxation or theft or fraud or all of them together), has no natural limits. Since Aristotle would also deny that political freedom could be found outside the small size of ancient republics (in which conviction he was followed by the American Anti-Federalists but opposed by the American Federalists),[29] he would have to view modern oligarchic states, not as communities of the free, but as extensive barbarian tyrannies.[30] To return, then, to my question from the beginning about a collective noun for oligarchs, we should perhaps, inspired by Aristotle, speak of a *globalization*, or *global corruption*, of oligarchs. For this word, as currently used, would capture all of modern oligarchy's corrupting effects: its worldwide extension, its destruction of difference and political freedom, its turning of everything into moneymaking and organized theft.

NOTES

1 *Politics* 1297a17–19. All translations of the *Politics* are taken from Peter Simpson, *The Politics of Aristotle* (Chapel Hill: University of North Carolina Press, 1997).
2 *Politics* 1297a36–8.
3 *Politics* 1317a40–18a3.
4 Craig Cooper, in his essay 'Oligarchy and the Rule of Law' in this same volume, mentions freedom of speech as characteristic of democracy. Aristotle does not and for good reason. Freedom of speech has not in any age been a feature of democracies any more than of oligarchies. The passage from Aeschines that Cooper quotes proves the point, for Aeschines warns his hearers to be on their guard against those 'whose speeches ... are contrary to the laws,' that is, who speak against democracy. Laws reflect the regime, as Aristotle himself noted (*Politics* 1281a34–8), and laws in a democracy are as biased towards democracy as laws in an oligarchy are towards oligarchy. Oligarchs could give the same advice to fellow oligarchs about those who speak against oligarchic laws. No regime of any kind can tolerate much opposition, verbal or otherwise, to its fundamental convictions. Freedom of speech is an ideological slogan, not an activating principle of political life.
5 *Politics* 1320b18–20.
6 *Politics* 1317a29–35.

7 *Politics* 1297a14–34.

8 *Politics* 1297b37–1298a3.

9 For the Articles of Confederation I have used Yale University's online Avalon Project, http://avalon.law.yale.edu/18th_century/artconf.asp (accessed 6 October 2009).

10 For the U.S. Constitution I have used Yale University's online Avalon Project, http://avalon.law.yale.edu/18th_century/usconst.asp (accessed 6 October 2009).

11 *Politics* 1300a31–b5.

12 The practice of having ballots and of naming candidates on a ballot is not specified in the Constitution, but it is not forbidden and must have become the norm very early on. The option of writing in any name not already printed on the ballot (a 'write-in' candidate), while always available, is of little significance. It does nothing to make the voting a case of all choosing from all as opposed to all choosing from some.

13 *Politics* 1271a9–18.

14 *Politics* 1303a13–16.

15 *Politics* 1273a35–b5.

16 Notable recent examples are the billions of dollars misappropriated in the oil for food scandal at the UN and the billions of dollars in U.S. military aid to Pakistan misappropriated by Pakistani officials to finance almost anything but the military.

17 *Politics* 1291b28–30, 1293a26–32.

18 *Politics* 1305b22–33.

19 The express opinion of Hamilton in *Federalist Papers* no. 9 and Madison in *Federalist Papers* no. 10, available at Yale's Avalon Project, http://avalon.law.yale.edu/subject_menus/fed.asp (accessed 6 October 2009).

20 The term may have been coined by Hamilton, and, since Hamilton was no friend of democracy, the fact that the term does not describe anything that can fairly be called democratic should come as no surprise. Jeff Sikkenga, in his essay 'Overcoming Oligarchy: Republicanism and the Right to Property in *The Federalist*' in this volume, regards Hamilton and the other authors of the *Federalist Papers* as men of wisdom and prudence whose thinking is much to be admired. The Anti-Federalists regarded them and proponents of the Constitution in general as deceivers and enemies of freedom. One has to read the writings of these Anti-Federalists to get a fair sense of what the Constitutional Convention was all about. As Aristotle's analysis of oligarchy well shows, the *Federalist Papers* are oligarchic propaganda.

21 To get a clear picture of the killing and plunder carried out by Henry VIII and his agents one has to turn to unconventional authors. I have used:

Gilbert Keith Chesterton, *A Short History of England* (London: Chatto and Windus, 1917); William Cobbett, *A History of the Protestant Reformation in England and Ireland* (London: Anne Cobbett, 1846); Eamon Duffy, *The Stripping of the Altars. Traditional Religion in England 1400–1580* (New Haven, CT: Yale University Press, 1992).

22 Alexis De Tocqueville, *L'Ancien Régime* [1856] (Paris: Les Éditions Gallimard, 1952, book 2, chaps. 2–5.

23 See in particular book 2 chapter 3 of de Tocqueville's *L'ancien régime*, and also R.W. and A.J. Carlyle, *A History of Medieval Political Theory in the West* (London: Blackwood and Sons, 1903–36). This work is probably best consulted by going first through the conclusions or summaries of its several volumes.

24 Article 6, for instance, of the French Declaration of the Rights of Man and of the Citizen (1789) reads: 'The law is the expression of the general will. All citizens have the right to take part, in person or by their representatives, in its formation. It must be the same for everyone whether it protects or penalizes. All citizens being equal in its eyes are equally admissible to all public dignities, offices, and employments, according to their ability, and with no other distinction than that of their virtues and talents.' This article does not, perhaps, strictly entail uniformity but it suggests it. Certainly it does nothing to favour difference. The text of the Declaration can be found at the Center for History and New Media of George Mason University, http://chnm.gmu.edu/revolution/d/295/ (accessed 6 October 2009).

25 Friedrich Heer, *The Holy Roman Empire*, trans. Janet Sondheimer (New York: Praeger, 1968), 279.

26 See the references to de Tocqueville and the two Carlyles in the earlier notes.

27 *Politics* 1257b40–58a18. This point is adverted to by Waller Newell in the concluding section of his essay in this volume, 'Oligarchy and *Oikonomia*: Aristotle's Ambivalent Assessment of Private Property.' Newell also contrasts the liberal commercial republic of the United States with the illiberal commercial republics now emerging in China and Russia. There are indeed two kinds of regime here, but Aristotle would regard both as kinds of oligarchy (for oligarchy has several kinds) and therefore as each bad in principle even if the first is less despotic than the second. Jeff Sikkenga in his essay quoted above also rightly notes the commercial acquisitiveness that marks modern states. The emancipation of acquisitiveness, which, as Sikkenga rightly notes, plays a decisive role in the defence of the U.S. Constitution propagated by the *Federalist*, does indeed seem to be what has made global oligarchy possible.

28 *Politics* 1257b23–30.
29 For the Federalists see Madison again in *Federalist Papers* no. 10, and for the Anti-Federalists the piece by Cato listed as the 14th of the *Antifederalist Papers*, http://www.wepin.com/articles/afp/afp14.html (accessed 6 October 2009).
30 *Politics* 1285a16–30, 1295a11–17, 1326a35–b24.

5 The Threat of Misguided Elites: Aristotle on Oligarchy

STEVEN C. SKULTETY

Introduction: The Nastiness of Aristotle's Oligarchs

In large, modern, democratic countries, the threat of oligarchy seems rather remote. For it appears that the best candidates for modern oligarchs are influential captains of industry, the unimaginably opulent owners and operators of large corporations, and well-known wealth fund managers. Yet, while citizens are obviously worried about the ups and downs of the complicated financial system in which such wealthy individuals play an important role, the super-affluent themselves do not seem to form any sort of cohesive political threat. Not only are their views scattered across the political spectrum, but they also do not seem terribly interested in politics. Indeed, if Hollywood and television are any guide to how most people imagine contemporary oligarchs, the rich look positively benign. Always background figures, they are inevitably sipping cocktails and watching polo matches, more or less relaxing, while a non-oligarchic protagonist furiously battles a tyrannical antagonist who was never satisfied with being a mere oligarch. Again, in the media at large, if there is a persistent worry expressed about our contemporary version of oligarchs, it is only that these well-heeled people have become too comfortable and insensitive to the struggles of their fellow citizens. They are not accused of sinister plotting, but chided for moral laxity.

It is quite a shock, then, to open Aristotle's *Politics* and find people called 'oligarchs' who, far from relaxing in the lap of luxury, are taking the oath: 'I will be hostile to the people and shall plan whatever evil [*kakon*] I can against them,' and forming constitutions whose very mission is, in part, 'to ill-treat the multitude, drive them out of the

town, and disperse them.'[1] Nor are these examples extreme exceptions: throughout Aristotle's analysis, oligarchs are noticeably disrup-
tive. Whenever they find themselves living in a city that does not
explicitly embrace their conception of justice, they almost always start
a civil war, and, unlike poor democrats who have antipathy only
toward the rich, Aristotle's oligarchs are just as ready to fight other oligarchs as they are the multitude.[2] Never content to play a supporting
role, these oligarchs are a quarrelsome lot of animated actors who
want to lead on the civic stage.

We could use such passages to argue that Aristotle has nothing to
teach the modern world about oligarchy. We might say that given the
cultural-historical milieu of fourth-century Athens, permeated with
memories of the horrendous life-and-death struggles of the fifth century (and, in particular, the Spartan-backed repressive rule of the
Thirty from 404–403 BCE), it makes sense that Aristotle would encum-
ber his oligarchs in this fashion. But times have changed. In the world
of large-scale nation-states with far different political terrains and histories, Aristotle's analysis can offer the reader little more than a
glimpse into a raucous world long passed.

Without a doubt, there are a number of historical relics in the *Politics* –
but I do not think that Aristotle's analysis of oligarchy is one of them.
Indeed, rather than thinking of their surprising militancy as a reason to
set them aside as historical curiosities, the shock of Aristotle's analysis
can serve as something of a wake-up call, demanding the reader to ask
whether he or she has not been lulled into a kind of complacency. Our
benign oligarchs may be far more pernicious than we are willing to
admit. Worse still, we might not be applying the term 'oligarchs' to the
correct group of people.

The Centrality of Belief about Merit

Why are Aristotle's oligarchs so pugnacious? To answer that question,
we first need to comprehend his conception of what exactly makes an
oligarch an oligarch. Unfortunately, Aristotle never provides an official definition of an oligarch, but we can piece together his conception
by collecting and comparing the various traits he ascribes to oligarchs
at different places in his work.[3]

The first, and most obvious, aspect of oligarchic identity is numerical. After all, the term 'oligarchy' is derived from the word *'oligos,'*
which means few, and in *Politics* 3.6, it is the numerical attribute of

rulers – whether they are 'one, few, or many' – that is put to use in distinguishing different kinds of constitutions. Aristotle uses this trait in his classificatory scheme because, in the world as we happen to find it, this numerical attribute often does an adequate job of picking out oligarchs from other political actors: walk into an average non-ideal city and ask to meet with the 'few' and you will probably end up speaking to oligarchs. By contrast, ask to meet with the 'many,' and you will probably end up speaking to democrats.[4]

Yet soon after using this attribute in his classification, Aristotle makes it clear that the numerical trait, while distinctive, does not provide a relevant answer to the question 'Who are these people?' He argues for this point in *Politics* 3.8 by asking the reader to engage in a thought experiment in which one city is ruled by a rich majority and another ruled by a poor minority. The former city, he maintains, should still be called an oligarchy because of the economic status of the rulers: the rulers, though a majority, are best identified by the fact that they are rich; similarly, the latter constitution should be called a democracy because the rulers are poor.

But neither the numerical nor economic trait, it turns out, is as critical to Aristotle's conception of oligarchs as its distinctive theory of distributive justice. Though oligarchic and democratic conceptions of merit are two instances of the universally held notion that a person's deserts should be proportional to his worth,[5] they employ quite different conceptions of worth: democrats determine a person's worth based on his free citizenship[6] and oligarchs measure it by wealth. A careful reading of *Politics* 3.8 shows that, of the three traits discussed so far, only the merit component really defines these political actors. For although Aristotle says that, 'What does distinguish democracy and oligarchy from one another is poverty and wealth' – which might sound like a clear endorsement of the centrality of the economic trait for identity – he goes on to finish his thought this way:

> Whenever some, whether a minority or a majority, rule because of their wealth [*dia plouton*], the constitution is necessarily [*anagkaion*] an oligarchy, and whenever the poor rule, it is necessarily a democracy. But it turns out, as we said, that the former are in fact few and the latter many. For only a few people are rich, but all share in freedom; and these are the reasons they both dispute [*di' has aitias amphisbētousin*] over the constitution.[7]

The numerical trait is obviously being downgraded severely ('whether a minority or majority'); more importantly, we see that the belief about merit is sharply upgraded above wealth. For notice that it is not the wealth of rulers per se that makes a city an oligarchy, but the fact that the city has people rule *because of* [*dia*] it. When citizens hold a belief that wealth $\underset{\cdot}{m}$erits rule, it is this fact about rulers which makes it necessary [*anagkaion*] to identify it as an oligarchy. Similarly, while it is distinctive of a democracy that it is controlled by the poor, it turns out that the fact that these 'all share in freedom' (the object of the democratic belief about merit) is most central. Wealth and freedom, not wealth and poverty, are the '*reasons* they both dispute over the constitution.'[8]

There is a rather striking passage in Aristotle's account of constitutional change that makes this same point. In the course of criticizing Plato's account of political transformations, Aristotle insists that it is the merit aspect of an oligarch's identity, and absolutely *not* his economic status, that defines the type of constitution that results from revolution:

> It is also absurd [*atopon*] to hold that a constitution changes into an oligarchy because the office holders are money lovers and acquirers of wealth, and not because those who are far superior in property holdings *think it unjust* for those who do not own anything to participate equally in the *polis* with those who do.[9]

I take this as yet more evidence that economic status is not helpful for giving an account of oligarchs as political actors. The fact that they are 'far superior in property holdings' will distinguish them in society. But though wealth is a distinctive property – and the fact that a person cannot be both rich and poor[10] helps to ensure that it is distinctive – it is not this trait which discloses the relevant political information.

Based on these reflections, we can concoct our own thought experiment inspired by *Politics* 3.8. Suppose Aristotle was confronted with a group of people who were poor, who made up the majority of inhabitants, and yet who also firmly believed that wealth entitled a person to rule. Aristotle, I believe, would insist that such people should be called oligarchs. Their belief about merit is the most central aspect of their political identity.[11]

Emotion and the *Haplōs* Mistake

But there must be more to an oligarch than his wealth-based conception of merit. After all, Aristotle depicts oligarchs as having a

fundamentally *despotic* attitude and uses this despotism to differentiate oligarchic constitutions from others. In *Politics* 3.7, Aristotle lays
out his famous six-fold classification of constitutions by making use
of the numerical distinction among rule by one, few, or many, as
well as a distinction between 'correct' and 'incorrect' rule. The latter
distinction is explained in 3.6 as follows. If rulers benefit themselves
first and foremost, and the community only coincidentally (if at all),
then their rule resembles that which a master takes toward his slave
and is 'incorrect' in a community of equals. On the other hand, if rulers look after themselves coincidentally (if at all), and look to the
welfare of the community first and foremost, then their rule is political and 'correct' among equals. Oligarchs, Aristotle claims, are rulers
who embrace this 'masterly' attitude that makes their constitution
incorrect.

But what explains such an 'incorrect' and despotic outlook? Surely
an oligarch's conception of merit is insufficient. After all, a person
can endorse oligarchic justice without thinking that the rich should
take the less fortunate for granted; indeed, many university adminis-
trators embrace this type of non-despotic oligarchic justice when –
keenly aware that some departments generate millions of dollars for
the school while others only spend money – they let some departments have more say in university decisions than others. This kind
of justice may be misguided, but that does not make it *despotic*. Moreover, this conception of justice in no way helps to explain the harsh
militancy of Aristotle's oligarchs that I described at the beginning of
this essay.[12]

To explain such behaviours and attitudes, I believe Aristotle attri-
butes two additional traits to ancient oligarchs, the first of which is the
emotion of arrogance. Because of the licence they were given during an
excessively privileged upbringing,[13] oligarchs characteristically suffer
from the emotional excess of hubris or arrogance.[14] This emotion, Aristotle thinks, especially in a political setting where it comes face to face
with many poor people who are envious, can apparently transform a
merely rich person into an oligarch who acts like a master:

> This results in a city coming into being that is made up of slaves and
> masters, rather than free people: the one group full of envy and the other
> full of arrogance. Nothing is further removed from a friendship and a
> community that is political. For community is friendly; when people are
> enemies, they do not wish to share even a journey in common.[15]

Arrogance and envy help to explain why oligarchs and democrats act more like oil and water than disinterested citizens ready to engage in constitutional debate.

But in addition to the emotion of arrogance, I think it is quite significant that Aristotle repeatedly mentions a distinct *conceptual* mistake that oligarchs make – an error I will call the '*haplōs*' mistake. In both *Politics* 3.9 and 5.1, we find the same succinct description of the origin of democratic and oligarchic beliefs: democracy originates from the inference that since people are equal in some *one* way (they are all free), they are equal, period [*haplōs*]; similarly, oligarchs think that inequality in one respect (being wealthy) means inequality in all respects.[16] The idea here is not simply a repetition of the claim that oligarchs and democrats adopt the wrong criterion of worth (freedom and wealth, rather than virtue), but rather that both groups have a predilection for making a particular invalid inference to reach these conclusions about justice.

In order to appreciate the contribution that the *haplōs* mistake makes to oligarchic identity, consider a rich person who merely begins with the incorrect belief that rule should be proportioned to financial contributions to the city. As I said before, we have no reason to accuse such a person of despotism. But now let us imagine that this same person is so wedded to the *haplōs* fallacy that he quite honestly cannot think of a *single* respect in which he and his wealthy peers are not better than poorer citizens. Go on to couple this inability to conceive of equality in *any* respect with a strong dose of emotional arrogance. What will be the result? Perhaps we should here recall Mill's apt observation that there are psychological conditions in which an astoundingly large 'difference in degree' can become 'a real difference in kind.'[17] For when a belief about wealth-based merit is coupled in a person's mind with the *haplōs* mistake and emotional arrogance, surely it becomes likely that he will assume that the group of ruling rich is better *in kind* from those who are not so privileged – and it is the belief that the ruling element is different in kind from the ruled element that makes an attitude resemble that which a master adopts toward slave.[18] With the addition of arrogance and the *haplōs* fallacy, we have transformed a person with merely a wealth-based conception of merit into someone who has profound disregard for those who lack resources.

Happiness and Oligarchic Deliberation

To this already complex portrait of the oligarch, Aristotle adds one last crucial feature: they possess a distinctive conception of happiness – a conception of the highest human good. While aristocrats take happiness to be the exercise of virtue, and democrats take it to be doing whatever one likes, each inhabitant of a city living 'according to his fancy,' Aristotle claims that the overarching goal for oligarchs is wealth acquisition.[19]

What difference will recognizing this distinctive conception of *eudaimonia* make to our understanding of oligarchs? Aristotle, I believe, wants to emphasize three things. First, in the case of both democrats and oligarchs, their different conceptions of happiness help to explain the origin and persistence of their different conceptions of merit. It is not clear that adopting a given conception of justice tells us much about a person's conception of happiness, but Aristotle suggests that knowing a person's conception of happiness helps to explain her conception of justice. Consider, for example, the following claim about democrats: 'In this way the second goal [of living as one likes] contributes to freedom based on equality.'[20] Note the direction of the causality: a democratic conception of justice does not lead one to live as one likes; rather, living as one likes leads one to a democratic conception of justice. In this capacity, then, telling the reader about an oligarch's conception of happiness is a way of explaining why oligarchs adopt their conception of merit; conceiving of wealth as the basis of desert emerges from the belief that it is the rich person who is genuinely flourishing as a human being.

Second, recognizing this conception of happiness allows us to appreciate the final end towards which oligarchs will want to orient the overarching political decisions that bear on citizens' common life together. Conceptions of justice influence decisions about who gets which honours and offices, and how rectificatory disputes should be resolved; but conceptions of happiness govern a far wider class of political considerations. For example, what festivals and celebrations should the city recognize? In what pursuits should young citizens be educated and encouraged? At which ultimate goal should political deliberators aim their policies? As is clear from his description of the ideal city in *Politics* 7 and 8, and his repeated criticisms of the Spartan constitution which aims at little more than military victory, Aristotle believes that different conceptions of happiness will lead to better or worse answers to the overarching questions that fall beyond the concerns of justice. Citizens who possess clashing conceptions of happiness, like democrats and oligarchs, are not merely advancing divergent policy positions on a narrowly defined subject, but embracing entirely different outlooks about the basic orientation of the polis.

The third – and what I take to be the most important – reason that Aristotle gives oligarchs a distinctive theory of *eudaimonia*, however, is to show that wealth seriously distorts the manner in which they weigh pros and cons in civic decision making. Wealth acquisition is not just one more mistaken conception of *eudaimonia* among others, but engenders a very special type of deliberative error.

But before describing this defect, it is necessary to issue a disclaimer: in criticizing wealth acquisition as a highest aim, Aristotle is not attacking the possession of wealth as such; he is not someone who treats money as the root of all evils. On the contrary, Aristotle insists that citizens must have enough money to run a successful household,[21] and it turns out that this is a rather considerable sum, especially for politically active citizens: they must have funds sufficient for meeting the needs of both family and friends, enabling the virtues of generosity and even magnificence, and allowing for the periodic performance of public services [*leitourgiai*] for the community.[22] Furthermore, ideally, a citizen should be able to adopt a civilized, leisurely life that is 'both free and temperate.'[23] A happy citizen should be wealthy enough to take advantage of a life 'free' from mere labour – and this is why Aristotle makes wealth a necessary (though not sufficient) good in a happy and well-lived life.[24]

Yet, despite this necessity, wealth has a major shortcoming as a highest good. Just as 'medicine aims at *unlimited* health, and each craft aims to achieve its end in an *unlimited* way,' so too the aim of wealth acquisition in the form of money is unlimited.[25] By itself, the fact that crafts do not generate their own limit does not imply that they are hopelessly unmanageable. When subordinated to another end, they can be circumscribed: indeed, Aristotle points out that wealth in the service of a properly run household has just such a limit,[26] and it is clear that wealth acquisition in a well-run city is similarly bounded. After all, properly run cities adopt the ultimate end of virtuous activity and, in Aristotle's ethical theory, virtue is a mean. Taken as a target, it demands attention to limits, boundaries, and avoiding excess.[27] When, on the other hand, possessing wealth is taken as an end, the goal becomes infinite.

Aristotle has a rather interesting account of both the causes and the effects of people taking wealth to be the highest end. He describes the cause this way: 'The reason they are so disposed [toward wealth] is that they are preoccupied with living, not with living well. And since their appetite for life is unlimited, they also want an unlimited amount of what sustains it.'[28] Notice that what lies behind money-lust is not so much selfishness or greediness as much as *aimlessness*: unencumbered by any legitimate notion of excellence, the person who merely accepts what life brings him is the one most easily seduced by the thought that you can never have enough money. For living, by itself, issues forth an unending string of desires, all of which request satisfaction in excess of what virtue recommends; as a result, 'since their gratification lies in excess, they seek the craft that produces the excess needed for gratification.'[29] Worse still, anyone who inhabits a household (which, for Aristotle, is the institution most concerned with life)[30] will daily see that there really is a great need for money.[31] Thus, even the most rudimentary social existence (let alone the opulent lifestyle to which oligarchs are exposed early in life) is capable of featuring desires that recommend the pursuit of limitless wealth.

The effect of taking money acquisition to be *eudaimonia* are two. First, Aristotle thinks that someone who devotes his life to money-making puts something like a category mistake at the heart of his life plan. After all, money is an instrumental good: it is only valuable inasmuch as it can be used to purchase something that is not money. Someone, therefore, who announces that wealth acquisition is his ultimate aim has, in fact, not really identified an ultimate aim at all. This is why Aristotle issues such a curt dismissal of wealth in his introductory survey of widely held conceptions of happiness: 'Clearly wealth is not the [highest] good we are seeking since it is merely useful for some other end.'[32] But besides conceptual incoherence, Aristotle thinks that someone who identifies wealth with *eudaimonia* suffers from some version of 'the Midas problem.' After a period, such a person is unable to appreciate the value of anything except insofar as it generates wealth. For example,

> the end of courage is not to produce wealth but to produce confidence in the face of danger; nor is it the end of generalship or medicine to do so, but rather victory and health. None the less, these people make all of these into forms of wealth acquisition in the belief that acquiring wealth is the end, and that everything ought to promote the end.[33]

Everything in an oligarch's life is reduced to an instrumental value which itself is never given direction.

But Aristotle's concern over citizens with this conception of *eudaimonia* is not limited to the worry that they might lead ethically monotone and conceptually confused lives. The political consequences of having such people serve as decision makers are equally problematic. On the one hand, if rulers take wealth acquisition to be the highest goal a human being can have, it will be difficult indeed to convince them that they should refrain from promoting some shameful, provocative, or even unjust action that would vastly increase the city's fortune. Again, and perhaps even more worryingly, it will be impossible to convince such rulers that the city has ever reached the point of being sufficiently rich – that a specific, limited goal has been attained, and that the pursuit for increasing wealth can stop.

As political actors operating under such a limitless conception of happiness, we might thus compare oligarchs to drivers who can always find new reasons to give the car more gas, but can find fewer and fewer reasons to step on the brake – with the inevitable result that the oligarchic political car is doomed to meet a curve at too great a speed. It is thus no surprise that a major theme of the middle books of the *Politics* is that unchecked oligarchs, behaving as oligarchs through and through, will always run their constitutions off the road. In the purist oligarchy where only the richest of rich have power, law disappears and the regime solidifies into a tyrannical 'dynasty.'[34] Such a dynasty is not an accidental result, but rather the inescapable result of trying to make the constitution fully embody an oligarchic conception of happiness.[35] Aristotle is quite adamant about this: it is oligarchs who take oligarchic virtue (i.e., wealth) as the one and only virtue that constitutes happiness who 'push the constitution to extremes.'[36] This also explains why the heart of Aristotle's advice to oligarchic partisans is that they abandon the attempt to make their constitutions as wealthy as possible and instead act more strategically to do 'the things that will enable [them] to *govern* oligarchically.'[37]

This, however, will be easier said than done; Aristotle is making a recommendation that *cuts against* the course oligarchs will want to take *qua* oligarchs. He is recommending that they act strategically *despite themselves*.[38] This explains why his recommendations for creating lawful forms of oligarchy never mention changing the souls of oligarchs, but rather outline strategies for isolating the influence of oligarchs.[39] Note too that Aristotle's 'middle regime' – the best constitution that most cities can realistically achieve – is not one in which the hearts and minds of oligarchs are reformed: rather, it is one in which the oligarchs are simply swamped with middle-class citizens.[40]

Oligarchy and Discriminatory Elitism

We now have collected all the components that constitute Aristotle's complex portrait of oligarchs. Oligarchs are people who believe that a person's worth is measured in money, are arrogant, believe that they are better in kind than the non-rich (and thus treat them despotically), and, finally, possess a limitless conception of human flourishing that both nourishes their conception of justice and continually motivates them to conceive of everything in the city as a tool of unending wealth creation.

But how shall we characterize the whole that is created from these parts? To answer this question, consider the figure of Cylon, who reportedly took an Olympic victory as a reason to aim at becoming tyrant of Athens in 632 BCE.[41] Here we have someone who is guilty of a particular kind of political fallacy: he begins with his success in one realm of activity – his superior ranking in the realm of sport – and then incorrectly infers that this higher standing in the non-political realm should translate into increased political importance. Now, elitism in general is simply the idea that a special group (the elites) is uniquely deserving of power and privilege in political life. But notice that Cylon is engaged in a special sort of *discriminatory* elitism in which he sets himself above others in the political arena because of a higher ranking in a realm that has no connection to political excellence.

I propose that the four characterological and intellectual properties discussed so far are supposed to show that oligarchs advocate a special breed of discriminatory elitism. First, oligarchs have a conception of human flourishing that blinds them to the fact that the realm of politics is *different in kind* from the realm of finance.[42] So, whereas Cylon mistakenly identified excellence in sport with excellence in politics, oligarchs mistakenly associate success in wealth acquisition with politics, and this mistaken conception of *eudaimonia* produces and entrenches an equally flawed conception of desert. But this is not the only similarity: Cylon did not wish merely to participate in Athenian government; he wanted to be an undisputed ruler who could *dominate* non-rulers – he was making a bid for tyranny. Yet this, as we have seen, resembles the oligarchs' desire: although they are not tyrants, their rule is despotic because they believe they should be able to dominate those they rule. In fact, there is a sense in which Aristotle's oligarchs have adopted a more extreme political outlook than even

Cylon: the *haplōs* mistake leads oligarchs from the premise of their inequality in wealth to the conclusion that no one could conceivably be their equal in *any* realm; it is as if Cylon took his inequality in athletic prowess to entail his superiority in everything from foot speed, to horse racing, to aesthetics, to philosophy, to political decision making.

With the components of their personalities identified, and the whole of their character revealed, we can at last appreciate why Aristotle's oligarchs are so pugnacious. These are not people who merely wish to relax in self-satisfaction, covering over their selfishness with a bit of political spin. On the contrary, Aristotle's oligarchs deeply believe that *true justice* is on their side, and that wealth accumulation is the only *credible* view of human success, and that to let lower sorts of people into the political decision-making process would be to let the incompetent push the city toward certain disaster. After all, from the perspective of Aristotle's oligarchs, only the rich comprehend all of what life has to offer: the poor do not understand how wealth works, they do not understand why wealth acquisition is so important for the city, and the poor will simply orient the city toward goals that waste money – that is, for the oligarch, unhappiness.

Oligarchs and the Continuing Threat of Contempt

Can we find anything in Aristotle's analysis of oligarchy that will help us to understand our own political situation? Political philosophers are often sceptical that Aristotle can aid us in political thought. His philosophy (it is said) is irrelevant because his conception of a flourishing community assumes that citizens inhabit small, homogeneous, conflict-free city-states, and his ethical theory elevates political participation to the status of a privileged ideal. Such a philosophy cannot be relevant for modern people who live in large, pluralistic nation-states, and for whom the political life is just one lifestyle choice among many others in civil society.

Regardless of what merit this argument has, it should be clear that Aristotle's analysis of oligarchy will not be rendered irrelevant because of it. Denying that Aristotle's positive vision is relevant in contemporary politics is perfectly compatible with an admission that he successfully analyses a *negative* condition that it is best to avoid. And, indeed, as we reflect on the details of Aristotle's account, it becomes clear that he is criticizing oligarchs for adopting an attitude that is strikingly ahistorical, and even apolitical. The very substance of his critique depicts oligarchy as a timeless, trans-historical mistake that can affect communities large and small, complex and simple. This is why, as soon as we ask whether there is any resemblance between Aristotle's oligarchs and those who inhabit the contemporary political realm, we are confronted with numerous similarities.

First, consider the politics of wealth. We have seen that Aristotle's oligarchs lead political lives exclusively centred upon money acquisition: rather than any idiosyncratic, historically bound ideal, it is wealth that defines their upbringing, their conception of worth, and even their conception of human happiness. Can there be any doubt that such money-centric citizens continue to be found within the political realm of modern nation-states? On the one hand, as Peter Simpson thoroughly analyses in his article for this volume, there is a great deal of evidence suggesting that 'money is the mother's milk of politics,' that large contributors to the two major parties have a disproportionately large say in determining who is picked to run in political races and what policies they advocate, and that elected politicians design political districts to act as money machines that lock them into perpetual re-election. On the other hand, even the specific components of Aristotle's unsavoury character sketch of oligarchs seem to be on regular display. While no one openly admits to having adopted an oligarchic conception of merit, it is hard to see how there is anything else behind the notion that 'you have to pay to play' in politics, or that you must have money 'to get your foot in the door.' Again, while no one wears a badge of self-proclaimed oligarchic arrogance, surely something like this fuels the notion that only those who travel extensively, who attend major national events, or who live in high-priced suburbs or cities are 'really living.' And, again, while no one calls it 'the *haplōs* mistake,' a move like this certainly helps to generate the familiar vocabulary of contempt that issues a distinction *in kind* between the poorer 'hicks' on the one hand, and the rich and trusted elites who stride atop the commanding heights, on the other. And, finally, as to whether there are people today who make money the ultimate goal in life, the answer seems painfully clear.

Yet the way in which Aristotle's analysis is relevant to contemporary politics extends beyond such a list of vague (albeit troubling) parallels. Rather, I think we can find within Aristotle's analysis three more specific lessons about oligarchs in contemporary political life. First, when worrying about the role of money in politics, it is tempting to think that this undue emphasis on wealth is the result of rampant greed, and that a less selfish citizenry would sufficiently inoculate political society against the proliferation of oligarchic types. Aristotle warns us that this is a misdiagnosis. He is, certainly, worried about the effect of greed on the polis[43] – but this, as we have seen, is not his problem with oligarchy. Rather than grabbing at power because of selfish lust, oligarchs are primarily driven by the distortion of an important truth: because of an arrogant belief that they are far more sophisticated than others, the *haplōs* mistake, and a misconceived conception of happiness and justice, they vastly overvalue what, in fact, *is* a valuable contribution to social welfare. This is why, despite their shared discriminatory outlook, Aristotle nevertheless makes a point of distinguishing Cylon from oligarchs. Whereas Cylon thinks that running speed legitimated political power – which seems so far-fetched as to be nothing more than a greedy power grab – Aristotle insists that the fight for political power among oligarchs, democrats, and aristocrats is based on plausible considerations: 'The dispute must be based on the things from which a *polis* is constituted. Hence the well-born, the free, and the rich reasonably lay claim to office.'[44]

This brings us to the second lesson. Readers will have noticed that Aristotle seems more interested in painting a psychological portrait of oligarchs than focusing on the abstract issues of what we would call 'constitutional law' or the 'legal rights and obligations' enshrined in oligarchies. This emphasis on political psychology makes sense: on the one hand, it is a matter of scholarly dispute as to whether the concepts of 'right' and 'obligation' can even be found in Aristotle's ethical or political thought;[45] but, second, the ancient conception of a constitution [*politeia*] was quite comprehensive, referring to the entire stable life pattern of a city, including norms that were written and unwritten, universal and particular, officially enacted and customarily adopted. Thus, when Aristotle considers oligarchy, he wants to do far more than describe this constitution's system [*taxis*] of offices and the procedures associated with them.[46] Rather, he thinks that the political scientist must reveal the entire outlook of those who are trying to order the city. Understanding the rulers in this way will help to explain why offices are set up the way they are, but will also shed light on the direction and orientation of the city beyond its merely official functions. Thus, Aristotle asks the political scientist to identify the *sort of person* who – to put it bluntly – is actually calling the shots in the city. This group, Aristotle says in *Politics* 3.6, this *politeuma*, is the constitution.[47]

If we want to understand the politics of a city as an Aristotelian, the question we must ask is not so much, 'What constitution does this city have?' but rather 'Who is the constitution here?'[48]

By emphasizing the role that character and outlook plays in politics, Aristotle offers us another lesson. Contemporary political philosophers strive to understand the ultimate conceptual foundations of current democratic constitutions; they articulate the procedural frameworks that best embody the crucial notions of justice, equal respect, and liberty. This is important work that needs to be done. But such worthwhile investigations will be incapable of protecting democracy from oligarchic threats if they neglect to ask Aristotle's question: 'At the end of the day, *who* does get to call the shots in this community? What is the best way to describe the outlook of people who end up being the *decision makers*?' Living in a country where rulers are determined by free and fair elections based on democratic principles in no way prevents permanent rule by Aristotelian oligarchs: just as the same team can win over and over again at a game with rules fair to all contestants, it is entirely possible to live in a society in which basic structures are democratic, but only oligarchs end up in office, year after year, election after election. Aristotle's analysis of oligarchy keeps us alive to this possibility.

Yet is there any reason to worry about this? Despite the influence of money in politics, despite the list of similarities I listed above, and even despite the recent, unprecedented relationships between democratic governments and businesses 'too large to fail,' it still sounds conspiratorial to claim that oligarchs are always the winners in the democratic game; the idea that the wealthy are controlling all major policy decisions sounds hyperbolic, even in the realm of money-soaked American politics. After all, we can think of many mega-rich citizens who have little political clout, and others of humble origin who went on to become political stars.

This brings us, however, to what is perhaps the deepest lesson of all in Aristotle's analysis of oligarchy: though wealth can be a good indicator of whether someone is an oligarch, oligarchy, in the end, does not really concern wealth. Fundamentally, Aristotle's oligarch is someone who believes that the contribution he is making to the city is the fundamental contribution. For, as he sees it, he is providing the very thing that makes human life flourish, and then concluding that only people like him deserve to steer the community toward happiness. Having chosen a limitless good as his highest end, and arrogant enough to make the *haplōs* mistake, the dangerous oligarchic character emerges.

Notice, though, that it need not be wealth that an oligarch seeks: any important, limitless good can serve as a misguided goal.[49] Consider, for example, what we call 'information.' An 'information economy' surely *does* depend on those who possess, store, and disseminate information. Now imagine an information savant who grew up surrounded by lavish intellectual and educational opportunities – a person who, at an early age, became aware of his superior ability at handling such things and correctly perceived that such acumen was crucial to the proper maintenance of society. After being praised and rewarded for his talents, can we not imagine a bit of arrogance moving in to help him make the *haplōs* conclusion that he and his information-savvy peers are simply in a different league – a different class – than those 'out in the sticks'? And will not such a person find it inconceivable that someone could deserve to be a political decision maker if he cannot even comprehend the demands of an information economy? Could this person imagine a point at which society had reached the point of having too much information? Here we have an infinite ideal, unlimited by any fixed political boundary. We could run the same thought experiment with health, security, trade, complex legal codes, and many other limitless goods that are crucial to the well-being of large, modern societies. Each can play exactly the same role that wealth plays for Aristotle's oligarchs; each has the potential to serve as the locus of an oligarchic outlook.

Aristotle might think that reducing greed and wealth inequality is beneficial for society, but he would not think it prevents oligarchic rule. Indeed, even among those who are quite selfless and of modest means, rigid discriminatory elitism can thrive. According to Aristotle, the only way to combat the threat of oligarchy effectively is to convince citizens to adopt a conception of happiness that is limited rather than unlimited, and steer young people away from the arrogant notion that early recognition by prestigious institutions legitimates the conclusion that they are better in kind than their peers. Without such a conception, and without such an upbringing, oligarchic governance within a democratic framework may be impossible to avoid.

NOTES

1 Aristotle, *Politics* 1310a9–10, 1311a10–15. All references to the *Politics* are based on W.D. Ross, *Aristotelis Politica* (Oxford: Oxford Classical Texts, 1957); references to the *Nicomachean Ethics* are based on I. Bywater,

Aristotelis Ethica Nicomachea (Oxford: Oxford Classical Texts, 1894). I take responsibility for all translations, though time and time again I find it nearly impossible to improve upon the elegant and accurate translations of Reeve and Irwin: *Aristotle: Politics*, trans. C.D.C. Reeve (Indianapolis: Hackett, 1998); *Aristotle: Nicomachean Ethics*, 2nd ed, trans. Terence Irwin (Indianapolis: Hackett, 1999).

2 *Politics* 1301a36–9, 1302a8–15.

3 My analysis of oligarchy is based upon previously published work. See Steven Skultety, 'Aristotle's Theory of Partisanship,' *Polis* 25, no. 2 (2008): 208–32.

4 *Politics* 1279b34–80a6.

5 *Nicomachean Ethics* 1131a25–7; *Politics* 1288a20, 1302b35.

6 In Athens, possessing the political prerogatives of citizenship by virtue of having been born of citizen parents was clearly an important status marker, especially for the poorest, landless citizens whose actual economic condition resembled the slaves. See Josiah Ober, 'Aristotle's Political Sociology,' in *Essays on the Foundations of Aristotelian Political Science*, ed. Carnes Lord and David K. O'Connor (Berkeley: University of California Press, 1991), 124.

7 *Politics* 1279b39–80a6.

8 For further discussion, see Skultety, 'Aristotle's Theory of Partisanship,' 213–15. My interpretation should be contrasted with Richard Mulgan, 'Aristotle on Oligarchy and Democracy,' in *A Companion to Aristotle's Politics*, ed. Keyt and Miller (Oxford: Oxford University Press, 1991), 316–17, and also Peter Simpson, *A Philosophical Commentary on the Politics of Aristotle* (Chapel Hill: University of North Carolina Press, 1998), 296–9. I believe that both of these interpretations focus too exclusively on the external features of few/many, rich/poor, free/unfree, well-born/low-born, and neglect what I take to be the most important feature of all: the internal belief of who deserves to rule.

9 *Politics* 1316a37–1316b2. Cf. *Rhetoric* 1396a.

10 *Politics* 1291b2–8.

11 At first it appears that *Politics* 1309b38–10a1 poses a problem for me: Aristotle claims that whenever the property of citizens is equalized in a democracy or oligarchy, the constitution is destroyed because it is impossible for these constitutions to exist without rich and poor. I do not think, however, that this passage (*contra* Ober, 'Aristotle's Political Sociology,' 120) is relevant to the definitions of democracy and oligarchy. In this passage Aristotle is encouraging partisans to make laws that preserve [*sōzei*] rather than destroy [*phtheirei*] their respective regimes: his point is that if democrats

liquidate the property of the rich they will quickly destabilize their democracy. Indeed, problems will result from the fact that the oligarchs – who will have lost their property and be economically poor – will now be furious *oligarchs*.

12 It should also be clear that a conception of merit based on inequality is not, by itself, sufficient to explain the intense oligarchic opposition to *isonomia* and *isēgoria* described by Craig Cooper in his 'Oligarchy and the Rule of Law' (included in this anthology). After all, Aristotle's conception of 'correct' justice itself embraces a form of geometric justice and thus sanctions inequality.

13 *Politics* 1295b15–18, 1310a23–6.

14 *Politics* 1295b12, 1295b23.

15 *Politics* 1295b19–25.

16 *Politics* 1280a8–23, 1301a30, 1283a26–9. I could just as easily have called this the 'for whom' mistake, for in these same passages Aristotle explains that democrats embrace 'equality' and oligarchs 'inequality,' but that they leave off the 'for whom' (1280a10–14).

17 J.S. Mill, *Utilitarianism*, ed. George Sher (Indianapolis: Hackett, 1979), 53.

18 *Politics* 1254b16–55a1.

19 *Politics* 1310a31–5, 1311a10. I disagree with Jeff Sikkenga (in his chapter in this volume) that for oligarchs 'wealth is honourable because it is the only means to a higher end'; in the passages Sikkenga cites Aristotle is describing cases where oligarchies are *mistakenly* called aristocracies.

20 *Politics* 1317b15.

21 *Politics* 1257b30–1.

22 For descriptions of generosity and magnificence, see *Nicomachean Ethics*, 1119b22–1123a33. For the need of a city to have wealthy citizens performing *leitourgiai*, see *Politics* 1328b5–15, 1329b36–1330a9.

23 *Politics* 1326b31–2.

24 Neither wealth, nor the freedom it enables, is sufficient for happiness: *Nicomachean Ethics* 1099b1. 'For Aristotle, being free is not itself a goal to be achieved but a prerequisite of attaining the ultimate end. One must live as a free person because, unless one is released from the constraint of acquiring life's necessities, one will not be able to acquire the virtues; even so, one might be free in this way and still fail to attain the ultimate end.' Richard Kraut, *Aristotle: Politics Books VII and VIII* (Oxford: Clarendon Press, 1997), 87.

25 *Politics* 1257b25–6.

26 *Politics* 1257b27–30.

27 *Nicomachean Ethics* 1106a14–07a27.

28 *Politics* 1257b41–2.

29 *Politics* 1258a6–7.
30 'The community naturally constituted to satisfy everyday needs, then, is the household.' *Politics* 1252b12–14.
31 *Politics* 1257b35–7.
32 *Nicomachean Ethics* 1096a6–7.
33 *Politics* 1258a10–14.
34 *Politics* 1292b10.
35 Indeed, Aristotle suggests that the logic of oligarchy itself leads to tyranny: if having more wealth is justification for excluding the poor from rule, then it seems that the wealthiest citizen is justified in excluding everyone from rule but himself. *Politics* 1283b13–18.
36 *Politics* 1309b19–21.
37 *Politics* 1310a22–3; cf. 1319b35–20a3.
38 Mulgan is exactly right to say the following: 'This illustrates an important distinction: the principles which support and preserve a constitution are not necessarily the same as those on which the constitution is itself based and which determine the distribution of power and the values of the ruling class. Indeed the dominant principles of the constitution may work against its continued existence ... To make their subjects contented and loyal, democrats must in certain respects become less democratic and oligarchs less oligarchic.' Richard G. Mulgan, *Aristotle's Political Theory* (Oxford: Oxford University Press, 1977), 131–2, cf. 133–4.
39 *Politics* 1292a39–b10. My reading should thus be contrasted with Sikkenga's; he believes Aristotle anticipates a psychological transformation of oligarchs in mixed constitutions.
40 *Politics* 1296b34–97a7.
41 Herodotus, *History*, 5.71. In Thucydides' account (*History of the Peloponnesian War*, 1.126), Cylon wins a victory but only seizes the Acropolis after making an inquiry at Delphi.
42 The *Politics* opens with an explicit declaration that each community aims at a distinct good (1252a1–3) and then, as I read it, sets out a thirteen-chapter-long argument for this thesis and the important corollary that communities differ in *kind*. Money (and everyday goods) is associated with the household community, while virtue is the good associated with the completely different kind of community, the polis. Notice that Aristotle feels so strongly about the distinction between business affairs and political affairs that he believes an ideal city should physically separate the business-related agora from the agora of leisure: *Politics* 1331a30–b2.
43 See Ryan Balot, *Greed and Injustice in Classical Athens* (Princeton, NJ: Princeton University Press, 2001), 22–57.

44 *Politics* 1283a14–15.

45 For the argument that Aristotle deployed a conception of rights in his political philosophy, see Fred Miller, Jr, *Nature, Justice, and Rights in Aristotle's
Politics*. Oxford: Oxford University Press, 1995); for the argument that Aristotle uses a notion of 'obligation' see Andres Rosler, *Political Authority and
Obligation in Aristotle* (Oxford: Oxford University Press, 2005). For a range
of critical views about whether such notions can be found in Aristotle's
political philosophy, see Malcolm Schofield, ed., *Sharing in the Constitution
(Aristotle's 'Politics': A Symposium). The Review of Metaphysics* 49, no. 4
(1996).

46 *Politics* 1278b8–9, 1289a15–20.

47 *Politics* 1278b11.

48 Broadly speaking, Aristotle's political science is a science of human beings
rather than an investigation into civic institutions and basic structures of
society that can be evaluated independently of citizens' character. For a
helpful discussion, see Richard Kraut, *Aristotle: Political Philosophy* (Oxford:
Oxford University Press, 2002), 433–7. This is not to say, of course, that
Aristotle ignores the institutional order of offices and procedures that
structure political life; indeed, see Peter Simpson's article in this anthology
for a detailed articulation of the institutional processes that distinguish oligarchies, Aristotelian and modern.

49 Aristotle himself suggests that many goods beside wealth can be the aim
of unlimited pursuit: 'For men consider any amount of virtue to be adequate, but wealth, goods, power, reputation, and all such things they seek
to excess without limit.' *Politics* 1323a35–7.

6 Thucydides and the Importance of Ideology in Conflict

LAURIE M. JOHNSON BAGBY

Thucydides is most often discussed as a proponent of realism. It is not difficult to discern in his work the stern, sober, and pessimistic understanding of human nature which is a hallmark of realism. Who can forget his view that most men make very little effort to investigate the truth,[1] or his claim that 'the absence of romance' will make his book more useful than those of his predecessors?[2] But as David Welch has pointed out, too often readers have taken a few statements from Thucydides to prove that he was a realist who looked only at relative power, who discounted factors such as politics and culture as unimportant trappings, and who disregarded moral and political claims as irrelevant to the outcome of any given clash.[3] In previous publications, I have disputed such narrow views of Thucydides, arguing that he is a realist, but a realist who does not discount the impact of other factors such as national character or the character of individual leaders in how conflicts proceed.[4] This chapter will further that argument and hopefully speak to the current debate between the neoconservatives, who advocate regime change as a way of winning the war against terror, and realists, who still wish to disregard ideology or belief systems as unimportant next to relative power.

One very significant layer of analysis which Thucydides develops in his *History* is the way of thinking associated with given regime types and how that way of thinking affected the decisions of leaders and the reactions of populations during the war. 'Ideology' is the most recognizable word we have today for describing this way of thinking. But the term's connection with twentieth-century totalitarianism makes its use both challenging and not quite accurate. Its use challenges the common view that political ideologies were fully articulated only in the twentieth century. At the same time, because of the term's association with mass politics via mass communications, it does not capture exactly what was going on in Thucydides' time. At any rate, Thucydides spends so much time in the *History* developing our understanding of ideology or *ways of thinking about regime type* that it becomes impossible to think that such considerations were, in his view, irrelevant.

The first thing we see in the *History* is Thucydides' tendency to characterize the nature of regimes as active or passive, conservative or daring. His characterization of regimes in this way is significant despite the fact, as Jeff Sikkenga points out in his chapter, that 'oligarchy has been eclipsed by democracy' in our world to the point that it is not even considered a possibility. Thucydides' characterization of regimes reflects a method that could be applied in other cases, taking into account any type of regime and how it affects national character and subsequent foreign policy. In his account of early history, Thucydides explains that when tyrannies ruled Greece, most states made 'safety the great aim of their policy ... Thus for a long time in Hellas do we find causes which make the states alike incapable of combination for great or national ends, or of any vigorous action of their own.'[5] Then Sparta put down the tyrannies, and Thucydides goes on to characterize Sparta and its soon-to-be chief rival, Athens, in very different terms. By virtue of its own good laws, he writes, Sparta gave its allies continuity of government and freedom from tyranny. When the Persians came to take over Greece, the Spartans naturally assumed leadership of the alliance that opposed them. Sparta fought on land and Athens took to the sea. So far the Spartans seemed heroic and responsible. But after the Greeks had repelled the Persians, the coalition began to fracture. Sparta was an oligarchy and established oligarchies wherever it had influence, but did not ask for tribute and held a loose grip on its allies. Athens was a democracy and imposed democracy wherever it could, depriving its allies of ships and imposing tribute on them, creating dependency. While the Athenians did not compel subject states in every case to become democracies, their policy was to do so wherever and whenever it was beneficial to them.

So we see that in Thucydides' accounts of the events between the end of the Persian Wars and the beginning of the Peloponnesian War, the two great states, Sparta and Athens, behaved very differently. Sparta acted similarly to the ancient tyrannies, aiming more at self-defence, preserving what it had rather than thinking to expand further. Athens, on the other hand, seemed to think of pressing its advantage at every turn. Thus importance of regime type and the corresponding way of thinking, though we cannot yet quite call it an 'ideology,' was important from the start in Thucydides' *History* and was to become ever more important.

The Spartan War Conference

The first lengthy treatment of differences in national character in Thucydides' *History* appears at the congress of the Peloponnesian confederacy at Sparta. The Corinthians, who had been attacked by the Athenians as they had battled Corcyra, and whose colony Potidaea (a tribute-paying ally of Athens) had likewise been besieged by Athens, came to Sparta to seek aid. But instead of humbly asking for help, the Corinthians blamed the Spartans for their reluctance to act in the past. Spartan reticence had only encouraged the Athenians to expand. They claimed, indeed, that the Spartans were the true source of the subjugation of Greece by Athens because they had remained passive while Athens grew ever larger. The Corinthians pointed out the differences between the two regimes:

> The Athenians are addicted to innovation, and their designs are characterized by swiftness alike in conception and execution; you have a genius for keeping what you have got, accompanied by a total want of invention, and when forced to act you never go far enough. Again, they are adventurous beyond their power, and daring beyond their judgment, and in danger they are sanguine; your wont is to attempt less than is justified by your power, to mistrust even what is sanctioned by your judgment, and to fancy that from danger there is no release. Further, there is a promptitude on their side against procrastination on yours; they are never at home, you are never from it: for they hope by their absence to extend their acquisitions, you fear by your advance to endanger what you have left behind.[6]

That the Spartans *were* procrastinators was proved by Thucydides in his depiction of their inaction at several key points in the conflict. Several cities, such as Melos, were more or less abandoned by the Spartans. The Corinthians, as we see, made an oblique reference to the Spartans' large slave population, the Helots, whose revolt they always had to fear and which often stopped them from acting quickly and aggressively.

But one thing the Corinthians failed to do was to tie these Spartan deficits directly to their form of government. Of course, the Corinthians shared that form of government, so they had good reason not to make the connection. After all, by their argument alone they prove that not all oligarchies lacked the resolve to fight. Instead, they ended their appeal to the Spartans on a more humble note, simply asking them to wake from their slumber and come to their aid now.

Next, the Athenian ambassadors spoke. They did not do much to dispel the notions of them that had been developed by the Corinthians. Their intention, wrote Thucydides, was to call attention to the great power of Athens, not to offer a defence of their country. They reminded the Spartans of the Athenian performance in the Persian Wars – that they met the enemy alone at the Battle of Marathon, that the Spartans came into the war late, when there was nothing left to lose. They agreed with the Corinthians that the Spartans' reluctance to take the lead in Greece left a power vacuum which Athens had to fill. They stated that they obtained their empire after the war, being compelled by fear, honour, and interest, and it was no longer safe to give up that empire because of the resentment it naturally stirred.[7] They clearly articulated the 'Athenian thesis' that it was a law of nature that the weaker are subject to the stronger. However, they went beyond this hard-headed realism to claim that they 'respect justice more than their position compels them to.'[8] Indeed, they point out, their attachment to the idea of equity had actually gotten them into trouble with their allies. Making a claim strangely reminiscent of our current debate over where and how to try terror suspects, the Athenians state they allowed non-Athenians to be tried by impartial Athenian courts in their disputes, and because of that, the subject states had come to expect impartial justice and were more offended when they did not get it than if they had never had it: 'But our subjects are so habituated to associate with us as equals, that any defeat whatever that clashes with their notions of justice, whether it proceeds from a legal judgment or from the power which our empire gives us, makes them forget to be grateful for being allowed to retain most of their possessions, and more vexed at a part being taken, than if we had from the first cast law aside and openly gratified our covetousness.'[9]

Here we see the Athenians making an attempt to attribute at least some of their actions, those that benefit their allies at any rate, to the fact that they were a democracy. But their main argument, that they were compelled by fear, honour, and interest to act as they did, is not portrayed as influenced by their regime type, but rather as a universal experience of human nature. At the end of their speech, the Athenians offered to take part in a process of arbitration, a proposal that a conventional state like Sparta would find hard to ignore. The Spartan King Archidamus, a 'wise and moderate' man, spoke next.[10] Archidamus epitomizes the Spartan character as described by the Corinthians. He urged the Spartans to slow down and at least delay war until better prepared. He counselled his people not to be ashamed of their character, because it is a wise moderation: 'We alone do not become insolent in success and give way less than others in misfortune.' He praised Spartan education as more manly and disciplined than that of the Athenians. He also pointed out that going to war without arbitration when it had been offered was unlawful. King Archidamus played by the traditional rules of the game, and was not ashamed of doing so. On the other hand, the Spartan Ephor Sthenelaidas briefly spoke in favour of declaring war, calling on Sparta to let Athens go no further, and to not betray her allies.

In the end, we know that the Spartans decided to declare war. This was done, wrote Thucydides, 'not so much because they were persuaded by the arguments of the allies, as because they feared the growth of the power of the Athenians, seeing most of Hellas already subject to them.'[11] This last statement might be taken as a sign that all the speeches were nothing but rhetoric, to be dismissed as irrelevant compared with the power imbalance that existed between Athens and Sparta. However, the speeches explain how the power imbalance occurred in the first place. Thucydides takes the time in his first book to go back to the root of the unequal relationship between Athens and Sparta. Both in his description of previous events and in his reporting of the speeches at the Spartan war conference, he shows that oligarchic Sparta, because of its more conservative nature, did not do everything it could during and after the Persian War to consolidate and expand its power. On the other hand, democratic Athens took advantage of every opportunity. The way that each nation thought, their way of looking at the world, influenced what they did in the years leading up to this imbalance. When confronted with that great imbalance, even the reluctant Spartans had to concede that now they must defend themselves and their allies. Thus, Thucydides' account does not treat the speeches as mere rhetoric, but as his explanation for how these two states came the point where armed conflict was inevitable.

Let us look at some specific ways in which aggressive Athens took advantage of reluctant Sparta. 'The way in which Athens came to be placed in the circumstances under which her power grew was this,' he begins.[12] After the Persian Wars, Athens took the town of Sestos, an act of aggression that should have set off an alarm at Sparta, but did not. The Athenians built their city back up and built walls around it. The Spartans sent ambassadors to Athens to ask that no walls be built, because this could be taken as an act of aggression, but had no intention of following through. Instead of honouring the Spartan request, Themistocles engaged in a lengthy deception to continue to build the walls and experienced no interference from Sparta. The walls made the defence of Athens easier so that Themistocles could send more men to sea to expand the empire. He took advantage of the widespread dislike of the Spartan commander Pausanias to urge more and more Greeks to look to Athens as the better leader.[13] Each step the Athenians took seemed to be a concerted effort to gain control over as much of Greece as they could, but the Spartans remained inactive. Instead of disputing this trend and trying to regain their influence, the Spartans were satisfied to let the Athenians handle the allies.

Athens began to subdue cities that preferred to remain independent. She took advantage of many cities' unwillingness to send men and ships and took their money instead, thereby robbing them of any ability to ultimately oppose Athenian power. The Spartans continued to do nothing. They were prevented by an earthquake (a bad omen) and a Helot revolt from coming to the aid of the Thracians. Sparta asked Athens for help in besieging Ithome, and the Athenians came. But at the last minute the Spartans changed their minds, fearful that the Athenians would try to foment democratic change in Ithome and take the city for themselves, and so they told the Athenians that they did not need them after all.

Athens then formally broke off its alliance with Sparta, and allied with Sparta's enemy Argos. Thucydides explains how Athens continued to manoeuvre toward outright empire, unafraid of offending the Spartans. Then Pericles became the leader of Athens, a man who 'opposed the Spartans in everything, and would have no concessions, but ever urged the Athenians on to war.'[14] He pointed out in his first speech to the Athenians that the Spartans lacked money and experience in sea battle. Also, their form of government, 'want of a single council-chamber requisite to prompt and vigorous action' often meant 'no action at all.'[15] In this way, Pericles pointed out the impact of Sparta's oligarchic government on their foreign policy.

Pericles' funeral oration tied the Athenian character directly to its democratic regime. After praising the Athenian constitution and laws for the amount of freedom they enabled ordinary people to have, he claimed that 'the freedom which we enjoy in our government extends also to our ordinary life. There, far from exercising a jealous surveillance over each other, we do not feel called upon to be angry with our neighbor for doing what he likes, or even to indulge in those injurious looks which cannot fail to be offensive, although they inflict no positive penalty.'[16] When it came to Athens' military policy, 'there also we differ from our antagonists. We throw open our city to the world, and never by alien acts exclude foreigners from any opportunity of learning or observing, although the eyes of an enemy may occasionally profit by our liberality … we Athenians advance unsupported into the territory of a neighbour, and fighting upon a foreign soil usually vanquish with ease men who are defending their homes.'[17] The Athenian democracy had created an open and dynamic culture, which resulted in a blessed way of life and great military strength, a strength that came not from regimentation and sacrifice, but from an overabundance of ability and love of country.

Thus it is clear that Thucydides thought that what we might call 'national character' was important in these early developments. At least twice he makes a direct connection between the national character of Sparta and its regime type, oligarchy. While it is true that Thucydides admired oligarchy, and could even be considered a member of the aristocracy in Athens, the argument he develops here shows that the more conservative nature of its oligarchic government left Sparta at a disadvantage next to the more daring nature of democratic Athens. Both Thucydides and various speakers point out the same differences between Athens and Sparta, and both attribute Athens' growth in power largely to Spartan reluctance. Sparta was all too ready to 'retire,' all too concerned with religion and traditional rules of conduct, all too constrained by its large population of slaves. Their form of government hindered them from making swift decisions. Clearly Thucydides thought that the types of regime these two states had, and their national characters, were vitally important to understanding their conflict. But we cannot yet say that these observations reveal competing 'ideologies,' at least not in the way we usually use that term. For that we must move to about five years into the conflict.

Corcyra

From the discussion above, we know that Thucydides thought that national character was an important factor in explaining how the war began. But how did the Greek world move from expressions of national differences and what we might call national pride to the hardened ideological positions of democracy versus oligarchy that characterized the latter part of the war? We know that the Athenians were proud of their democracy, and that they had taken many measures to prevent oligarchic elements from gaining power. Athenian democrats, writes Alford, 'were more explicitly concerned with mitigating another type of oligarchy: the control of the polis by families of great wealth and influence.'[18] They combated this threat by rotating citizens in and out of a myriad of brief stints in administrative positions. With about 40,000 citizens, 'virtually every citizen would serve as a magistrate, about half would sit on the council, and of those who sat on the council better than 70 per cent (roughly 365 out of 500) would serve as president of Athens for a day.'[19] It was precisely at the time of the Peloponnesian War that Greeks started thinking in terms of democracy versus oligarchy, that is, in *ideological* terms. If we take Thucydides as our chief guide on this question, it was in the fifth year of the war that the Greeks moved from awareness of the differences caused by national character and regime type to full-blown ideological divides. 'Reflections on differences among political structures and the values embodied in each are not found before the fifth century, in Pindar (*Pyth.* 2.85–88) and in the so-called *Constitutional Debate* in Herodotus, and do not become ideologies until the 420's,' writes Martin Ostwald. 'The terms "democracy" and "oligarchy" are both first attested in Herodotus, and they assume political ideological overtones for the first known time in Thucydides' account of the civil war in Korkyra.'[20]

The Corcyraean civil war took place in 427 BCE. Thucydides' account of it takes place in Book 3 of the *History*, in which he also includes his accounts of the Mytilenaean Debate and the Plataean Dialogue. These two events set the stage for his treatment of the trend toward ideological thinking most fully represented by his description of the Corcyraean civil war. Diodotus's argument, for instance, turns away from the previous Athenian rhetorical strategy, still employed by Cleon, that appealed to common notions of the way all states acted. Cleon emphasized Athenian self-interest, the deterrence power of punishing the Mytilenaeans, and also the injustice of their actions. As Marc Cogan points out, Cleon also assumes that 'the only significant agents with which one deals are states as a *whole*.'[21] Diodotus's speech, which ultimately prevails, introduces a new dimension:

Only consider what a blunder you would commit in doing as Cleon recommends. As things are at present, in all the cities the people is your
friend, and either does not revolt with the oligarchy, or, if forced to do
so, becomes at once the enemy of the insurgents; so that in the war with
the hostile city you have the masses on your side.[22]

Diodotus warns the Athenians not to punish their benefactors, and
thus to send a message to other nations that they will not punish the
people but instead will encourage them to revolt. He introduces the
idea that Athens' interests may lie in encouraging the democratic faction in cities against the oligarchs there. Cogan points out that in the
subsequent Plataean Debate, Thucydides introduces for the first time
the accusation of 'Atticizing' which is made by the Thebans against
the Plataeans. The crime of identifying with Athens and its democracy
outweighs all the Plataeans' previous heroic actions during the Persian Wars. This shows that 'Oligarchs, too, were aware of the distinction of democrats and oligarchs, and to the oligarchs in Thucydides'
history, the concept of Atticism came to stand for the international
form of Athenian democracy and the dangerous influence they believed it exercised.'[23]

Thucydides' treatment of the Corcyraean civil war is particularly
noteworthy because it is here that he gives us his most extended remarks, in his own voice, about this type of ideological conflict in Corcyra and elsewhere. Corcyra was a colony of Corinth (Corinth was an
oligarchy and an ally of Sparta). The split between Corcyra and Corinth had come in 435 BCE when Corcyra had refused to come to the aid
of one of its colonies, Epidamnus, during disputes between the democrats and the oligarchs there. When Corinth did come to the aid of Epidamnus (specifically the aid of the democrats there), this angered the
Corcyraeans, who split with Corinth and sought an alliance with Corinth's rival, Athens. The spark that started the Corcyraean civil war
was the return of some prisoners that the Corinthians had taken in
this conflict over Epidamnus before the Peloponnesian War had been
declared. The prisoners had been ransomed, but the real reason the
prisoners were allowed to return to Corcyra was to agitate for a return
to an alliance with Corinth. At this time this did not seem to include a
demand to change governments and adopt an oligarchy. The government of Corcyra, at the start of the conflict, appears to have been democratic. Indeed, though a colony of Corinth, it had probably been
democratic even prior to 435, when the struggle over Epidamnus

occurred. Donald Kagan reasons that 'a change from aristocracy to democracy could hardly have come about so swiftly without a serious struggle. Since none of our sources says a word about such a civil conflict, although a lengthy and detailed account of the civil war of 427 such as Thucydides gives would demand an account of such recent troubles, we must believe that the government of Corcyra was democratic in the years before 435 as well. We may not, therefore, explain Corcyra's behavior toward Epidamnus by oligarchic or aristocratic sympathies.'[24]

An Athenian ship arrived at Corcyra at the same time as a Corinthian ship, both with envoys. The Corcyraeans, after deliberating, voted to remain allied with Athens but to 'be friends of the Peloponnesians as they had been formerly.'[25] So Corinth's first attempt to make the government of Corcyra revoke its alliance with Athens by activating dissatisfied elements within Corcyra appears to have failed. The government stayed with Athens and acted to try to appease both sides. But this did not stop the returned prisoners from trying to stir up more trouble. They charged a Proxenus of Athens and leader of the commons, Peithias, with trying to enslave Corcyra to the Athenians. After being acquitted, Peithias turned the tables and charged five of the richest oligarchs with impiety. They were convicted of the crime, but because the fine was quite large, 'they seated themselves in the temples, to be allowed to pay it by installments.'[26] When the oligarchs learned that Peithias, who was a senator, was going to try to persuade the senate to make offensive and defensive alliance with Athens, they 'banded together armed with daggers, and suddenly bursting into the senate killed Peithias and sixty others, senators and private persons; some few only of the party of Peithias taking refuge in the Athenian galley, which had not yet departed.'[27]

Again, the government of Corcyra tried to recover from the actions of these two battling factions. In an assembly, the Corcyraeans voted not to receive representatives of either Corinth or Athens unless they came together peacefully in the same ship. They also sent off envoys to Athens to explain their decision. But upon arriving in Athens, these envoys were arrested as revolutionaries. A Corinthian ship arrived at Corcyra with Spartan representatives, and now the oligarchic party saw its chance, emboldened by the Spartan presence, and attacked the commons and got the better of them. Both sides were clearly aligned into fighting forces now, and each took refuge in a different part of the city, the commons in the Acropolis and higher parts, and the oligarchs in the marketplace (where most of them lived) and the adjoining harbour.[28] At this point, the government of Corcyra ceased to be an important actor in this conflict, and the battling factions became all-important. In ensuing battles, the democrats gained the advantage.

Then, twelve Athenian ships arrived at Corcyra. The Athenian general Nicostratus attempted to negotiate a peace settlement between the two sides and get them to accept an offensive and defensive alliance with Athens. But his very presence was now too much of a temptation for the democrats, who came up with their own proposal. They would keep five of the Athenian ships with their crews in exchange for five of theirs, as a show of force and solidarity against Corinth. Nicostratus agreed, and immediately the democratic side seized the opportunity to politicize this act and proposed that members of the oligarchic faction be the ones to man the ships that Athens would take back. Of course the oligarchs believed that this was a ploy to arrest them and take them to Athens for trial (it probably was). The oligarchs once again employed the traditional defence of 'seating themselves as suppliants in the temple of the Dioscuri.' Another four hundred seated themselves at the temple of Hera, fearing for their lives.[29] Normally, this act would place them off-limits to any type of molestation. But the democrats made them leave the temple and carried them over to a small island facing the temple, with provisions.

Now, fifty-three Peloponnesian ships arrived, with the aim of making sure that Corcyra remained under their control. The Corcyraeans armed sixty of their own ships to meet them, even though the Athenian ships were still there, and asked to be the first to attack. But the Corcyraean forces were unable to cope with the Peloponnesian fleet. The Athenian ships did their best to keep the enemy off as they retreated. True to form, the Spartans did not take full advantage of this situation. Instead of taking the city, upon hearing that a fleet of sixty Athenian ships was approaching Corcyra, they took thirteen Corcyraean ships they had captured and left. Without the protection of the Spartans, and with the arrival of the Athenian fleet to back up the democratic party, the Corcyraean oligarchs who were prisoners were in grave danger.

It is at this point that Thucydides turns from a fairly objective narration of important events at Corcyra to an impassioned description of the violence that ensued and his own analysis of it. The commons persuaded some of the oligarchs to stand trial, but promptly sentenced all of them to death. Understanding their situation, those who had refused to go to trial now began to kill themselves. 'The mass of the suppliants who had refused to do so, on seeing what was taking place, slew each other there in the consecrated ground; while some hanged themselves upon the trees, and others destroyed themselves as they were severally able.'[30] The Athenian ships led by Eurymedon stayed for seven days, and during those days, the 'Corcyraeans were engaged in butchering those of their fellow-citizens whom they regarded as their enemies: and although the crime imputed was that of attempting to put down the democracy, some were slain also for private hatred, others by their debtors because of the monies owed to them.'[31] Fathers killed sons. Suppliants were killed in the temples where they had taken refuge. This means that literally nothing was considered sacred, not family ties, and not long-standing religious beliefs and customs. As Clifford Orwin points out, 'standing by one's *philoi*, ones "dear ones" – originally, one's kin, later one's friends – was the true north of the Greek moral compass. Its collapse represents the dissolution of the living bedrock of life as usual in the Greek city.'[32]

Thucydides turns away from an analysis of the specifics of Corcyra at this point and discusses how this instance of ideological violence was just the first of many that would tear Greece apart. 'Later on, one may say, the whole Hellenic world was convulsed; struggles being everywhere made by the popular chiefs to bring in the Athenians, and by the oligarchs to introduce the Lacedaemonians. In peace there would have been neither the pretext nor the wish to make such an invitation; but in war, with an alliance always at the command of either faction for the hurt of their adversaries and their own corresponding advantage, opportunities for bringing in the foreigner were never wanting to the revolutionary parties.'[33] This aspect of the conflict was completely new to the Greek world, the 'unprecedented sort of alliance,' not between governments or states, 'but of state with party.'[34] It was unprecedented, too, in that the alliances were 'politically homogeneous; they might be made, initially, with political factions rather than with the governments of the states; and their purpose (to the faction calling in the great power) was to cause harm to the opposing political party. The last would certainly have been an *incidental* result of all previous alliances between states, but the alliances described by Thucydides in 3.82.1 were the first which aimed specifically at influencing internal politics.'[35]

Thucydides' analysis of this new situation reveals an understanding of what had changed and what had remained the same. What had changed was the virulence with which people attacked each other and

persisted in their violence, in their zeal to hurt their ideological enemies. In this zeal, Thucydides finds neither the oligarchs nor the democrats deficient – both are more than capable of deadly fervour. This
is what he is getting at when he emphasizes the fact that the democrats disregarded all religious conventions, dragging suppliants from
temples and even killing them inside temples, or when he mentions
that fathers killed sons. Simply put, party or faction became more
sacred than religion or family. He also masterfully describes the radicalization of thought and language that comes in the wake of full-
blown ideological conflict:

> Words had to change their ordinary meaning and to take that which was
> now given them. Reckless audacity came to be considered the courage of
> a loyal ally; prudent hesitation, specious cowardice; moderation was
> held to be a cloak for unmanliness; ability to see all sides of a question in-
> aptness to act on any. Frantic violence became the attribute of manliness;
> cautious plotting, a justifiable means of self-defense. The advocate of
> extreme measures was always trustworthy; his opponent a man to be
> suspected. To succeed in a plot was to have a shrewd head, to divine a
> plot a still shrewder; but to try to provide against having to do either was
> to break up your party and to be afraid of your adversaries.[36]

Again, Thucydides does not distinguish between democracy and oligarchy when it comes to the inversion of values and the perversion of
language. Both 'parties' were capable of this radicalization. It was the
phenomena of ideological factions itself, made extreme by war, and
enabled by the great powers, that became so dangerous. On the other
hand, while the intervention into internal affairs of states on behalf of
ideological parties was something new, some things about the ensuing
conflicts did remain the same. Just as he had made clear in his treatment
of the Plague of Athens, Thucydides states that what men would never
think to do in peace they thought perfectly acceptable to do in war. The
pressures of war, and its temptations, pushed people into extreme violence and disregard for all moral and religious rules. In this case, war
supplied the context in which these extreme and bloodthirsty factions
could emerge and thrive. And the consequences that people experienced
in the wake of this domestic violence were likewise timeless:

> The sufferings which revolution entailed upon the cities were many and
> terrible, such as have occurred and always will occur, as long as the

nature of mankind remains the same; though in a severer or milder form, and varying in their symptoms, according to the variety of the particular cases. In peace and prosperity states and individuals have better senti-ments, because they do not find themselves suddenly confronted with imperious necessities; but war takes away the easy supply of daily wants, and so proves a rough master, that brings most men's characters to a level with their fortunes.[37]

Thucydides also notes that the desire for power, a universal and timeless desire, lay at the heart of all such actions:

The cause of all these evils was the lust for power arising from greed and ambition; and from these passions proceeded the violence of parties once engaged in contention. The leaders in the cities, each provided with the fairest professions, on the one side with the cry of political equality of the people, on the other of a moderate aristocracy, sought prizes for them-selves in those public interests which they pretended to cherish.[38]

Note again that both democrats and oligarchs were equally capable of extreme behaviour. In a different context oligarchies were more conservative, reticent, moderate, or wise than democracies, but not at the height of these ideological battles. There, ambition became a com-mon human attribute that transcended regime type and which, as Jeff Sikkenga points out in his chapter, the American founders recognized as a transcendent and universal part of human nature. Thucydides ar-gues that the leaders of both sides were motivated by lust for power, greed, and ambition. Does this mean that we should not take the impact of ideology on these conflicts seriously after all? Should we see all such claims as 'mere rhetoric' to be disregarded in favour of the 'true motives' that correspond with universal human nature? This would be an over-reading of Thucydides' analysis. If he did not think ideology was an important factor in these conflicts, *simply* a 'cloak' for deeper motivations, he would not have described the radicalization of thoughts and words during *staseis*. This does not mean that one must dismiss what remains the same – the fact that many people, perhaps especially at the top, were motivated by self-interest, and saw such conflicts as opportunities to aggrandize themselves. To not see both factors as important would be, for instance, to read the French Revolu-tion as either a completely ideological event, in which even the leaders of the Terror were entirely motivated by the partisan vision, or to see the French Revolution as a completely political event, in which ideology was mere window dressing to everyone involved. Obviously both views are untenable abstractions from the reality of the Revolution, and such would certainly be the case if we read Thucydides as being an advocate of only one part of his explanation for the civil conflicts that engulfed the Greek world.

In the course of the history of Corcyra we can see the turn from a world in which it was possible for an oligarchic city to create a democratic colony, or for a democratic party to call for help from an oligarchic power, to a situation in which such ideological juxtapositions would become unthinkable. The ultimate victim was any degree of civilized relations among these cities. Near the end of his analysis of the Corcyraean civil war, Thucydides laments, 'Indeed men too often take upon themselves in the prosecution of their revenge to set the example of doing away with those general laws to which all alike can look for salvation in adversity, instead of allowing them to subsist against the day of danger when their aid may be required.'[39]

As if to underscore the decisive influence the great powers had in bringing this situation about, at the very end of his account of the civil war, Thucydides observes that about 600 of the oligarchic faction from Corcyra who had gone into exile took the occasion of Athens' departure to start wreaking havoc again. They invaded the country, burning their ships so that there was no turning back, and fortified a position on Mount Istone from which they were able to gain control of much of the countryside and continually harass the city. This last observation, once again, illustrates the extreme and even foolish fervour the oligarchs had for their cause. If they were simply motivated by greed, they probably would not have burned their ships and left themselves with nothing to lose.

The Oligarchic Coup of the Four Hundred

The last book of Thucydides' *History* contains the sad but fascinating tale of how Athens went from a democracy, to an oligarchy, to a mixed regime with strong oligarchic elements. Along the way, we find a raging competition for which side could produce the most revolts and counter-revolts within their opponents' allies. We also find a contending or shadow government made up of some of the Athenian military stationed away from the city. Then there is the incredible Alcibiades, who seems truly free of ideology even in a highly ideological world, and who works for Sparta, Persia, and Athens, depending upon the day and time. In addition, we have some of Thucydides' most forthright comments on democracy and oligarchy. Book 8 leaves the history of the Peloponnesian War incomplete, and in some ways it is the least coherent of the books, as it is obviously less polished and itself incomplete. But in some ways, it is Thucydides' best writing. The situation in Athens and in the rest of the Greek world is so fluid, so complex, so inexplicable, that it takes a master like Thucydides to report on it, untangle it, and help us make sense of it.

The change in Athens' government occurred in the wake of the ruinous Sicilian Expedition. Much of the Athenian fighting force, certainly a great deal of its navy, had been destroyed in this debacle, and the Athenians were afraid that the Sicilian forces would now come after them, along with the Peloponnesians and their allies the Persians. But, true to their nature, the Athenians decided to fight to the last, and began to prepare accordingly. Thucydides commented that this was 'the way of a democracy, in the panic of the moment they were ready to be as prudent as possible.'[40] Finally departing from character, the Spartans could see their advantage and 'now resolved to throw themselves without reserve into the war.'[41] They would soon be joined with the Sicilians and in a precarious alliance with the Persian King Darius to finish Athens. Athens' allies were deserting them, and neutral cities were now joining Sparta. The Athenian ally Chios was a centre point, with Athens attempting to maintain control by supporting the democrats there, and Sparta seeking its overthrow (with the help of Alcibiades) by appealing to its oligarchs to revolt, change the government of the city, and make an alliance with Sparta. Indeed, Alcibiades' mission at this time was to encourage as many oligarchic revolutions as possible in Athens' allies.

On the island of Samos, however, the opposite was true. Thucydides reports on 'the rising of the commons at Samos against the upper classes, in concert with some Athenians, who were there in three vessels. The Samian commons put to death some two hundred in all of the upper classes, and banished four hundred more, and themselves took their land and houses; after which the Athenians decreed their independence, being now sure of their fidelity, and the commons henceforth governed the city.'[42] This island was to become a staging ground for some of Athens' most important actions in this latter phase of the war, and a centre point in the factional conflict to take place within Athens itself.

After talking with the Persian general Tissaphernes, who was working with Spartans and providing them pay, in order to show the Athenians at Samos how valuable he was, Alcibiades sent word to them that if only Athens' 'rascally democracy' was replaced with an oligarchy, he would be glad to come home and bring Tissaphernes' friendship with him. The chief men in the army at Samos 'at once embraced the idea of subverting the democracy.'[43] Word of this got around the military leaders at Samos, and it was then proposed to the army as a whole: Alcibiades would deliver Tissaphernes' support if they would get rid of the democracy and restore him. Thucydides explains that the upper class within the army liked the proposal because they wanted power, and the lower class within the army liked it because they wanted the Persian's pay. 'When the Athenians at Samos found that he [Alcibiades] had influence with Tissaphernes, principally of their own motion (though partly also through Alcibiades himself sending word to their chief men to tell the best men in the army, that if there were only an oligarchy in the place of the rascally democracy that had banished him, he would be glad to return to his country and to make Tissaphernes their friend), the captains and chief men in the armament at once embraced the idea of subverting the democracy.'[44]

The Athenian general at Samos, Phrynicus, did not like the deal. He 'rightly' thought that Alcibiades only wanted to change his country's institutions in order to get recalled. Phrynichus knew that offering oligarchy to the allied states now 'would not make the rebels come in any the sooner, or confirm the loyal in their allegiance; as the allies would never prefer servitude with an oligarchy or democracy to freedom with the constitution which they actually enjoyed, to whichever type it belonged. Besides, the cities thought that the so-called better classes would prove just as oppressive as the commons, as being those who originated, proposed, and for the most part benefited from the acts of the commons injurious to the confederates. Indeed, if it depended on the better classes, the confederates would be put to death without trial and with violence; while the commons were their refuge and the chastiser of these men. This he positively knew that the cities had learned by experience, and that such was their opinion.'[45]

This is one of Thucydides' few statements, albeit through the lens of one particular actor, about the value of democratic versus oligarchic government for the allied cities. We can see, at least in the context of this war, with its raging battle over the allegiance of allied states, that Phrynicus, and perhaps Thucydides himself, thought that what mattered more to the allies at this point was freedom from the control of either great power, rather than the form of government. The ideas that Thucydides puts into the mind of Phrynicus here reveal that both oligarchies and democracies could be oppressive or provide good government, but also that the general opinion was that rebels would stand a better chance, once captured, in the hands of an Athenian democracy than an Athenian oligarchy.

Despite the opinion of Phrynicus, the oligarchic partisans on Samos formed a political club or party, 'and openly told the mass of the armament that the king would be their friend and would provide them with money, if Alcibiades were restored, and the democracy abolished. The multitude, if at first irritated by these intrigues, were nevertheless kept quiet by the advantageous prospect of the pay from the king; and the oligarchic conspirators, after making this communication to the people, now re-examined the proposals of Alcibiades among themselves, with most of their associates.'[46] The members of this oligarchic club accepted Alcibiades' proposition and sent Pisander to Athens to ask for Alcibiades' restoration.[47]

Some first-rate intrigue then occurred, as Phrynichus tried to forestall Alcibiades' restoration by letting the Spartans in on Alcibiades' plot to take the Persian alliance away from them. The Spartan general, Astyochus, did not do what Phrynicus thought he would do with this information, instead telling it to Alcibiades and the Persian general Tissaphernes. Phrynicus tried again, ramping up the accusations, and once again Astyochus told Alcibiades and Tissaphernes. Alcibiades also sent the men at Samos a letter letting them know of Phrynicus's intrigues. But this backfired – Phrynicus's men believed that Alcibiades was the most likely liar. Thus hard-pressed, Phrynichus fortified Samos and boosted his defences as much as possible.

Meanwhile, the ambassadors from Samos to Athens presented their plan on behalf of Alcibiades, telling them that 'if Alcibiades were recalled and the democratic constitution changed, they would have the king as their ally, and would be able to overcome the Peloponnesians.'[48] Several speakers opposed this proposal about changing Athens into an oligarchy. But Pisander asked them one question: 'In the face of the fact that the Peloponnesians had as many ships as their own confronting them at sea, more cities in alliance with them, and the king and Tissaphernes to supply them with money, of which the Athenians had none left, had he any hope of saving the state, unless some one could induce the king to come over to their side?' None of them could offer him any hope. 'This we cannot have unless we have a more moderate form of government, and put the offices into fewer hands, and so gain the king's confidence, and forthwith restore Alcibiades, who is the only man living that can bring this about. The safety of the state, not the form of its government, is for the moment the most pressing question, as we can always change afterwards whatever we do not like.'[49]

After hearing Pisander's argument, the people of Athens gave way, but Thucydides noted that they promised themselves that they would be able to change the government back some day. So they sent Pisander to go see what deal he could make with Alcibiades and Tissaphernes. Alcibiades, however, did not conclude the deal with Tissaphernes. In order to hide the fact that he had been bluffing about how much influence he had with Tissaphernes, he requested so many concessions from the Athenians on behalf of the Persian general that the Athenians finally withdrew their proposal of alliance. This was alright with the king, says Thucydides, since his goal had been to strengthen Athens so that the two enemies could continue to weaken each other to his benefit. Instead of making a treaty with Athens, he sent the Spartans their pay and concluded a third treaty with them. For their part, the Athenians at Samos decided to leave Alcibiades alone because he refused to join them, and he 'was not the man for an oligarchy.'[50]

The Athenians, now in the midst of stasis themselves, found it impossible to act militarily with any degree of effectiveness. When Pisander and the other oligarchs who had gone with him returned to Samos from negotiations with Tissaphernes, they made every effort to bolster their influence with the Athenian army stationed there 'and instigated the upper class in Samos to join them in establishing an oligarchy in the city, the very form of government which a party of them had lately risen to avoid.'[51] The Athenians at Samos sent envoys, including Pisander, back to Athens, establishing oligarchies along the way. However, their attempts to do so often backfired, according to Thucydides, because once they received a 'moderate government and liberty of action' they went on to insist on freedom (from Athens) instead of being seduced by the Athenians' 'show of reform.'[52]

Pisander and the rest of the embassy from Samos reached Athens and found that their oligarchic associates there had already assassinated an enemy of Alcibiades and killed other 'obnoxious' people, and demanded that 'no pay should be given except to persons serving in the war, and that not more than five thousand should share in the government, and those such as were most able to serve the state in person and in purse.'[53] The government of the Five Thousand, wrote Thucydides, was a mere 'catchword for the multitude.' The oligarchic conspirators of approximately 400 men would really run the government. For the entire time the Four Hundred governed, the Five Thousand was a myth, but most people did not know whether they existed or not. The people saw the numbers of the conspirators, and thought of the potential of 5,000 of them, and kept their mouths shut out of fear. Opponents were killed, and mistrust reigned, because no one could be sure if their friends were really part of the Five Thousand or not. Divided about what they thought, the common people did not oppose the actions of the few.[54]

Pisander moved quickly. He called an assembly at which the democratic institutions were officially abolished. He moved to elect ten commissioners who would frame a new constitution. He called an assembly and moved that 'any Athenian might propose with impunity whatever measure he pleased, heavy penalties being imposed upon any who should indict for illegality, or otherwise molest him for doing so.'[55] After this, he was able to propose an end to any pay for holding offices, and that five men would be elected presidents. They would elect one hundred and each of the one hundred would elect three more, which would then constitute the four hundred who would 'convene the five thousand whenever they pleased.'[56] Then, writes Thucydides, they ruled the city by force. But they did not recall Alcibiades.

Thucydides takes the time at this juncture to comment on the quality of these oligarchic leaders, and his appraisal of them probably speaks volumes about his own aristocratic background and leanings. Pisander was thought to be the chief strategist behind all of these actions because he put forward most of the proposals. But Antiphon, 'one of the best men of his day,' was most crucially important, the real brains behind the plan. He had 'a head to contrive measures and a tongue to recommend them, [but] did not willingly come forward in the assembly or upon any public scene.'[57] He stayed in the shadows, looked down upon by the multitude 'because of his talent.' Nevertheless, his advice was crucial at aiding other more outspoken leaders like Pisander. When the Four Hundred were overthrown, writes Thucydides, he made the best defence of himself of 'any known up to my time' (he was killed anyway). Here Thucydides makes the connection between oligarchy and a greater concentration of virtue or wisdom which, as Jeremy Neill states in his chapter in this volume, Aristotle later made more systematically. Thucydides also mentions Phrynichus and Theramenes as men of great ability and enthusiasm for the oligarchy.

> Conducted by so many and by such sagacious heads, the enterprise, great as it was, not unnaturally went forward; although it was no light matter to deprive the Athenian people of its freedom, almost a hundred years after the deposition of the tyrants, when it had been not only not subject to any during the whole of that period, but accustomed during more than half of it to rule over subjects of its own.[58]

The oligarchs were unopposed. They put to death some men (but, Thucydides says, not that many) and imprisoned and banished others they thought might be a threat. King Agis, who tried to take advantage of the city's turmoil at this time, met with united force and was repelled. Seeing no real dissent in Athens of which he could take advantage, he turned his attention to establishing a peace between Athens and Sparta. In a dramatic twist, while the government of Athens was now oligarchic, the people of Samos and the Athenian forces there had rebelled against their oligarchy of 300 previously established there 'and lived together under a democratic government for the future.'[59] Some of the rulers were killed and some were banished. Most were given amnesty, and accepted the restored democracy there. Having heard all sorts of rumours about the excesses of the oligarchs at Athens, the army now swore their opposition to Athens' government of the Four Hundred. 'The struggle now was between the army trying to force a democracy upon the city, and the Four Hundred an oligarchy upon the camp [Samos].'[60] The soldiers at Samos decided to operate a second Athenian government at Samos, using their fleet, which was most of the Athenian fleet, in order to collect tribute from Athens' subject cities. 'The home government had done wrong in abolishing the institutions of their ancestors, while the army maintained the said institutions, and would try to force the home government to do likewise.'[61] Despite this change, they wanted to guarantee Alcibiades his security and recall him in exchange for his obtaining the alliance of the King of Persia. This army continued the war effort against Sparta while the government of the Four Hundred at Athens was attempting to sue for peace with Sparta. Athens also sent ambassadors to Samos to set the record straight about how they had behaved during the takeover and their reasons for action.

The Athenians at Samos elected Alcibiades their general and handed all affairs over to him, still hoping he could bring Tissaphernes' support with him. 'There was now not a man in the army who would have exchanged his present hopes of safety and vengeance upon the Four Hundred for any consideration whatever.'[62] Then 'Alcibiades for the first time did the state a service and one of the most signal kind.'[63] After ignoring the explanations of envoys from Athens, the troops at Samos were ready to vote to invade their own city in order to abolish the oligarchy, but Alcibiades strongly opposed it. In a masterful rhetorical manoeuvre, he offered, as a way out, that he did not object to the government of the Five Thousand and that it should be put in place of the Four Hundred. This proposal was carried back to Athens by the envoys who had been sent to Samos. It resonated there, as some leaders of the oligarchy began to say that 'the Five Thousand must be shown to exist not merely in name but in reality, and the constitution placed upon a fairer basis.'[64] Now oligarchs began to compete for influence and popularity, a tendency which Thucydides remarks is a 'line of conduct so surely fatal to oligarchies that arise out of democracies.'[65] In reality, he says, this was now a competition for who would become leader of the people. The more loyal oligarchs, meanwhile, attempted to send rather desperate messages of reconciliation to Sparta, which were rebuffed, and the clamour was on to restore the democracy. 'For instead of saying in so many words "all who wished the commons to govern," they still disguised themselves under the name of the Five Thousand; being afraid that these might really exist, and that they might be speaking to one of their number and get into trouble through ignorance.'[66]

The Athenians, in the midst of what amounted to a democratic revolution going on in their city, were compelled to try to defend Euboea against the Peloponnesians and were roundly defeated because of their lack of composure. This caused even more political chaos at home:

When the news of what had happened in Euboea reached Athens a panic ensued such as they had never before known. Neither the disaster in Sicily, great as it seemed at the time, nor any other had ever so much alarmed them. The camp at Samos was in revolt; they had no more ships or men to man them; they were at discord among themselves and might at any moment come to blows; and a disaster of this magnitude coming on the top of all, by which they lost their fleet, and worst of all Euboea, which was of more value to them than Attica, could not occur without throwing them into the deepest despondency.[67]

· But in the midst of this crippling turmoil, 'as on so many other occasions the Lacedaemonians proved the most convenient people in the world for the Athenians to be at war with. The wide difference between the two characters, the slowness and want of energy of the Lacedaemonians as contrasted with the dash and enterprise of their opponents, proved of the greatest service, especially to a maritime empire like Athens.'[68]

The Four Hundred were deposed and government was handed over to the Five Thousand. All who could furnish a suit of armour would be included. No one would receive pay for any office. At this juncture, Thucydides makes his most definitive statement of approval for any form of government, and it is not clearly democratic or oligarchic, but what might be called 'mixed.' This statement foreshadows Aristotle's endorsement of the mixed regime or polity, which, Jeremy Neill in his chapter points out, is also 'similar to the political ideals of the American founders.' 'It was during the first period of this constitution that the Athenians appear to have enjoyed the best government that they ever did, at least in my time,' wrote Thucydides. 'For the fusion of the high and the low was effected with judgment, and this was what first enabled the state to rise up her head after her manifold disasters.'[69] Thucydides says that with this action 'the oligarchy and the troubles at Athens ended,' so he must not have thought of this government as an oligarchy.[70]

The Athenians reconciled with Alciabiades and the troops at Samos and resolved to fight the war as vigorously as they could. The Athenians rallied and, for a time, had the Peloponnesians on the defensive again. This is where Thucydides' *History* ends. Of course, we know that the Peloponnesians soon got the upper hand and defeated Athens, but it is noteworthy that near the end of his work, Thucydides praises the mixed government of the Five Thousand as the best government Athens had had in his lifetime.

Thucydides' Politics

Through this analysis we have seen that Thucydides does not think that the only thing necessary to explaining the war is relative power, as strict realists would have us believe. His account of the war is in fact full of analysis that acknowledges the importance of national differences and that recognizes the advent of new ways of expressing and advocating those differences that in modern language are best described as ideological. This view, that the ideology that is produced by any given regime type matters a great deal, has notable current resonances. It resonates with a new type of warfare that involves the subversion of the enemy via what we might now call 'regime change,' and describes the internal ideological battles within Athens and its military. This way of looking at regime type and ideology was reflected well in the Bush administration's policy of democratic regime change, while the Obama administration has unsuccessfully attempted to disassociate itself with this policy. The idea advocated by the Bush administration was that regime type more or less determined ideology and thus foreign policy. From that point of view, the Muslim extremism that led to terrorist attacks stemmed from the closed systems, such as theocracies or de facto dictatorships, that ruled states like Iran and Syria. This view still leads some observers to hope that the uprisings against the former regimes currently underway will, if they topple the governments, usher in a more Western-friendly foreign policy and begin a process that unravels the old power structures in the Middle East.

While today we can certainly find advocates for liberal democracy who believe that it brings peace in its wake, we cannot so confidently find in Thucydides an advocate of any regime type or corresponding ideology as a solution to the disaster of war. There are certain parts of the *History* that seem to speak to his allegiance to or at least admiration for particular types of regimes, but the problem is that he expresses this admiration about more than one type. In Book 1, as we have seen, Thucydides mentions the ancient tyrannies and indicates that most Athenians do not really understand this history.[71] And in Book 6, we find him praising tyranny, or at least what he considers to be wise or benevolent tyranny. Thucydides makes a digression to correct the Athenians' misconceptions about the demise of the old tyranny of the Pisistratids (mid-fifth century BCE) by which Athens had been governed prior to the Persian Wars. In it he gives his own opinion about the value of at least that particular tyranny, an opinion that has led some to think that perhaps tyranny or monarchy was Thucydides' preferred form of government:

> Indeed, generally their government was not grievous to the multitude, or in any way odious in practice; and these tyrants cultivated wisdom and

virtue as much as any, and without exacting from the Athenians more than a twentieth of their income, splendidly adorned their city, and carried on their wars, and provided sacrifices for the temples. For the rest, the city was left in full enjoyment of its existing laws, except that care was always taken to have the offices in the hands of some one of the family.[72]

Thomas Hobbes, in the introductory material to his own translation of Thucydides' *History*, made much of the ancient historian's family connections, including the possibility that he was related to the Pisistratids, and concludes that Thucydides' noble birth and aristocratic leanings made him a supporter of monarchy. In Hobbes's view, it was also clear that 'he least of all liked the democracy.'[73] Of course, it is characteristic of Hobbes more than Thucydides to find the historian's chief admiration aimed at monarchy rather than oligarchy. Michael Palmer argues that rather than being a direct endorsement of a type of government, Thucydides is alluding to the mistake the Athenians were making regarding Alcibiades. 'Just as the tyranny of the Pisistratids does not deserve the calumny of the many, Alcibiades does not deserve their blame. Thucydides' primary intention in correcting the common opinion about the Athenian tyrants and would-be tyrannicides is to correct the common opinion regarding Alcibiades and his relations with the Athenian democracy.'[74] Because of where this story is brought in, it is difficult to deny this is Thucydides' intention, and because Alcibiades at this time is a leader attempting to lead a democracy, we have to say that Thucydides' focus here is on the individual and not on the type of regime. Just as the Pisistratids could offer wise and moderate government under a tyranny, so might Alcibiades have offered the government the Athenians needed under a democracy.

Given that Thucydides spends no more time praising tyranny, we can move on to other more likely possibilities. Thucydides was an Athenian, and Athens was, for most of the time in which he wrote, a democracy. It is commonly acknowledged that Thucydides had a great admiration for Pericles, the first man in Athens at the outbreak of the Peloponnesian War, and approved of his strategy for fighting the war. But would Thucydides endorse the democratic regime type as better, smarter, more likely to bring stability and peace, such as would today's advocates of democratic regime change? After his speech in which he lays out his strategy to defeat Sparta, Thucydides assesses Pericles as being a man who could control the democracy when no one else could (except perhaps Alcibiades, as we have seen, if he had been given the chance). He notes that the public anger toward him for the hardships of the war led the people to fine Pericles; 'however, according to the way of the multitude, they again elected him general and committed all their affairs to his hands.' Pericles advised them with a measured and limited war strategy, but after his death they did the opposite, 'allowing private ambitions and private interests, in matters apparently quite foreign to the war, to lead them into projects unjust both to themselves and to their allies – projects whose success would only conduce to the honour and advantage of private persons, and whose failure entailed certain disaster on the country in the war.'[75] While Pericles held sway in Athens, 'what was nominally a democracy became in his hands government by the first citizen. With his successors it was different. More on a level with one another, and each grasping at supremacy, they ended by committing even the conduct of state affairs to the whims of the multitude.'[76] Thucydides specifically cites the Sicilian Expedition as one of the 'blunders' that Athens committed after Pericles' death. He refers to Pericles' 'genius,' which had given the Athenians so many resources that it was difficult to lose despite themselves, but lose they did.

Clearly, Thucydides sees Pericles as the exception to the rule in democracy. Martha C. Taylor provides an analysis of Thucydides' description of the government of the Four Hundred that took over Athens in the spring of 411 and disagrees with those scholars who see Thucydides as an advocate of democracy. Such scholars tend to view the Athenian oligarchy as the result of a violent and oppressive takeover that forced the Athenian *demos* into retreat. But in depicting the event in this way, argues Taylor, they ignore what Thucydides actually says about the government as well as the people's response to it. 'In fact, Thucydides takes great care to charge the Athenian people themselves with a large share of responsibility for the oligarchy. Some embrace it outright for the sake of money. Others accept it with only a token reluctance. Thucydides shows few, if any, resisting oligarchy and defending the traditional regime. The Athenian democrats in Thucydides' account do not do well by their democracy.'[77] That is, Taylor believes that Thucydides uses the oligarchic coup as an opportunity to praise the character of the oligarchy and to criticize the foibles of democracy, the latter being so easily cowed by the possible presence of the Five Thousand, and so easily tempted by the lure of Persian pay.

In fact, Thucydides gives us many indications that he is no uncritical admirer of democracy, despite the fact that he lives in one, and thus that he would not be an uncritical advocate of spreading democracy as a means of achieving peace. This really should not come as a surprise, considering that he himself was a general, exiled from Athens by the people fairly early on in the war for failing to stop the fall of Amphipolus (though he said he had not been able to arrive in time to save it). He has speakers as opposed as Cleon and Diodotus point out the weakness of the decision-making powers of the demos.[78] Indeed, he has Diodotus say that the people 'visit the disasters into which the whim of the moment may have led you, upon the single person of your advisor, not upon yourselves, his numerous companions in error,' and suggest that the best counsellor of the people must 'lie in order to be believed.'[79] He shows how leaders like Cleon, who are rash and prone to bad decisions, can continue to hold undue influence in democracies.[80] Writing of the start of the Sicilian Expedition, Thucydides says of Cleon that 'as the multitude is wont to do, the more Cleon shrank from the expedition and tried to back out of what he had said, the more they encouraged Nicias to hand over his command, and clamoured at Cleon to go.'[81] He frequently notes the volatility, lack of wisdom and foresight, the blind ambition of the people, and the ease at which they could be swayed to change their minds on crucial issues. These are the negative qualities of democracy that, as Jeff Sikkenga points out, the American founders took to heart when rejecting democracy as an option for the new nation.

What about oligarchy? Thucydides came from an aristocratic background. There is evidence to suggest that 'among the branches of Thucydides' family-tree the names of Miltiades, Kimon, and the son of Melesias are conspicuous.'[82] Thucydides can be found praising the Spartans and allies like the Chians, who shared the oligarchic form of government: 'Indeed, after the Lacedaemonians, the Chians are the only people that I have known who knew how to be wise in prosperity, and who ordered their city the more securely the greater it grew.'[83] But really, Thucydides' most definitive endorsement of any form of government occurs in reference to what Hobbes refers to as a government that mixed the few and the many. As we have seen, his endorsement comes in Book 8: 'It was during the first period of this constitution that the Athenians appear to have enjoyed the best government that they ever did, at least in my time. For the fusion of the high and low was effected with judgment, and this was what first enabled the state to raise up her head after her manifold disasters.'[84]

Despite this last evidence, we may never know exactly Thucydides' own political leanings, but we can confidently say that for Thucydides, ideology – particularly the democratic and oligarchic ideologies that came to the fore in his time – was an important factor in explaining the cause and unfolding of the war. To that extent, he would agree with those who reject the realist 'black box' view of nation-states. However, he would not agree that regime type *determines* foreign policy, especially in a predictably peaceful direction. In his analysis Thucydides acknowledges both the desire for power of individuals and nations as well as ideological zeal as strong motivations for doing violence. He treats international violence as an essentially insoluble part of the human condition. Hence Thucydides is still a realist, but a realist who does not see the desire for power as the only important reason why nations go to war. In his work we see for perhaps the first time the power of political ideas to pit nation against nation, as well as to divide countries and plunge them into the worst kind of civil strife.

NOTES

1 Thucydides, *The Complete Writings of Thucydides: The Peloponnesian War* trans. Richard Crawley (New York: The Modern Library, 1951), 1.20.3.
2 *The Peloponnesian War* 1.22.4.
3 David A. Welch, 'Why International Relations Theorists Should Stop Reading Thucydides,' *Review of International Studies* 29 (2003): 301–19.
4 See Laurie M. Johnson, *Thucydides, Hobbes, and the Interpretation of Realism* (DeKalb, IL: Northern Illinois University Press, 1993), and Laurie M. Johnson Bagby, 'The Use and Abuse of Thucydides in International Relations,' *International Organization* 48, no. 1 (1994): 131–53.
5 *The Peloponnesian War* 1.17.
6 *The Peloponnesian War* 1.70.2–5.
7 *The Peloponnesian War* 1.75.3–4.
8 *The Peloponnesian War* 1.76.2–3.
9 *The Peloponnesian War* 1.77.3–4.
10 *The Peloponnesian War* 1.79.2.
11 *The Peloponnesian War* 1.88.
12 *The Peloponnesian War* 1.89.1–2.
13 *The Peloponnesian War* 1.95.1–2.
14 *The Peloponnesian War* 1.127.3.
15 *The Peloponnesian War* 1.141.6–7.

16 *The Peloponnesian War* 2.37.2–3.
17 *The Peloponnesian War* 2.34.1–3.
18 C.F. Alford, 'The "Iron Law of Oligarchy" in the Athenian Polis ... and Today,' *Canadian Journal of Political Science* 18, no. 2 (1985): 296.
19 Ibid., 303.
20 Martin Ostwald, 'Oligarchy and Oligarchs in Ancient Greece,' in *Polis and Politics*, ed. Pernille Flensted-Jensen, Thomas Heine Nielsen, and Lene Rubinstein (Copenhagen: Museum Tusculanum Press, 2000), 386.
21 Marc Cogan, 'Plataea, and Corcyra Ideology and Policy in Thucydides, Book Three,' *Phoenix* 35, no. 1 (1981): 8.
22 *The Peloponnesian War* 3.47.1–3.
23 Cogan, 'Plataea, and Corcyra Ideology and Policy in Thucydides, Book Three,' 17.
24 Donald Kagan, *The Outbreak of the Peloponnesian War* (Ithaca, NY: Cornell University Press, 2006), 208–9.
25 *The Peloponnesian War* 3.70.2–4.
26 *The Peloponnesian War* 3.70.5–6.
27 *The Peloponnesian War* 3.70.6.
28 *The Peloponnesian War* 3.72.2–3.
29 *The Peloponnesian War* 3.75.3–5.
30 *The Peloponnesian War* 3.81.3–4.
31 *The Peloponnesian War* 3.81.4–5.
32 Clifford Orwin, 'Stasis and Plague: Thucydides on the Dissolution of Society,' *The Journal of Politics* 50, no. 4 (1988): 836.
33 *The Peloponnesian War* 3.82.1–2.
34 Cogan, 'Plataea, and Corcyra Ideology and Policy in Thucydides, Book Three,' 2.
35 Ibid., 4.
36 *The Peloponnesian War* 3.82.4–5.
37 *The Peloponnesian War* 3.82.2–3.
38 *The Peloponnesian War* 3.82.8.
39 *The Peloponnesian War* 3.84.3.
40 *The Peloponnesian War* 8.1.4.
41 *The Peloponnesian War* 8.2.4.
42 *The Peloponnesian War* 8.21.
43 *The Peloponnesian War* 8.47.2.
44 *The Peloponnesian War* 8.47.2.
45 *The Peloponnesian War* 8.48.4–7.
46 *The Peloponnesian War* 8.48.2–4.
47 *The Peloponnesian War* 8.49.
48 *The Peloponnesian War* 8.53.1–2.
49 *The Peloponnesian War* 8.53.2.

50 *The Peloponnesian War* 8.63.4.

51 *The Peloponnesian War* 8.63.4.

52 *The Peloponnesian War* 8.64.5.

53 *The Peloponnesian War* 8.65.3.

54 *The Peloponnesian War* 8.66.

55 *The Peloponnesian War* 8.67.3.

56 *The Peloponnesian War* 8.67.3.

57 *The Peloponnesian War* 8.25.29.

58 *The Peloponnesian War* 8.68.4.

59 *The Peloponnesian War* 8.73.6.

60 *The Peloponnesian War* 8.76.1–2.

61 Ibid.

62 *The Peloponnesian War* 8.82.1–2.

63 *The Peloponnesian War* 8.86.4–5.

64 *The Peloponnesian War* 8.89.3.

65 *The Peloponnesian War* 8.89.3.

66 *The Peloponnesian War* 8.92.11.

67 *The Peloponnesian War* 8.96.1–3.

68 *The Peloponnesian War* 8.96.5.

69 *The Peloponnesian War* 8.97.2–3.

70 *The Peloponnesian War* 8.98.4.

71 *The Peloponnesian War* 1.20.

72 *The Peloponnesian War* 6.54.5–6.

73 Thomas Hobbes, *Hobbes's Thucydides*, trans. Richard Schlatter (New Brunswick, NJ: Rutgers University Press, 1975), 13.

74 Michael Palmer, 'Alcibiades and the Question of Tyranny in Thucydides,' *Canadian Journal of Political Science* 15, no. 1 (1982): 115.

75 *The Peloponnesian War* 2.65.7–8.

76 *The Peloponnesian War* 2.65.10–11.

77 Martha C. Taylor, 'Implicating the Demos: A Reading of Thucydides on the Rise of the Four Hundred,' *The Journal of Hellenic Studies* 122 (2002): 94.

78 *The Peloponnesian War* 3.38,42.

79 *The Peloponnesian War* 3.43.2–3. See Laurie M. Johnson Bagby, 'Rethinking the Diodotean Argument,' *Interpretation: A Journal of Political Philosophy* 18, no. 1 (1990): 53–62.

80 *The Peloponnesian War* 4.21.3.

81 *The Peloponnesian War* 4.28.3–4.

82 Malcolm F. McGregor, 'The Politics of the Historian Thucydides,' *Phoenix* 10, no. 3 (1956): 94.

83 *The Peloponnesian War* 8.24.4–5.

84 *The Peloponnesian War* 8.97.2.

7 Oligarchs and Democrats

LEAH BRADSHAW

Oligarchy is not a term heard much in the discourse on contemporary politics, although it is a useful one. Oligarchy in the classical understanding given to us by Plato and Aristotle is the rule of the rich. It belongs in a hierarchy of regime typologies, each of which is defined according to the dominant social force that underpins the form of government. In the descent of regimes catalogued in Book 8 of Plato's *Republic*, oligarchy sits squarely in the middle, between timocracy (the rule of the warrior types) and democracy (the rule of the many). At the extremes of the hierarchy are the best regime, the utopian rule of philosopher-kings, and the worst, tyranny. Interestingly for us contemporary liberal democrats, oligarchy is identified by Aristotle as a *better* form of rule than democracy in some respects. I want to explore the connection in this paper between oligarchy and moderation. Starting from the categorizations in Plato and Aristotle, I compare the rule of the rich in this classical context with John Locke's *Second Treatise on Government*, in which Locke identifies the pursuit of wealth and property as the foundation of the modern representative state. I believe that Locke really elevates the oligarchic state to the best regime, counting upon state protection of money and property to provide political stability. The paper will argue that Locke's project fails, ultimately, for reasons identified in the classical teachings of Plato and Aristotle. Pursuit of wealth may be a reasonable goal, when it is understood as a necessary support for political community, but the sanction of unlimited acquisition leads to political ruin. It does so, first, because it prohibits the cultivation of *moderation* and in fact disparages moderation as an unnecessary restraint upon entrepreneurship, and it does so, second, because the push toward accumulation bursts the boundaries of the political community and pushes toward empire and global markets. As we well know in the West, the notion that markets will regulate themselves, and that the pursuit of wealth will automatically result in a more peaceful and just world, is under serious assault. As the *Economist* noted in its 2009 end-of-year account of the state of things in the capitalist world, 'the eighteenth century was optimistic that business could bring prosperity; and that prosperity, in its turn, could bring enlightenment,' but 'people [now] fear that mankind is failing to manage [material progress] properly – with the result that, in important ways, their children may not be better off than they are. The forests are disappearing; the ice is melting; social bonds are crumbling; life is becoming a dismal slog in an ugly world.'[1]

Socrates had no illusions about progress. When Socrates engages Glaucon in Book 7 of the *Republic* in a discussion about the types of regime, he warns that 'for everything that has come into being, there is decay.'[2] Socrates has just spent a considerable amount of time with his young friends, building a 'city in speech' in which they have been thinking together about what a perfectly just state might look like. By the end of this discussion, Socrates has cautioned the rest that in thinking about this city, they were doing so for the sake of a pattern for the just man.[3] One can know something about justice but there is no perfectly just city in the real world, and no matter how one may try to construct a just state, factionalism will tear the state apart. In the real world, the tendency of most people is to gravitate toward the enhancement of their private estates, pulling the state toward 'money-making and the possession of land, houses, gold and silver,'[4] although there are those few for whom the possession of private goods is not paramount. These are the timocrats, warrior-citizens whom Socrates describes as 'spirited and simpler men,'[5] men for whom the pursuit of honour and victory in battle is more important than the security that is required for a life of acquisition.[6] There is something admirable about these honour-seekers, whose dedication to a good that goes beyond their own private benefit leads them toward a public-spiritedness, but there is a kind of vacuity in their pursuit. Readiness for war is a uniting, but not necessarily just, pursuit, and one suited to the young and the brave, and it is difficult to maintain a state in a permanent condition of aggression.[7] One can see that warriors do not have pure motives for honour and likely will use their positions of public valour to enhance their own estates: 'They will harvest pleasures stealthily, running away from the law like boys from a father.'[8]

The lure of comfort and wealth is strong, and we can understand that this is a perpetual problem in politics. Interestingly, in the *Republic*, Socrates identifies the slide from timocratic honour into the love of money and possession as a feminization of ends. Timocratic men first 'seek out expenditures for themselves and pervert the laws in that direction; they themselves and their wives disobey them.'[9] The more preoccupied the rulers become with moneymaking, the less they are focused on civic honour. 'There is no other transformation,' says Socrates, 'so quick and so sure from a young man who loves honour to one who loves money.'[10] The regime shifts from one that reveres honour and victory in war to one that reveres the man of wealth. The regime becomes an oligarchy when access to ruling office is defined by the possession of a fixed assessment of money. The rule of money is by definition an inferior regime type to timocracy, because whereas timocracy is the rule of the warrior for the benefit of the whole city, the rule of oligarchs is for their own benefit. Oligarchy is *really* 'two cities,' one of the rich and one of the poor.[11]

Socrates' condemnation of oligarchy is harsh. Oligarchies allow for wide differences between the rich and the poor. An oligarch is a sort of 'squalid man,' seeking always to maximize his own profit, with no care for the broader public good. 'The stingy man is a poor contestant when with his private means he competes for some victory or any other noble object of ambition in a city; he's not willing to spend money for the sake of good reputation in such contests. Afraid to awaken the spendthrift desires and to summon them to an alliance and a love of victory, he makes war like an oligarch, with a few of his troops, is defeated most of the time, and stays rich.'[12] Measured against the self-sacrificing courage of the timocrat in time of battle, the oligarch appears an effete and cautious type, preferring to increase his stores of private wealth, even at the cost of his city. The oligarch is really *anti-political*, using the city for the enhancement of private ends.

Socrates is unequivocal that 'it is not possible to honour wealth in a city and at the same time adequately to maintain moderation among the citizens.'[13] The poor build up resentments against the unjust privileging of the rich, and they will plot against this injustice. An oligarchic city will 'fall sick and do battle with itself' as the poor demand a share in rule, and this is how democracy comes into being out of oligarchy. The transition from oligarchy to democracy is not one toward a greater virtue; it is actually a further decline. The poor rise up against the rich with a demand for rule, but what they desire is a greater share in the pleasures afforded by wealth, not a return to the public-spirited military culture of the timocracy. Democracy appeals not only to the poor and the excluded, but to the offspring of oligarchs who have been raised in luxury and privilege and are bored by the mendacity of a life of wealth. A young man, raised in wealth, may taste the honey of 'wild fiery beasts' and may well be enticed by the call to freedom and licence, and so 'begins his change from an oligarchic regime within himself to a democratic one.'[14]

Socrates' picture of the decline of regimes is a sobering one. Without the structure of discipline and dedication to the state, these young men will drift toward satisfying base pleasures. In Socrates' characterization of the decline of regimes, the 'stingy' oligarchic father produces an immoderate, democratic son who will be drawn to 'insolence, anarchy, and wastefulness.'[15] Too much money and too little instruction in responsibility and virtue will lead to the indulgence of base passions, and for the sake of gratifying these passions, the young will 'take away and distribute the parental property.'[16] Socrates' chronicle of this decline puts one in mind of the afflictions of contemporary Western democracy. The indulgence in drugs, pornography, cosmetic surgery, and entertainment may be symptomatic of the necessary dissipation of oligarchic political structures. Too much affluence with no coherent thought of an end for which that pursuit of affluence is intended will inevitably be directed toward the baser desires of the body.

How many times in the contemporary world have we heard stories of collapsed financial empires in the hands of indulged children? The father works his way up the ladder of success, establishes great wealth, produces a family to whom he gives all the luxuries and advantages that he himself did not have, and the children repay him by driving his wealth into obscurity. The message is that oligarchic tendencies have a temporarily moderating effect, because someone who is out to acquire wealth and property can apply enormous discipline to the task. The problem is that acquisition is not a meaningful end in itself, and without the tempering effect of education and philanthropy, the oligarchic regime will degenerate. Democracy is even more precarious than oligarchy, because democracy is a regime in which *all* desires are fostered, even those most base. The democratic 'son' likely will treat the oligarchic 'father' with contempt, calling his fiscal moderation a kind of 'cowardliness,' accusing that his measured and orderly expenditure is 'rustic and illiberal.'[17] Of course, from what Socrates has already told us about oligarchy, the son is largely right in his accusations. He is wrong in that he chooses unbridled freedom as the alternative. If he had had a proper education from the father, he might well reject the oligarchic pursuit, but in favour of virtue or even civic pride, not freedom.

Central to this story that Socrates tells of oligarchy and its pitfalls is his conviction that the pursuit of money can never gratify certain longings that are integral to human beings, and particularly to men. Honour is a more manly pursuit than money, and virtue the highest pursuit of all. One cannot expect virtue to rule in politics, but it is possible though the cultivation of public honours (particularly in war) to ground a city, or a state, in a sense of common purpose that transcends private gain. Once a city turns to the reward of wealth and acquisition, it will degenerate rapidly into two cities of the rich and the poor, and it will have the added problem of spirited young men for whom the management of wealth is a less than gratifying life project.

Aristotle has much to say about oligarchies too. He does not measure his regime typologies against the standard of 'perfect justice,' so his views on oligarchy appear to be more charitable. Most people, Aristotle says, think that regimes in ancient Greece are either democracies or oligarchies, and in claiming this, they make a simple distinction between the rule of the many and the rule of the few.[18] Aristotle compares oligarchies and democracies, respectively, to aristocracies and polities, the latter divided also by rule by the few, rule by the many, except that the ruling principle in these latter regimes is a kind of virtue, not monopoly on wealth. From Aristotle's perspective, political virtue is a dedication to the common good of the city. Neither oligarchs nor democrats have the common weal as a priority. In fact, Aristotle would rather define oligarchies and democracies *exclusively* within the terms of who owns what. 'Democracy exists when the free and poor, being a majority, have authority to rule; oligarchy, when the wealthy and better born have authority and are few.'[19] Aristotle spends a great deal of time in *The Politics* speaking to the issues of oligarchies and democracies because, while these types of regime may be deficient from the standpoint of virtue, they are in fact the most common kinds of political arrangement in the ancient Greek polis. Much of Aristotle's project, then, evolves on how one can make the best of a practical situation. How can one mitigate the excesses peculiar to oligarchies and democracies so that these types of regime can be better rather than worse?

Although Aristotle's general distinction between oligarchies and democracies pertains to the rule of the few versus the rule of the many, he points out that who the few and the many are, and hence the entitlement to rule, can vary from one context to another. The majority in a democracy can consist of farmers, craftsmen, the 'marketing element,' or the 'fishing element.'[20] Oligarchies can have regulations stipulating that only the very rich can hold office, they can have rules whereby some offices are held by election, they can be dynasties in which the son automatically succeeds the father in positions of rule, and so on. Despite the general definition of oligarchy and democracy, in other words, there can be a wide variety of institutional forms characterizing either oligarchy or democracy. If we pay too much attention to the institutional structures, we may mistake a democracy for an oligarchy, or vice versa. Just because there are elections does not mean we are living in a democracy. Just because the wealthy seem to have a lot of power does not mean that we do not live in a democracy. 'It should not be overlooked,' Aristotle says, 'that it has happened in many places that, although the regime insofar as it is based on the laws is not a popular one, it is governed in popular fashion as a result of the character and upbringing of the citizens. Similarly, it has happened elsewhere that the regime insofar as it is based on the laws tends toward the popular, but through the citizens' upbringing and habits tends to be oligarchically run.'[21] Aristotle's message is that to understand whether a city (or state) is an oligarchy or a democracy, we look to what we might now call 'socialization,' and to the configuration of wealth and power among the citizens, not necessarily to the legal and constitutional structures. The kind of oligarchy that is *closest* to democracy is one in which a large number of people own property 'but in lesser amounts and not overly much' and participation in the ruling offices is open to anyone who possesses property.[22]

As in the *Republic*, Aristotle identifies the principal sites of contestation in politics to be ones concerning honour and money. The people may perceive that political power is unjustly co-opted by the wealthy. In an oligarchy, the specific dangers are twofold: the oligarchs may be fearful of the encroachment by the people, but they are also in competition with one another. Aristotle runs through a number of 'case studies' of acrimony among the ruling oligarchs, resulting in one of the oligarchs culling the favour of the people to overthrow his adversary.[23] Oligarchies may run into difficulty if they are forced into a state of war, and since they do not have support of the people, they may have to rely on mercenaries, who likely will turn on them at some point. Common problems in oligarchies in general are the expenditure of private wealth in 'wanton living'[24] and manipulating or paying off the courts for preferential treatment in private matters.[25]

The downfall of oligarchic regimes for Aristotle is tied explicitly to the failure of moderation. Moderation for Aristotle is an ethical virtue, one cultivated by thought and habit. Specifically with respect to accumulation, Aristotle says that for everything there is a use-value, an exchange value, and a 'business value.'[26] A shoe is to cover a foot, not to make money. In a community of many people, one can see plainly that things would be exchanged as a matter of efficiency. Exchange, Aristotle tells us, is 'not contrary to nature,' because it supports a kind of self-sufficiency. If I make shoes, I may trade a pair of shoes for someone else's wine. The invention of money, Aristotle conjectures, arose reasonably enough 'as the assistance of foreigners became greater in importing what [the community] was in need of and exporting what is surplus.'[27] Implied in this passage is the clear association of money with the abandonment of the idea of the polis as a self-sufficient community. Money opens up one to the world.

Business, or commerce, is made possible only with the introduction of money, and for Aristotle 'the expertise that is according to nature is something different: this is expertise in household management, while the other is commercial expertise, which is productive of wealth not in every way but in trafficking in goods.'[28] Business activity, for Aristotle, is an *unnatural* although reasonable engagement, and its unnaturalness stems from its lack of limit. Acquisition is a necessary and even admirable pursuit within the proper boundaries, and those boundaries are the sustenance of the household (in the private realm), leaving enough leisure and prosperity so that one might attend to higher pursuits, like political engagement, or thinking. Accumulators are 'serious about living, but not about living well; and since that desire of theirs is without limit, they also desire what is productive of unlimited things.'[29] Aristotle anticipates the popular charge: 'If you are so smart, why aren't you rich?' Thales, the philosopher, was reproached by others for his poverty and his 'uselessness,' whereupon Thales decided to enlist his knowledge to make a profit for himself. Because of his knowledge of astronomy, Thales predicted a rich olive harvest, and so he borrowed some money and bought up a lot of olive presses at a low rate. As predicted, the harvest was bountiful and Thales became a rich man, thus proving to his critics 'how easy it is for philosophers to become wealthy if they so wish, but this is not what they are serious about.'[30]

For Aristotle, the problem with 'business activity' is precisely its lack of boundaries. Industry does not remain constant, and once one encourages the unlimited desire of accumulation, this boundlessness is likely to spiral downward into the gratification of other desires. Too many possessions seem to be connected to the desire for bodily gratifications, and if there are no 'natural limits' on the pursuit of desires, it is only a matter of time (or generation) that the industrious and the rational become decadent and self-indulgent. 'As gratification consists in excess, [the business types] seek the sort that is productive of the excessive characteristic of gratification; and if they are unable to satisfy it through expertise in business they attempt this in some other fashion, using each sort of capacity in a way not according to nature.'[31]

What are Aristotle's prescriptions for arresting the degeneration of oligarchy? The kind of oligarchy that is closest to democracy, without actually becoming democracy, seems in some way to be Aristotle's preferred state among those that he thinks are practically possible. Since it is a fact that most people prefer to take care of their own interests, and their own private affairs, perhaps it is best to manage a state with a view to this reality. It does not help much to condemn acquisition and property from the standards of virtue or honour, but it may help to teach moderation in these pursuits. 'Thus it is the greatest good fortune,' Aristotle writes, 'for those who are engaged in politics to have a middling and sufficient property, because where some possess very many things, and others nothing, either [rule of] the people in its extreme form must come into being, or – as a result of both these excesses – tyranny. For tyranny arises from the most headstrong sort of democracy and from oligarchy, but much less often from the middling sorts [of regime].'[32] To build and sustain such a regime, midway between oligarchy and democracy, is very difficult. The tendency is for one element – either the wealthy or the poor – to become dominant and to 'overstep the middle path, and conduct the regime to suit itself.'[33] Aristotle's general advice is that revolutions always occur in regimes in which there is the 'disproportionate growth of a part.'[34]

Moderation is the key to political stability (not justice). Aristotle is just as wary of the rule of wealth as Socrates, it seems, but perhaps more pragmatic in looking to its management rather than chastisement. It is always a mistake in politics to reward the rich with too much and deceive the people. 'For in time from things falsely good there must result a true evil, and the aggrandizements of the wealthy are more ruinous to the polity than those of the people.'[35] The most trustworthy person in the regime, Aristotle says, is the middling sort: he who has neither too much nor too little. We might see this to be Aristotle's premonition of the importance of the 'middle class' to modern democratic states. Waller Newell, in his contribution to this volume, takes this up in his judgment through Aristotle that 'ameliorating the tension between haves and have-nots is the indispensable pre-condition for establishing an environment of minimal stability and civic order.' Newell notes that this teaching of Aristotle's can be seen mirrored in modern liberal democracies, where 'the success of the middle class in advancing itself economically has been viewed as a bellwether for the health of the liberal democratic regime altogether, giving the average person a stake in its stability and success.' (Newell does not mention the fact that the disappearance of the middle class, and the growing polarization between the rich and the poor both inside developed countries and between the developed and developing world, is of grave concern.)

The ancient caution against the accumulation of wealth is not one taken seriously by modern liberal democrats for the most part. John Locke, in the seventeenth century, lays the foundations for representative government grounded in the endorsement of unlimited accumulation. Rejecting the classical typologies of politics (rule of the one, the few or the many, based on a variety of ends such as honour, money, power), Locke as we know begins from the premise that we as human beings are by nature solitary and acquisitive creatures. The earth was given by God to all mankind in common, yet Locke establishes that all men have a God-given right to property. Because every man has a property in his own person, 'the labour of his body and the work of his hands, we may say, are properly his.'[36] Labour affords an entitlement to private property by mixing human ingenuity and effort to nature. God gave the world to men in common, but it is clear in Locke that God gave it especially to the 'industrious and the rational.'[37] For those who might complain about appropriation, Locke admonishes that 'he that had as good left for his improvement, as was already taken up, need not complain, ought not to meddle with what was already improved by another's labour.'[38]

There is in Locke's construction an initial curtailment on acquisition in the provision that no man can appropriate more than he can use, for this would lead to spoilage. 'As much as anyone can make use of to any advantage of life before it spoils, so much he may by his labour fix a property in; whatever is beyond this, is more than his share and belongs to others.'[39] Spoilage, however, is not a brake on accumulation, for people can figure out barter and trade, so that it becomes possible to accumulate a lot without spoilage. Locke argues that people agreed 'tacitly' even prior to lawful government to the use of money as a medium of exchange. Currency does not spoil. So for Locke, 'it is plain that men have agreed to a disproportionate and unequal possession of the earth, they having, by tacit and voluntary consent, found out a way how a man may fairly possess more land than he himself can use the product of, by receiving in exchange for the overplus gold and silver, which may be hoarded up without injury to anyone ... this partage of things in an inequality of private possessions, men have made practicable out of the bounds of society, and without compact.'[40]

In Locke's construction, the industrious and the rational are rewarded, even in the natural state, by applying their wiles to property and acquisition. Labour is the key to success for human beings, and 'labour puts the difference of value on everything,' but labour combined with money is the key to abundance, expansion, and progress.[41] In Locke's story about the origins of government, the acrimony that develops between the 'haves' and the 'have-nots' is central. Despite what Locke has argued are the natural foundations of acquisition and property, and the tacit agreement to unequal possession, there are those wayward (and probably lazy) human beings who invade the rightful property of others, thus putting all of mankind into a state of war. Government arises as a contract among the majority of peaceful acquisitors willing to put themselves under the rule of law so as to ensure that their labour power and their industriousness are protected from invasion by transgressors.

Locke writes that government 'has direct jurisdiction only over the land, and reaches the possessor of it (before he has actually incorporated himself in the society) only as he dwells upon, and enjoys that.'[42] And Locke famously pronounces that 'the great and chief end of men's uniting together into commonwealths, and putting themselves under government, is the preservation of their property. To which in the state of nature there are many things wanting.'[43] There is much debate in the Locke scholarship regarding Locke's understanding of commonwealth, but I find wholly persuasive those accounts that emphasize the centrality of property, and the encouragement of expansion and unlimited accumulation. As C.B. Macpherson famously declared, property is the core of Locke's political theory, but property transformed by *money* is the key to truly understanding his intent. 'Locke saw money as not merely a medium of exchange but as capital. Indeed its function as a medium of exchange was seen as subordinate to its function as capital, for in [Locke's] view the purpose of agriculture, industry and commerce was the accumulation of capital. And the purpose of capital was not to provide a consumable income for its owners, but to beget further capital by profitable investment.'[44]

Government exists, in Locke's view, for the protection of the industrious, the rational, and the acquisitive. The rule of law, backed up by force, and formulated in the consensual structure of representative institutions, will ensure that these ends are promoted. The legislative branch of government, elected by the majority, will be subjected to periodic renewal, so that those who are elected do not become accustomed to political power and abuse their authority. By instituting a rotation of office, one ensures that legislators return to their private (acquisitive) lives and therefore will be unlikely to draft laws that militate against their private interests. 'It is a mistake to think, that the supreme or legislative power of any commonwealth, can do what it will, and dispose of the estates of the subject arbitrarily, or take any part of them at pleasure. This is not so much to be feared in governments where the legislative consists, wholly or in part, in assemblies which are variable, whose members, upon the dissolution of the assembly, are subjects under the common laws of their country, equally with the rest.'[45]

The commonwealth requires executive as well as legislative power, partly for reasons of expediency (it is unwieldy to assume that an elected legislature can deliberate on all matters at all times), partly as a mechanism for punishment of transgressors within the state, and partly to deal with the problem of foreign relations and the ever-present possibility of foreign aggression. Locke concedes that war for example may sometimes be necessary, and it may require executive decision. Executive power can be wielded for the 'public good,' but that public good is always tied back to the protection of the *private* good of property. In discussing the causes and cures for dissolution of the commonwealth, Locke reiterates that 'the reason why men enter into society, is the preservation of their property; and the end why they chuse and authorize a legislative is, that there may be laws made, and rules set, as guards and fences to the properties of all members of the society, to limit the power, and moderate the dominion, of every part and member of the society.'[46]

Locke's use of the term 'moderation' is interesting to us, because it is vastly different from the meaning imparted to the word by Aristotle. Locke, it appears, hopes to encourage the pursuit of wealth in a political arrangement regulated by law. 'Moderation' is a task assumed by the state, which has the power of execution to punish transgressors who would seek to exert dominion over others and their property. Aristotelian moderation is actively discouraged, indeed considered almost unholy in Locke's commonwealth, since God gave the earth to the 'industrious and the rational.' Business activity and accumulation for Locke are activities that emerge in the natural condition anterior to the construction of state and law; so in Locke's understanding, they are *natural* human pursuits. In Locke's story of the stages from state of nature, to state of war, to civil society, money is described as a characteristic of the natural condition, even if it required the tacit consent of people. Furthermore, Locke tells us that 'it is plain, that men have agreed to a disproportionate and unequal possession of the earth,' since they found out a way 'how a man may fairly possess more land than he himself can use the product of, by receiving in exchange for the overplus gold and silver, which may be hoarded up without injury to any one.'[47]

Locke's commonwealth looks like an oligarchy in the terms that the ancient philosophers described such a regime. As Aristotle advises, one can have laws that 'tend toward the popular, but through the citizens' upbringing and habits tend to be oligarchically run.' Locke, we might argue, hopes to entrench oligarchic 'stinginess' (frugality, acquisition, careful hoarding) as a way of life, and arrest its decline into the kind of excesses identified by Plato and Aristotle. Throughout Locke's *Second Treatise*, we are presented with images of the Protestant work ethic. Hard-working men increase their bounty, thereby making the world a better place for us all. As Edward Andrew notes, 'Locke painted the charming portrait of rational and industrious proprietors, eschewing waste and unjust greed, cutting down the primal forest and creating, from the God-forsaken wild and waste, cultivated and smiling fields of golden wheat. All individuals benefit from progress and the enlargement of holdings and the rational exploitation of natural and human resources.'[48] Accumulation is an incentive for industry and imagination. Locke, despite his endorsement of 'business activity' and unlimited accumulation, does seem to have a sense that restraint, born out of the abhorrence of waste rather than any moral twinges regarding excess, will exercise itself in the new expansionist state. But does this work? How does Locke deal with the two specific dangers identified in Plato and Aristotle as the most common causes of the dissolution of oligarchies: the resentment of the poor and decadence of the offspring, both catalysts for the transition from oligarchy to democracy?

Plato and Aristotle had identified oligarchies as precarious states because they really are cities divided against themselves, in that they are cities of the rich and poor. Aristotle had warned that 'revolutions always occur in regimes in which there is a disproportionate growth of a part.' In Locke's commonwealth, there is encouragement of disproportion because accumulation is sanctioned and inheritance laws are protected. Some can accumulate vast amounts of wealth, they can use that wealth to employ the labour of others, and they can hand on their wealth to their descendants.[49] The genius of Locke's plan lies in the persuasiveness of his argument that in the state of nature, prior to political contract, people agreed to the unequal possession of the earth, as soon as they tacitly agreed to the use of money. According to Locke, people think that inequality is *fair*. It is fair because it rests, in Locke's story, upon varying levels of industry and applied reason. Part of the story is that anyone can become unequal if he or she works hard enough, and smart enough. In the classical understanding of the democratic pressures on oligarchy, Plato and Aristotle are emphatic that democrats are not protesting oligarchic injustice because it is categorically unjust; they protest it because they want access to the opportunity to become unequal. If Locke succeeds in building a commonwealth in which the opportunity to become unequal is promised to all, this may well set off democratic resistance, but those aspiring to inequality would have to discount the disadvantages accruing to them by inheritance and vast accumulation.

The 'poor' will not revolt as long as they can be persuaded that they have the opportunity to become rich. In addition, Locke constructs government in such a way that resistance is impossible, and can be cut off swiftly by executive power. Should the legislative arm of government 'endeavor to take away and destroy the property of the people,' it puts itself into a state of war with the people, and it devolves to the people to disband the government and constitute a new one. Locke is adamant that even in this case, people are not thrust back into a 'natural' condition, but rather into the pre-contractual (but social) condition of property rights, sanction of unequal possession and agreement to money.[50]

To summarize, for Locke, government by consent, with election, sanctioned by the natural right to property and the defense of 'natural' inequality and unlimited accumulation, are all bulwarks against the erosion of oligarchy into the excesses of democracy, as the ancients understood that degeneration. Jeff Sikkenga, elsewhere in this volume, makes the argument that in the American experiment (articulated through 'Publius') it is precisely this Lockean turn toward acquisition (coupled with the separation of powers in government), and away from the militaristic ambition of the honour seeker, that provides the foundation for a secure contemporary oligarchy, immune to the decay chronicled by the classical thinkers. As Sikkenga writes: 'Sober industriousness will be excited into economic avarice while many of the more ambitious forms of acquisitiveness will be channeled away from politics into building economic empires ... the right to property will be exercised with greater vigour, and the love of power will be turned into a more economically beneficial passion.'

Locke's provisions for staving off the democratic revolution against oligarchic privilege are ingenious, but his formulations may work only as long as disparities between the rich and the less rich are not glaringly huge. This is why Aristotle cautions that the most successful oligarchies are those where a lot of people have a middling sort of wealth. There seems little in Locke's vision that would adhere to this advice. If we look at the contemporary picture of capitalism, as Edward Andrew does, we may have little in the way of optimism that Locke's defence of modern oligarchy works, and may find that Aristotle's warnings are prescient. In fact, the 'two cities' of the rich and the poor may now extend in a global oligarchy to the divide between the industrialized parts of the world and everyone else. Locke argued that efficiency of production, the conquest of nature by human ingenuity and the division of labour, is always good, because it produces greater wealth, thus benefiting the whole of mankind. But there are challenges to this view. Drawing on the work of Amartya Sen, Andrew writes that we know that in the developing world small farms with family labour are more productive, and a better buffer against mass starvation and drought, than large capital-intensive farms subsidized by Western capital and dependent on wage labour. 'Locke's assumption that large and unequal land holdings are most efficient tends to be unquestioned in the industrial world but is highly questionable in Asia and Latin America. Hands employed and directed by managers tend to be less productive than small owners working for themselves.'[51] Andrew's indictment of Locke, and his support for 'small owners working for themselves' echoes a strong current in Aristotle's defence of property attached intimately to the pride in one's own. As Waller Newell has suggested in his chapter in this volume (albeit in the context of Aristotle's critique of communism, not capitalism), property and family are intimately connected in Aristotle's understanding, and 'the household with its concomitants of family ties and private property is at the heart of the love of one's own.' Embedded in Aristotle's defence of property is his conviction that people will care more for what is their own than they will for either that which is held in common or that which is owned by another.

And what of the problem of moral degeneration? Plato and Aristotle emphasize that the endorsement of 'business activity' and accumulation without end is problematic *because* the unlimited pursuit of wealth opens the gates to the unlimited pursuit of all kinds of desires. People who have lots of money look for ways to spend it, and most people with a lot of money will spend it on luxuries, pleasures, entertainment distractions, and what Aristotle describes as 'wanton living.' The oligarch in the making may be a 'stingy' sort, a hoarder, but the oligarch in decline is a spendthrift and decadent character. Accumulation fails to breed moderation and in actuality encourages immoderation in all things. Thomas Pangle writes that Locke was very much concerned with moral education, but that Locke's moral education was an 'enlightened self-interest grounded in rational self-control.'[52] Recognizing that this is a difficult task, Locke encouraged an 'artificial implantation, beginning when very young, of habits of self-control, resting initially on fear of the parents, and eventually on a reconstruction of the natural lust for power, together with a modulation of the natural desires for liberty and pleasure.'[53] These are all measures to prevent the slide from the parsimonious disposition of the oligarch into the free and non-discriminating freedom of the democrat. Locke wanted people to be *civil*, not political, to be industrious and rational, not self-indulgent and hedonistic, to be peaceful moneymakers, not glory-seeking political warriors. Pangle thinks this does not work. It does not work because one cannot in the end cultivate the character virtue of moderation out of an ethos of unlimited accumulation. Property and money have to be curtailed by something *outside their own momentum.* Pangle calls for a reinvigorated political virtue in America, one based on 'a heritage of civic virtues, virtues of gratitude and generosity, of struggle at home and abroad, of sacrifice for freedom rather than mere enjoyment of freedom, of faith in the one God whose oneness inspires and helps weld our oneness as a nation.'[54] Together, Pangle calls these things a 'new infusion of classical republican inspiration.'[55] In Plato's terms, this is sort of like steering the ship back up the grid from oligarchy to timocracy. Can you turn an oligarchic sensibility, once already degenerating into corruption, and accustomed to luxury, comfort, and lack of external discipline, into the disposition of a 'plain and simple' man, the timocratic soldier? Far more likely is the democratic dissolution laid out by the classical thinkers.

We have considered arguments that the problem of oligarchic degeneration can be subdued by the construction of natural right, property, industry, and institutional checks on ambition (John Locke, and Sikkenga in this volume), or, conversely, by the redirection of acquisitive desire into a higher end of civic responsibility (Pangle), and found them to be unpersuasive. The republican project (either through Locke or 'Publius') to subdue oligarchic ambition in the quiet and peaceful business of acquisition has not worked. Property is power, and those who pursue property as an end in itself will seek to expand it indefinitely. Thomas Pangle recognizes this and seeks to redress the problem by redirecting people's passions toward a more focused *political* loyalty to the political integrity of the state. The problem with this 'solution' is that it rests upon the sustaining of a civic virtue grounded in love of country and the willingness to prepare for defence and war. The indulgences of democrats in the modern West, their habituation into a life of luxury and plenitude, and their taste for cosmopolitanism are unlikely to be curtailed by an appeal to the ascetic loyalties that Pangle identifies. Neither *commercial* nor *civic* republicanism addresses the fundamental problem with oligarchy targeted by Socrates and Aristotle, and that is the problem of *desire*. Socrates seems unrelenting in his prediction that the desires of human beings will inevitably drag us down into dissolution and decay, but Aristotle may be more instructive for those of us who hope for political reform. He believes that the *natural* inclinations of most people tend toward their own self-interest, their own property, and their own families. If Aristotle is right, then a successful political community must build upon these natural inclinations and must work to prevent then from corrupting into their unnatural counterparts. Acquisition

for the sake of maintaining one's family and one's community is a
good and natural thing, but acquisition as an end in itself cannot be
the sole end for which we are intended. We have to think about the
kinds of households and communities we want to live in, and these
considerations inform a moderation of our acquisitive impulses.
Locke and his contemporary enthusiasts try to persuade us that we do
not need to think about moderation as a virtue in the modern liberal
democratic republic, but despite Locke's innovative thinking, greed is
what it has always been. Giving free reign to accumulation is a bad
idea. It is a bad idea because it leads to great inequalities, always a
source of injustice and political instability. It is also a bad idea because
it fosters the free reign of other pursuits, like pleasure and power.
Aristotle's modest, but persuasive, remedy for greed is the oligarchic
regime *tending* toward the democratic, with a large number of people
holding property, but not too much property.

NOTES

1 'The Idea of Progress,' *The Economist*, December 2009, 38.
2 Plato, *Republic*, trans. Allan Bloom (New York: Basic Books, 1979), 546a.
3 Plato, *Republic* 472c.
4 Plato, *Republic* 547b.
5 Plato, *Republic* 547e.
6 Plato, *Republic* 548c.
7 Machiavelli of course disagrees with this indictment of the warrior-rule. In
   The Prince, he defines politics as the art of making war, or readying for
   war. 'A ruler must think only of military matters, and in times of peace, he
   should be even more preoccupied with them than in times of war.' Machiavelli, *The Prince*, in *Machiavelli: Selected Political Writings*, trans. David
   Wootton (Indianapolis and Cambridge: Hackett, 1994), ch. 14, 46. Yet Machiavelli seems to identify the 'timocratic' decline in much the same way
   as Socrates. If 'heaven should smile' on a state in such a manner that it felt
   no necessity to go to war, then 'idleness would lead to internal divisions or
   effeminacy; either of these, or both of them together, would bring about its
   collapse.' Machiavelli, *The Prince*, ch. 6, 101.
8 Plato, *Republic* 548b.
9 Plato, *Republic* 550d.
10 Plato, *Republic* 553d.
11 Plato, *Republic* 551d.

12 Plato, *Republic* 555a. Kant famously predicted that modern democracies would be less inclined to war with one another than other kinds of states, because the launching of war requires the consent of the citizens, and since the citizens are largely preoccupied with advancing their private wealth, and are interested in maintaining open channels of trade and commerce, they will be less likely to advocate for war. 'The spirit of commerce' writes Kant, 'sooner or later takes hold of every people, and it cannot exist side by side with war. And of all the powers (or means) at the disposal of the power of the state, *financial* power can probably be relied on most. Thus states find themselves compelled to promote the noble cause of peace, though not exactly from motives of morality.' Immanuel Kant, 'Perpetual Peace,' in *Kant's Political Writings*, trans. H.S. Reiss (Cambridge and London: Cambridge University Press, 1970), 114.

13 Plato, *Republic* 555c.

14 Plato, *Republic* 559e.

15 Plato, *Republic* 561a.

16 Plato, *Republic* 574a.

17 Plato, *Republic* 560d.

18 Aristotle, *The Politics*, trans. Carnes Lord (Chicago and London: University of Chicago Press, 1984), 1290a10–20.

19 Aristotle, *Politics* 1290b15–20.

20 Aristotle, *Politics* 1291b15–25.

21 Aristotle, *Politics* 1292b10–20.

22 Aristotle, *Politics* 1293a10–15.

23 Aristotle, *Politics* 1305b.

24 Aristotle, *Politics* 1305b40.

25 Aristotle, *Politics* 1306a30–40.

26 Aristotle, *Politics* 1257a15.

27 Aristotle, *Politics* 1257a30. We are reminded here of the discussion of the 'city of sows' in Book 2 of Plato's *Republic*. Socrates and his companions set about building a 'healthy' city based on the satisfaction of needs, and the division of labour according to innate ability ('from each according to his ability, to each according to his needs,' Karl Marx) but Glaucon objects that such a city fails to satisfy human longings for luxury, embellishment, splendour. A city is more than a place for sustenance. Socrates concedes that they will now go on to consider 'not only how a city, but how a luxurious city, comes into being. Perhaps that's not bad either. For in considering such a city, too, we could probably see in what way justice *and* injustice grows in cities.' Plato, *Republic* 372e. It might be the case, then, that money is introduced only when the city transcends its 'natural' boundaries of

need, and hence the introduction of money is coincidental with the advent of the 'feverish city' and injustice. Plato, *Republic* 372e.

28 Aristotle, *Politics* 1257b20.

29 Aristotle, *Politics* 1258a1.

30 Aristotle, *Politics* 1259a5–20.

31 Aristotle, *Politics* 1258a5. Ryan Balot offers an excellent account of the links in Aristotle's thought between excessive accumulation and the excesses of other desires. 'Aristotle's fundamental interest in discussing acquisition, then, is not with the economy in its own right, but with desire, greed, and self-control – all of them seen against the background of Aristotle's account of human flourishing and well being (*eudaimonia*) in the *Ethics*.' Ryan Balot, *Greed and Injustice in Classical Athens* (Princeton, NJ: Princeton University Press, 2001), 43.

32 Aristotle, *Politics* 1295b35–1296a10.

33 Aristotle, *Politics* 1296b20–30.

34 Aristotle, *Politics* 1302b30–40.

35 Aristotle, *Politics* 1297a1–10.

36 John Locke, *The Second Treatise of Government* (Indianapolis, IN: Hackett, 1980), 19.

37 Ibid., 21.

38 Ibid., 23.

39 Ibid., 20–1.

40 Ibid., 29.

41 Ibid., 25.

42 Ibid., 64.

43 Ibid., 66.

44 C.B. Macpherson, *The Political Theory of Possessive Individualism* (London, Oxford, and New York: Oxford University Press, 1962), 207.

45 Locke, *Second Treatise*, 73.

46 Ibid., 111.

47 Ibid., 29.

48 Edward Andrew, *Shylock's Rights: A Grammar of Lockian Claims* (Toronto: University of Toronto Press, 1988), 132.

49 In fact, one could argue that inheritance, or the prospect of it, is the principal glue that holds the nuclear family together, in Locke's understanding. The family is not 'natural' for Locke – it is contractual – and while the child may owe his parents some honour for nurturing and raising him, he has no binding obligation to his parents once he is an adult. Locke says clearly, however, 'there is another power ordinarily in the father, whereby he has a tie on the obedience of his children ... and this is the power men

generally have to bestow their estates on who please them best; the possession of the father being the expectation and inheritance of the children ... it
is commonly in the father's power to bestow it with a more sparing or liberal hand, according as the behavior of this or that child hath comported
with his will and humor.' Locke, *Second Treatise*, 41.

50 Ibid., 111.
51 Edward Andrew, 'A Note on "Locke's Great Art of Government," ' *Canadian Journal of Political Science* 42, no. 2 (2009): 518.
52 Thomas Pangle, *The Ennobling of Democracy: The Challenge of the Postmodern
Age* (Baltimore and London: Johns Hopkins University Press, 1992), 167.
53 Ibid., 168.
54 Ibid., 180.
55 There is a considerable amount of literature on the classical republican
antidote to the excesses of liberal individualism. I am sceptical about this
cure. See Leah Bradshaw, 'Republic to Empire,' Annual Meeting of the
Canadian Political Science Association, Canadian Congress, Carleton University, June 2009. Also see Waller Newell, 'Machiavelli's Model of a Liberal Empire: The Evolution of Rome,' in *Enduring Empire: Ancient Lessons
for Global Politics*, ed. David Edward Tabachnick and Toivo Koivukoski
(Toronto: University of Toronto Press, 2009), 164–84.

8 A Shortage of Men: Wealth, Rank, and Recognition in Cicero's Civic Education

GEOFFREY KELLOW

Cicero worried about prosperity. Considering the tension between material wealth and moral worth, he famously contended that he preferred 'a man that lacks money to money that lacks a man.'[1] That such a sentiment found its clearest expression in Cicero's text on duty is no coincidence. The greatest of Rome's republican politicians put the dilemma in even starker terms later in the same work. Employing an anecdote about the Elder Cato, the very embodiment of Roman virtues, Cicero illustrated the conflict between avarice and honour with a terrible clarity:

> Externals are compared, on the other hand, when glory is preferred to riches, or urban income to rural. The words of the Elder Cato belong to this class of comparison. Someone asked him what was the most profitable activity for a family estate. He replied, 'To graze herds well' 'And what next' 'To graze them adequately' And what third? 'To graze them, though poorly' and what fourth? 'To plough' Then when the question was asked, 'What about money lending?' Cato's reply was 'What about killing someone?'[2]

In its brutal succinctness, the legendary censor's response revealed the depth of Cicero's concern with the rising influence of money on the young men of Rome. Cicero understood the importance of youth to the future of the struggling republic. His later works, some written in exile as the republic crumbled, return repeatedly to the relationship between Roman education and republican virtues. Indeed, Cicero begins his dialogue *De Re Publica* with a passage that closely mirrors the Catonic exchange from *De Officiis*. In the exchange from *De Re Publica* a young student, Tubero, initiates a conversation with the august general Scipio Africanus by posing a question about a recently sighted *parhelion* or sun dog. With this odd question, Cicero restates the central failing of Roman education. To ask a great general about astronomy indicates a profound failure of recognition. Tubero does not know what to ask of his superiors because he does not understand the character of their superiority.

The Catonic exchange presents the same essential characteristic. Cato's unfortunate partner in dialogue, because of his failure to recognize his elder's nature, does not know what to ask. In the first exchange, Cicero positions philosophy at otherworldly odds with the city. In the second, Cicero places business, an all-too-worldly obsession, even more at odds with the city. Common to both exchanges, a youthful interlocutor is unable to discern the true nature of his partner in conversation. The ill-considered question, either ethereal or avaricious, represents a failure of recognition rooted in the education of youth. To ask the austere Cato about money or the noble Scipio about astronomy suggests that the young can no longer recognize virtue among their elders. They can discern public prestige but cannot distinguish between its various and competing substances. In particular, Cicero worried that when Roman youth looked to their elders, they were unable to discriminate successfully between a Cato or Scipio and the rising class of wealthy oligarchs. They could not differentiate between the virtuous republican elite and the increasingly prosperous imperial elite. As a result, when they looked for mentors, the central pillar of Roman civic education, these youth gravitated towards the ostentation of wealth instead of the nobility of virtue.

The Decline of Roman Education

According to Cicero, Rome shared the fate of its virtues; the two thrived or failed together. Both depended on the character of citizens and inevitably upon the character of Rome's students. The precipitous decline in the *mos maiorum*, in the inherited life lived within the moral virtues and the civic modes of revered ancestors, spelled the doom of both citizen and state. In his later writing especially, Cicero returned often to the consequences for the Republic that this moral and civic decline heralded. In his own most private life, Cicero wrote from amid these consequences. The most telling of these, the ostensible purpose of his writing *De Officiis*, concerned the fate of his son Marcus.

Since they were young boys, Marcus, along with his cousin Quintus, were Cicero's special educational project.[3] Initially, Cicero took on the education of the boys out of dissatisfaction with the quality of Roman schooling. However, as the boys grew older their education inevitably involved professional teachers. Away from Cicero's tutelage, first Quintus and then (albeit to a lesser extent) young Marcus turned against Cicero and towards Caesar. In the case of Quintus, the turn ultimately led him to side with Caesar against Pompey and possibly even to conspire against his uncle.[4] The corruption of son and nephew painfully demonstrated to Cicero the decline of Roman education. For a son to consider turning against his father was outrage enough to the *mos maiorum*,[5] but to turn against Cicero in particular, who had done so much to protect and preserve the Republic, added immeasurably to his concerns for Rome's future.[6]

Preoccupied with these concerns, both political and paternal, Cicero turned to the connection between morals, education, and politics. At the beginning of Book 5 of *De Re Publica*, Cicero quotes Ennius: 'The Roman state stands upon the morals and men of old.'[7] To the extent that the teachers of Quintus and Marcus, and of the youth of Rome in general, failed to pass on the lessons and lives of the past, Cicero charged them with undermining the very foundation of Republican government. Cicero contended that in the time of Rome's material thriving the structures of the Republic remained but had been deprived of the morals and the men that once filled them. In the place of the *mos maiorum* stood only the empty husk of the old Republic.

> What remains of the morals of antiquity, upon which Ennius said that the Roman state stood? We see that they are so outworn in oblivion that they are not only not cherished but are now unknown. What am I to say about the men? The morals themselves have passed away through a shortage of men; and we must defend ourselves like people being tried for a capital crime. It is because of our own vices, not because of some bad luck, that we preserve the commonwealth in name alone but have long ago lost its substance.[8]

Cicero lamented the passing of the morals of Rome's republican past but also suggested the means of their recovery. The decline of Roman morals derived from the failure of those morals to be lived by men. They did not fail because of inherent flaws, but because they were inadequately lived; they perished of a 'shortage of men.' For

Cicero, Roman restoration depended on the education of men back into the ways of life that once nourished and sustained republican government.

'A shortage of men' and not the shortcomings of institutions explained the centrality of civic education to Cicero's political project. The particular character of Cicero's writing, especially the dialogue form, sought to remedy that shortage in both the short and long term. His dialogues sought to resurrect the character, conduct, and convictions of Cato the Elder, Crassus, and Scipio. In his own voice, in vivid first-person and epistolary prose, Cicero sought to incarnate Rome's virtues. The overall political project of his later writings aimed at revivifying the richly ancestral cultural context of the Republic. Cicero sought to repopulate the cultural milieu of his prospective pupils and inconstant son with the heroes of his own Roman antiquity. He wrote to repopulate the educational stage with a forgotten aristocracy of virtue. Cicero recounted his own education in Book I of *De Officiis*:

> I myself, whatever assistance I have given the republic, if I have indeed given any, came to public life trained and equipped by my teachers and their teachings. Not only when they are alive and present do such men educate and instruct their assiduous students; they continue the same task after death by means of their writings, which they leave as memorials.[9]

By portraying a lost aristocracy in conversation, Cicero sought with the written word to rectify the shortage of great men needed to teach the young. In his dialogues, Cicero constructed out of his imagination a community of men for the youth of Rome to look to and from whom to draw a fuller knowledge of duty and virtue. Cicero hoped to teach his prospective audience, through the experience of his dialogues and letters, to recognize among their leaders their own era's great men.

The apparent novelty and even peculiarity of Cicero's endeavour make more sense when placed within the practical context of Roman education in the late Republic. In the early and middle periods of Latin antiquity most of Rome's prosperous sons, if not quite all, acquired their education in the home. A son's education was primarily the responsibility, a deeply respected and serious duty, of the paterfamilias.[10] However, by the time of Cicero's own youth, education had almost entirely deserted the home. The explicitly civic education of a young Roman man began in adolescence with his initiation into adulthood, symbolized by the removal of his juvenile *toga praetexta* and its replacement with the *toga virilis* of manhood. Officially presented to the forum, the young pupil and new man received a formal training and introduction into oratory, law, and public life, the *tirocinium fori*.[11] For Cicero, this stage of learning marked the moment the rot had truly set in.

Cicero believed education in the Roman forum constituted the crucible that forged the great leaders of the past. Of his own schooling Cicero recalled

> In fact, public life was my education, and practical experience of the laws and institutions of the state and the custom of the country was my schoolmaster. (*De Oratore*, III.xx.74–5)[12]

The public life of the failing republic taught a very different lesson. Cicero considered the contemporary Roman forum and saw a narrow and socially destructive education that had displaced the expansive civic education he had received from the likes of Crassus and Scaevola. Education in the Roman forum of the late Republic increasingly consisted of sophistical showmanship and empty contests characterized by ornate language and rhetorical flourish.[13] Teachers trained solely in sophisticated and persuasive speech replaced the mentors of the past, educators but also lawyers, statesmen and orators in their own right. These new teachers, unschooled in the moral and political traditions of Rome, offered only the simulacrum of a true education in oratory; the new teachers of rhetoric taught only the appearance and not the substance of civic virtue. Of them Cicero lamented:

> My reason for dwelling on these points is because the whole of this department has been abandoned by the orators, who are the players that act real life, and has been taken over by the actors who only mimic reality.[14]

The consequences of such a teaching seemed obvious to Cicero. A narrow rhetorical training transformed the already deeply agonistic character of politics and law. The search for the best answer to a given problem or the correct verdict in a given proceeding gave way to an unqualified desire for victory. These rhetorical contests undermined the Roman forum as a venue of education. The larger interests of Rome and their deep connection to education were lost in the competition between speakers and for students. For Cicero, the fault attributed to the displacement of true orators echoed the critique of wealth-seeking presented in the Catonic anecdote in *De Officiis*. Cato's ersatz pupil inquired after the good life when he really sought the rich life. The actors who 'mimic reality' enter the arena of politics, the Roman forum, pursuing not justice but victory. Both group's actions and objectives manifest a break with the civic imperative that ideally undergirds both forms of discourse.

Unfortunately, the structure of Roman education lent itself to such distortions. The education in public life in the Roman forum involved learning and practising oratory in front of crowds of other young men. Here, in institutionalized form, Cicero found a situation catastrophically close to that warned of by Plato (*Republic* 491e–492b). Popularly praised rather than condemned, sophistical speech became the crucial element of Roman education. Cicero himself admitted as much in *Brutus*, acknowledging 'the orator who inflames the court accomplishes far more than the one who merely instructs it.'[15] Each victory on the part of an ethically constricted oratory further narrowed political outcomes and equally narrowed students.

Cicero further condemned the teachers of rhetoric not only for the reckless and mercenary way in which they taught but also for the non-technical social curriculum they offered. In place of the *mos maiorum* and the *artes liberales*, Cicero accused Roman rhetoricians of teaching a politically and morally corrosive love of luxury and a concomitant valorization of greed. In Cicero's own poignant estimation, in moving from republic to incipient empire, from the austerity republics demanded to the luxury empire enabled, the Romans succumbed to their own success.[16] Granting this, Cicero rejected the notion that Rome's virtues relied on constant military readiness.[17] Instead, in periods of either war or peace, Cicero contended that the conjunction of prosperity with a political legitimation of luxury constituted the true threat to civic virtue. Describing the situation, in the passage mentioned at this essay's outset, Cicero quotes Themistocles:

'I myself,' he replied, 'prefer a man that lacks money to money that lacks a man.' And yet, conduct has been corrupted and depraved by admiration for riches. What does someone else's great wealth concern any one of us? It may perhaps help him who has it. It does not always even do that; but grant that it does. He may, it is true, be better provided; but how will he be more honorable?[18]

Cicero lamented more than just the corrosive consequences of a social system that valued luxury over industry and indulgence over duty.[19] Indeed, Cicero hints at a deeper dilemma, the possible hostility of money to manhood. In the short term, it may corrupt; in the long term, Cicero feared that the admiration of riches undermines the very sources of Roman virtue.

Money, and in particular luxury, aggravates the shortage of men because of the role of emulation in Roman education. The pairing of a young man with an older and established mentor in the forum comprised the key element of Roman civic education. The lives and life-styles of those admired and valued within the context of the Roman forum constituted a critical component of the social curriculum. The mimetic structure of such an education inevitably magnified the negative consequences of the admiration of riches. As a result, to some extent the teachers of rhetoric were running behind the curve. They taught how to praise and become that which had already become praiseworthy in the eyes of the Roman citizenry. Cicero both feared and acknowledged that students increasingly sought to emulate not the wise and the just, not those who best embodied civic virtues, but the ostentation and opulence of the wealthy. Worse still, they tended to conflate the former with the latter. To Cicero, the young seemed increasingly unable to distinguish between wealth and virtue, to comprehend that only the latter quality suited one for rule. As such, Roman students were likely to select the wrong mentors and as citizens, the wrong leaders.

Much of modern civic education, in liberal democracies at least, rejects emulative models rooted in narrative histories. The displacement of so-called 'great men' accounts of history by more strictly normative visions of civic education necessarily precludes the possibility of an emulative education. More precisely, it precludes the possibility of an emulative *civic* education. However, if the civic stage is depopulated, replacing models of civic character with rules of conduct, the propensity to emulate reorients to whatever public models remain. For Cicero the process of maturing demanded that we tie our lives to those of our ancestors, to the public figures of our past. As he declares in *Orator*,

To be ignorant of what occurred before you were born is to remain always a child. For what is the worth of human life, unless it is woven into the life of our ancestors by the records of history?[20]

Liberal modernity, with its instinctive prejudice in favour of the present, short-circuits the emulative education ancestors provide. As a result, the modern student seeks to emulate those public figures, hardly august ancestors, who remain. On this account, the lamentable lessons of celebrity culture are a consequence not simply of the rise of wealth but the forced retreat of virtue. Countless elements of the media weave the lives of the young into the ways of life and codes of (mis)conduct of celebrities. There is no equivalent apparatus for our civic virtues, lived first by increasingly unknown ancestors.

The Status of the Student

The expansion of Roman rule made possible both the rise of Cicero and the decline of the old ways he admired. Roman virtue made possible the political and material success that created the conditions for its own undermining. Virtuous men unwittingly paved the way for wealthy men. Among his own generation, Cicero saw fewer and fewer men suited for leadership. Even his great friend and noble tyrannicide Brutus appeared to Cicero to have succumbed to the lure of riches at the cost of character.[21] Despite this, Cicero denied that the expansion of Rome inevitably entailed the corrosion of Roman virtue. Rome's virtues endured in the substance, however currently corrupted, of its citizenry. Those citizens, as Cicero understood them, retained a capacity for virtuous self-rule; more fundamentally still, they were 'born for justice.'

In perhaps the single greatest break from the Attic influences on his thought, Cicero posited what, on the surface at least, appears to be a fundamentally and even radically egalitarian account of the person:

> If distorted habits and false opinions did not twist weak minds and bend them in any direction no one would be so like himself as all people would be like all others. Thus, whatever definition of a human being one adopts is equally valid for all human beings.[22]

Ciceronian equality, as posited in this passage, possesses some peculiar characteristics. First and most readily apparent to the modern reader is the language and imagery of what Christianity would subsequently characterize as humanity's 'fallenness.' Nonetheless, setting aside the influence Cicero exerted on the Early Roman Church and most especially Saint Augustine, a close reckoning of Cicero's account reveals key differences between the Ciceronian student and the Augustinian soul. Of these none is more important than the strictly definitional and original character of Ciceronian equality. According to Cicero, in key respects an original neonatal equality does not endure as human beings grow and mature. Cicero never suggests that human qualities and faculties remain identical in proportion and expression across humanity in its development. Undeniably, man has most in common with man, but commonality does not entail an equal apportioning of these characteristics across mankind.[23]

Cicero's account of human nature encompasses both commonality and difference but rejects a simple or deep equality. In terms of commonality, Cicero contends that human beings share a common core of innate abilities and even innate beliefs. However, these characteristics and beliefs are possessed and realized to differing degrees across the species. Of primary importance among these characteristics is a capacity for reason, a capacity that all human beings participate in. Returning to De Legibus, Cicero writes:

> All the same things are grasped by the senses; and the things that are impressed upon the mind, the rudiments of understanding which I mentioned before, are impressed similarly on all humans, and language, the interpreter of the mind, may differ in words but is identical in ideas. There is no person of any nation who cannot reach virtue with the aid of a guide.[24]

A careful reading of this passage reveals key elements of Cicero's conception of the pupil and his education. The claim that every person contains the rudiments of rational comprehension and of the seeds of virtue stands at the centre of Cicero's account of the citizen. This claim recurs across Cicero's philosophic oeuvre. In De Finibus, characterizing nature's gift of virtue to humanity, he writes: 'But of virtue itself she merely gave the germ and no more.'[25] This metaphor of rudiment and seed fundamentally transforms the task of the civic educator. All humans possess a basic substance out of which virtue and intellect are 'grown' by the educator.[26] More importantly, the seed remains available, open to circumstances conducive to growth and receptive to a change in the educational or political climate. Cicero's dialogues seek to recover the depleted soil, the men and morals of old, and the ground that will allow the seed of civic virtue and political prudence to thrive again.

Cicero maintained that the republican population retained a common capacity for virtue. Civic education aimed at inculcating this capacity in all while drawing out those whose particular portion of virtue suited them for republican rule. A common heritage of reason and virtue constituted one-half of Cicero's dyadic account of the student and citizen. While he posited broad commonalities across the species, Cicero also asserts that politically relevant differences of ability exist within the species:

> For just as there are enormous bodily differences (for some, as we see, their strength is the speed that they can run, for others the might with which they wrestle: again, some have figures that are dignified, others that are graceful) similarly there are still greater differences in men's spirits.[27]

According to Cicero, each human being possesses a dual persona. On one hand, they are deeply similar to all other human beings. The degree to which they share qualities make them more like each other than like any other animal; this is their species persona. However, within the species there are tremendous differences, both moral and political. These differences create the second persona, that of the individual.[28] Recognizing and responding to the particular admixture of virtues within this second persona constituted a key task of the educator. Recognizing among Rome's potential leaders the superior admixture of civic virtue of a potential leader's second persona constituted the key task of the citizen. Cicero's account of the student, citizen, and statesman mirrors the delicate balance between the equality encouraged by the structures of the Roman Republic and the recognition of difference and superiority that it depended on. This equality and difference further sets novel tasks in the way of a Roman recovery.

Statesmen and Teachers

As Rome expanded, the immediate task of the Roman educator became ever more distant from that described by Cicero's Attic precursors. Cicero's civic educator increasingly diverted his focus from those great in spirit, the potential statesmen. Instead, Cicero's ideal educator turned towards the continually swelling ranks of those who were destined for a slimmer share in rule. The education of ordinary citizens gained central significance by virtue of their role in the selection, by means formal and informal, of those who were to rule them. Cicero aimed at educating the populace to be ruled as opposed to tyrannized.[29] Cicero acknowledges as much in *De Re Publica* when he has Scipio describe the primary task of the people. Scipio observes that a free people do not rule; they choose those who will rule. Cicero's Scipio suggests that the republican virtue of ordinary citizens expresses itself through their capacity to entrust themselves to the best men:

> But if a free people chooses the men to whom to entrust itself (and it will choose the best people if it wants to be safe), then surely the safety of the citizens is found in the deliberations of the best men. That is particularly true because nature has made sure not only that men outstanding for virtue and courage rule over weaker people, but that the weaker people willingly obey the best.[30]

Scipio further contends that republics do not depend on the judgment of the best men. After all, the judgments of the best men must almost invariably be correct as a consequence of their nature. Instead, success or failure hinges on the judgment of the population who must entrust themselves to the great. Successful republican government depends on the political judgment of the ordinary citizen. It is on popular discernment alone that a republican aristocracy, a natural aristocracy of the best men, as opposed to a wealthy oligarchy, depends. If the popular character of the citizenry is incapable of recognizing the naturally best then the best will be unable to rule on their behalf. This act of discernment, the recognition of the few among the many *by the many*, is the critical task of civic education.[31]

    This ability to discern is twice challenged in Cicero's Rome. Most obviously, Cicero contends the rise of a wealth-obsessed oligarchy means there are fewer virtuous men to whom the citizens can entrust themselves. Moreover, as such men become rarer, the declining ability of the citizen to recognize qualities they are rarely exposed to further undermines the process of recognition. For the weak to 'willingly obey the best,'[32] they must be able to recognize the best; they must be familiar with what is best. The Ciceronian student learns to distinguish oligarch from aristocrat through an education both in *and* by the latter. The Republic thrived when the political horizon was filled with a robust sense of Rome's history. It thrived when the Senate was filled with the best men and when the ordinary citizen, through familiarity with the worthy, recognized and entrusted himself only to those who embodied Roman virtue.

In Cicero's civic education the statesman is the captivating and illuminating example that draws the people upwards towards virtue. The true statesman prompts a recognition of his superior nature by speaking through the elements, the commonalities, he shares with the citizenry. He transcribes the Ciceronian dual personas onto the political, as the individual deeply connected to the common. Considering the expression of this civic reality in rhetoric, Cicero contends 'the very cardinal sin is to depart from the language of everyday life, and the usage approved by the sense of the community.'[33] Speaking in ordinary language allows the statesman to communicate what he shares with the citizenry and convey their share in virtues that he more perfectly embodies.[34] By acting and speaking in a manner that conveys both commonality and superiority, the statesman embodies the Ciceronian dual personas and in so embodying encourages emulation among the citizens, similar to that first practised when they don the *toga virilis* in the Roman forum. Moreover, by speaking in common language the statesman allows himself to be recognized in the fullness of his nature and consequently entrusted with rule.

The recognition of the superior facilitated by the common is the crucial pedagogic element in the celestial encounter between the two Scipios in *Scipio's Dream*. In *Scipio's Dream*, during his sublunar encounter with his illustrious grandfather, the younger Scipio Africanus turns his face back to the earth. Despite his ascent, he seems captivated by the quotidian concerns of mundane existence. The elder Scipio, who exists above it all, repeatedly chides him: 'I wonder how long your mind will be fixed on the ground?'[35] The elder Scipio draws the younger Africanus to the divine in himself, draws him upward:

> Therefore look on high if you wish; contemplate this dwelling and eternal home; and do not give yourself to the words of the mob, and do not place your hope in human rewards: virtue itself by its own allurements should draw you towards true honor.[36]

Contemplating the divine in his ancestor initially draws Scipio towards it and away from the base. At first Scipio is dazzled by the apparition; he is dumbfounded and even frightened. Eventually his gaze steadies upwards in contemplation of his illustrious ancestor. As he focuses, the intergenerational dialogue turns to virtue, a quality shared between the Scipii. The grandson's recognition of his grand-father's greater portion thereof draws him upward. In Scipio this pull is not towards the heavens, not yet at least,[37] but towards recognition of the true nature he shares, to some extent, with those superior to him in virtue. In the city, the statesman stands in the same position as the elder Scipio. The citizenry dimly share and are drawn toward the virtue that shines bright in the natural aristocrat, the best of men. Conversely, in the enduring temptation to turn his gaze downward the younger Scipio expresses the confusion that confronts the citizen in an age of oligarchs and aristocrats. The oligarch appeals to another set of commonalities and another set of differences. The oligarch draws us downward, to the things of the world that he possesses more fully. In his metaxic dilemma,[38] the younger Scipio finds himself torn, like Cicero's fellow citizens, between the higher and lower, between the transcendent and the immanent, between the virtues of aristocratic ancestors and the wealth of oligarchic contemporaries. That which is common provides the grounds for both appeals. Cicero's civic education speaks through humanity's common virtues, that which is both higher and yet held to some degree by all.

A Shortage of Men and the Education of Aristocrats

Cicero's understanding of the education of the citizen seems on the surface to be relatively undemanding.[39] For the individual and ordinary citizens this may be a fair account of Cicero's position. Their education is in virtue, but its aim is not primarily the practice of the highest virtue but the ability to recognize such virtue in others. However, returning attention to Cicero's initial diagnosis of the cause of the decline of civic virtue in Rome, 'the shortage of men,' reveals necessary conditions for civic education that are quite demanding. Cicero contends that civic virtue is dependent on men of stature whose conduct, comportment, and character they seek to emulate; a state that lacks such men will lack civic virtue. The generation of such men explains the peculiar exhortative character of Cicero's epistolary prose, a character most apparent in his letters to the younger M. Cicero but also present in his letters to Brutus. *De Officiis* in particular reads like an instruction manual for *both* civic virtue and political success. It is the complex interplay of these moral and political imperatives that marks the most significant modern return to Cicero's concerns, Machiavelli's *The Prince*. Machiavelli corrupts Cicero's message of duty almost absolutely. However, he retains not merely important elements of the style of *De Officiis*[40] but equally Cicero's concern with the exemplary significance of the statesman. The barbaric spectacle of Machiavelli's Borgias would have appalled Cicero, but he would have recognized in it the political reality Machiavelli seized upon. *De Officiis*, like *The Prince*, takes for granted the presence of young and ambitious men.[41] It begins with the assumption that the young find themselves drawn to politics. Machiavelli also echoes Cicero in appealing to that which prince and populace have in common. Where Machiavelli departs from Cicero is in the substance of that commonality. Where Cicero appealed to the common inheritance of virtue, Machiavelli appeals to and speaks through the universal experience of the passions.

De Officiis assumes as its most urgent task the pulling of such pupils towards republican virtue and away from the thrall of Caesar and later Antony. Cicero realized that this challenge demanded an encounter with greatness, an alternative republican greatness. The education of young men, especially the politically gifted, depended on the elements of recognition and resonance already present in the education of the ordinary citizen. For Cicero, the particular promise of such men consisted in their potential to move from being the subject of virtue, those in whom the virtue of others resonates, into an object of such recognition and a source of such resonance.

For Cicero the education of a natural aristocracy, able to compete for the attention of the politically decisive republican populace, demanded that they virtuously match the profile and prominence of the wealthy oligarch. However, Cicero maintained such new statesmen must attain prominence in a manner informed by the virtue they share, that calls the citizen up rather than bringing the statesman down. To this end, Cicero commended the *artes liberales*:[42] history, literature, rhetoric, law, and philosophy. The orator schooled in all these would stand above all others in the forum. Cicero insisted that the genuine orator must have knowledge of the 'whole of the contents of the life of mankind.'[43] The genuine orator would speak of the political in a manner that both appealed to citizens and helped constitute a community of virtue. Indeed, Cicero maintained in *De Oratore* that learned discourse constituted the original source of political community:

> To come, however, at length to the highest achievements of eloquence, what other power could have been strong enough either to gather scattered

humanity into one place, or to lead it out of its brutish existence in the wilderness up to our present condition of civilization as men and as citizens, or after the establishment of social communities, to give shape to laws, tribunals and civic rights?[44]

According to Cicero, humanity emerges from its scattered and brutish existence through the twinned phenomena of resonance and recognition. Ciceronian oratory, grounded in the *artes liberales*, constitutes the resonating instrument by which those suited for rule draw to themselves the discerning attention of those suited to being ruled. Oratory both provides the grounds for discernment and in its own public expression provides the education that permits discernment. The aristocrat, through oratory, teaches the nature of the great and evidences it. In his dual existence, as both lesson and teacher, he further reinstantiates the duality. Expressing publicly the relationship between that which is shared and that which is unique, at the heart of Cicero's account of humanity, the statesman embodies the principle of Roman republican government.[45]

Like the practice of oratory, the instructional nature of Cicero's writing aimed at a two-fold purpose. Cicero's dialogues sought to morally and politically elevate individuals distinct in their portion of virtue. It aimed to create in them a new class of great men, equal in stature to those who formerly peopled the Republic, living and thereby sustaining its virtues. Cicero hoped this new group of both virtuous and successful men would repopulate the Roman forum and retake the role of mentor to those newly donning the *toga virilis*. Ultimately, through the process of resonant virtue and its recognition, such men would prompt emulation, which would permit the process started by Cicero's dialogues to return to its true home, the Roman forum.

Conclusion

Cicero sought to re-establish a Republican aristocracy because he saw in it the only alternative to an oligarchy based on the valorization of wealth and luxury. He recognized the threat that this division posed to the Roman Republic. He saw in Roman prosperity the temptation to equate wealth with virtue, worse still to prefer wealth to virtue. This same temptation presents similar challenges to modern free market societies. In modern free market societies, especially in a relatively pacific age of globalized trade, the most conspicuous symbols of success are material. The market provides the most readily apparent demonstrations of aptitude and industry if not civic virtue. More than this, the market in its materiality emphasizes an alternative commonality. Like virtue, material needs, comforts, even luxury and their affiliated desires are shared by all humanity. Those who speak to these desires, who embody their fulfilment, cannot fail to resonate with their fellow citizens. For Cicero and ourselves, the Themistoclean distinction between a man without money and money without a man remains compelling. Nonetheless, the spectacle that money makes possible, the public stages that money can access, makes it much more difficult to discern the absence of a man.

We have only selectively carried Cicero's assumptions into the present. Cicero's assertion of an initial equality, a capacity for both reason and virtue, deepens and expands in liberal democracies. The central premise of representative politics depends on a principle of democratic discernment not dissimilar to that described by Cicero's Scipio. At the same time, perhaps out of respect for the autonomy that a deepened estimation and respect for natural equality seems to demand, we have neglected the question that the younger Scipio's celestial grandfather insists on asking: Why with all that is worth looking up to, do you continue to look down?[46] The politics of prosperity, for Cicero and ourselves, push the civic horizon and the citizen's gaze downward, to the material, the concrete, and the immediate. Cicero recognizes that the political stage invariably fills with one sort of men or another; prosperity tends to push forward an oligarchy of wealth, the exemplars of the material, and undermines an aristocracy of virtue. The stage of late Republican Rome, like that of late liberal modernity, is a tilted venue. Cicero's institutions share with ours a confusion whereby the principles of original construction are mistaken for the prosperity they make possible. In institutions of politics and market, in the contest of recognition and resonance between worthy aristocrat and the wealthy oligarch, the satisfying spectacle and not the superior citizen too often carries the day.

NOTES

1 Cicero, *De Officiis,* trans. and ed. M. Griffin and E.M. Atkins (New York: Cambridge University Press, 1991), I.71.
2 Cicero, *De Officiis* II.89.

3 Aubrey Gwynn, *Roman Education from Cicero to Quintillian*, 2nd ed. (New York: Russell and Russell, 1964), 80.

4 Manfred Fuhrmann, *Cicero and the Roman Republic*, trans. W.E. Yuill (Oxford: Blackwell Publishers, 1990), 156.

5 Elizabeth Rawson, *Cicero A Portrait* (London: Penguin, 1975), 251.

6 For Plato's discussion of the same transformation among Athenian youth, see Leah Bradshaw, 'Oligarchs and Democrats' in this volume.

7 Cicero, *On the Commonwealth and On the Laws*, trans. James Zetzel (New York: Cambridge University Press 1999), V.1.

8 Cicero, *De Re Publica* V.2.

9 Cicero, *De Officiis* I.155–6.

10 H.I. Marrou, *A History of Education in Antiquity*, trans. George Lamb (London: Sheed and Ward, 1956), 232.

11 Ibid., 236.

12 Of course Cicero typically overstates the case; compare his remarks in *Orator* 12: 'I confess that whatever ability I possess as an orator comes, not from the workshops of the rhetoricians, but from the spacious grounds of the Academy.'

13 Stanley F. Bonner, *Education in Ancient Rome* (London: Metheun, 1977), 332.

14 Cicero, *De Oratore*, 2 vols., trans. E.W. Sutton (Cambridge, MA: Harvard University Press, 1942). *De Oratore* III.lvi.241.

15 Cicero, *Brutus*, 89, quoted in Bonner, *Education in Ancient Rome*, 85.

16 T.N. Mitchell, 'Cicero on the Moral Crisis of the late Republic' *Hermathena* 136 (1984): 27.

17 Ibid., 26.

18 Cicero, *De Officiis* II.71.

19 In *Tusculan Disputations* Cicero went further, suggesting that luxury posed a threat to not merely virtue but masculinity. For Cicero's account of the feminizing effects of luxury, see Christopher J. Berry, *The Idea of Luxury* (Cambridge: Cambridge University Press, 1994), 84.

20 Cicero, *Orator*, trans. H.M. Hubbell (Cambridge: Harvard University Press, 1962), 120.

21 Cicero, *Cicero's Letter's to Atticus*, trans. D.R. Shackleton Bailey (Harmondsworth: Penguin, 1978), V.i.5–6.

22 Cicero, *De Legibus* I.30. We will see this assertion echoed in strikingly similar terms in both Rousseau and Smith, whose debt to Cicero's educational thought is substantial and conspicuous in their own.

23 Leo Strauss, *Natural Right and History* (Chicago: University of Chicago Press, 1953), 135.

24 Cicero, *De Legibus* I.30.

25 Cicero, *De Finibus*, trans. H. Rackham (Cambridge: Harvard University Press, 1967), V.xxi.60.

26 Maryanne C. Horowitz, 'The Stoic Synthesis of Natural Law in Man: Four Themes,' *Journal of the History of Ideas* 35 (1974): 14.

27 Cicero, *De Officiis* I.107.

28 Ibid.

29 As a result, to some extent Cicero's specifically political education is closer to Aristotle than to Plato; see *Politics*, 1259.

30 Cicero, *De Re Publica* I.51.

31 Cicero, *De Re Publica* V.8.

32 Ibid.

33 Cicero, *De Oratore* I.iii.8.

34 Gary Remer, 'Political Oratory and Conversation,' *Political Theory* 27 (1999): 54.

35 Cicero, *De Re Publica* VI.17.

36 Cicero, *De Re Publica* VI.25.

37 Cicero, *De Re Publica* VI.26.

38 See Plato, *Laws* 644e.

39 For an interpretation that sees citizen education as almost *completely* undemanding, see Cary J. Nederman, 'War, Peace and Republican Virtue: Patriotism and the Neglected Legacy of Cicero,' in *Instilling Ethics*, ed. Norma Thompson (Lanham, MD: Rowman and Littlefield), 17–29.

40 J. Jackson Barlow, 'The Fox and the Lion: Machiavelli Replies to Cicero,' *History of Political Thought* 20 (1999): 629.

41 Ibid.

42 Gwynn, *Roman Education*, 118.

43 Cicero, *De Oratore* III.xvi.54–5.

44 Cicero, *De Oratore* I.viii.33–4.

45 For Aristotle's treatment of the same element of education, see Waller Newell's 'Oligarchy and Oikonomia' in this volume.

46 Cicero, *De Re Publica* 6.19.

9 On Oligarchy: An Ontological Account

TOIVO KOIVUKOSKI

> Wealth is the good; wealth tends to the general enjoyment, it is there sim-
> ply to be disposed of, and it ensures for every one the consciousness of
> his particular self.
>
> – G.W.F. Hegel, *Phenomenology of Spirit*[1]

> We must not regard a citizen as belonging just to himself; we must rather
> regard the citizen as belonging to the city.
>
> – Aristotle, *Politics*[2]

The sense of substance in classical Greek philosophy can be understood as the forms that define a rational order overarching the flux of
being, which when it coughs up injustice, bad luck, or unintended
consequences does so within the measure of an order inscribed in reason itself, an order that is both more perfect and more enduring than
any actual governing regime or effort at the management of things.
Real being, or *ousia* in the lexicon of classical philosophy, has substance because it is stable and self-subsistent. That is to say that within
the ontologies of Plato and Aristotle, what is considered real are those
aspects of a thing that do not change.[3] In physical terms, this substance is what a thing is made of. In ethical terms, *ousia* is what a person is made of.[4] This also bears on what we mean when we identify
particular regimes according to the forms or purposes of the distributions of power within them, which within classical political theory are
of an unchanging variety.

And yet, curiously, if we consider the political situations of those
two theorists, these distinguishing concepts of stable categories and

self-subsistent purposes were brought forth by an environment that pulsed with passion, greed, hope beyond limit, violence, and imperial ambitions. If Plato and Aristotle presented ontologies that made rational substance out of *ousia* – understood as both that which underlies a person's substance as well as the very being of beings – then what provoked them to that common attribution was a critical composure towards the frantic compulsions of their time and place.

In this chapter I would like to call attention to two dimensions of oligarchy, one of them quite clear and manifest, pertaining to the tension between oligarchy and democracy, the other inherently rather more amorphous, reflecting on a certain misunderstanding of substance that underlies the self-legitimation of oligarchs: what is really a dissemblance identifying the appearance of fortune that accompanies the accumulation of wealth with a supposed right to rule. First, in terms of what is clear, I would point to Aristotle's extended analysis in the *Politics* of oligarchy in its contested relation to democracy. If one were to characterize this treatment in general terms, it is that oligarchical regimes work to depoliticize power by conflating the properly political with economic necessity. When this collapse of what is for Aristotle an architectonic distinction occurs, public life starts to take on qualities that ought to be circumscribed within the private sphere – the privations of which include the urgent insistences of biological life and the patterns of violence routinely employed to manage the economic life of humankind.[5]

As acquisition comes to the fore as the driving determination of life within a political community, the public goods that are constitutive of that association[6] unravel into the appetites of each and every individual. What community remains is reduced to the bond of the cabal, indistinguishable from the society of criminals.[7] In the absence of common goods that would transcend what are strictly private interests, the body politic is rocked this way and that in torturous agitations, moved by an unsteady mix of hunger pains on the one hand and the anxious protection or reclamation of property on the other. An oligarchy is in this sense a body politic motivated by the stomach, with what remains of reason in public discourse reduced to an instrumental rationality that would preserve and increase one's own property, irrespective of the needs of others.

This lack of a common good is what makes oligarchies so unstable and prone to violence – for if political power is merely a possession, like an estate, then one seizure may appear as legitimate as another. Thus the idea behind Proudhon's infamous appraisal of property as theft informs every counter-oligarchic revolution, which in its founding act of violent levelling generates the necessary conditions for a counter-democratic revolution, and so on, and again and again.[8] This sort of vengeful politics – what Nietzsche would have called the politics of resentment[9] – had characterized much of Athens' political history up until Aristotle's time, which swung pendulum-like from democratic to oligarchic extremes: in the violent aftermath of the Peloponnesian War lurching towards oligarchy, then back to a retributive democracy, in each case with a class taking power exclusively for its own, so that the other class would not have its share.[10]

The class conflict that intermittently rocked the ancient Greek world can be traced as far back as the *Iliad*, to Thersites' mutinous critique of the warlord class of Achaean rulers, whom he identifies as vulgar war profiteers, and of whom he asks simply what more they might need.[11] And yet, the crucial point that makes the conflict between the privileged rich and the demos more than a matter of bare economic necessity, which would in that case offer the simple solution of an egalitarian society where all are secured with the necessities of life and no more – something like the first just city described in Plato's *Republic* – is that material wealth may be appreciated as more than mere stuff. Certainly this was true for the Greek warlords, for whom the cuts of meat served and war-booty claimed implied their relative rights to rule and the virtues that would make them deserving.[12] Similarly, when Glaucon turns up his nose at the pastoral justice of a city bound together by the simple needs of human beings for one another,[13] asking 'Where are the relishes?'[14] we suspect that he means something more than condiments.

The unsettling effects of concentrations of wealth in society have to do precisely with how such excesses are interpreted. It is because wealth is elevated from article of necessity to an attributed symbolic value that what should be the basis of social order – namely a society's capacity to sustain itself by regenerating its own substance – becomes instead an incendiary element.[15]

In this sense, the inherently contested questions of who is virtuous and who has the right to rule are grafted onto the possession of the material goods of life, with the sense of compulsion that attends the realm of necessity then inflected into public deliberations. Similarly reflective matters concerning the interpretation of value, such as one finds in the appreciation of aesthetic objects, are infused with an interest in power. Whatever worldly things may be taken to represent, whether beauty, or fetish, or ancestral authority, or so forth, the elevation of superlative wealth as a representative point of distinction inserts these unsettling questions directly into a social order, making for a destabilizing combination of chance and perceived legitimacy.

The see-saw contest between the rich and poor for rule was a regular spectacle in classical Athens. Aristotle devotes considerable attention to oligarchy as a class of regime;[16] and it is likely that the political situation of Athens, with its uneasy alterations between democratic and oligarchic governments, informed the currency of the philosopher's interest and at least partly explains the extent of his treatment. Yet given the prominence of the topic in the *Politics*, there is correspondingly little scholarship on this aspect of Aristotle's political science.[17] This may be simply because his treatment of oligarchy is outwardly straightforward: that it belongs to the unjust class of regimes because its rulers are motivated by private interests, specifically for the increase and security of their wealth; that it conflates economic privilege with the right to political rule; that it depends upon an unequal distribution of wealth (for otherwise superlative wealth could not serve as a source of power) and, therefore, tends to undercut the possibility of a robust middle class; and perhaps most importantly in Aristotle's view, that the disparity between the ultra-rich few and the impoverished many within a society contributes to overall political instability, with class divisions giving rise to factionalism, and power thus tending to cycle violently between the oligarchs and the people, both likewise motivated by the crude demand to get more for themselves by taking from the others.

Contra such a violent cycling of regimes, Aristotle's practical and ontological preference for a stable polis is fairly clear; the stratagem is even carried to the extreme position of encouraging the reform of tyrannies through their stabilization.[18] In the case of the other two unjust regimes in his classification, democracy and oligarchy, the general thrust of his argument is to reconcile the two through a moderate policy of redistributive taxation and enfranchisement, effectively aiming to produce a politically engaged middle class. This would not have been a new idea even at the time; in its central features the modest plan resembles Solon's reforms, which describe a middle-broadening of the base of political participation, saving a good portion of the population of citizens from enslavement to an oligarchic class, while avoiding retributive, wholesale appropriations of property and political legitimacy.[19]

Overall, as a matter of philosophic intent, the preservation of regimes is of high priority for Aristotle. It seems as if, for him, revolution is more damaging to a political community than the deprivals of
an unjust government. At an extreme of the good as stability position,
he recommends attempting to preserve unjust regimes, even codifying
their principles of inheritance (however happenstance the rule that results) as if in order to raise an immanent code of lawfulness from
within the unjust regime. In lieu of stabilization and reform, the unjust
regime would otherwise harm itself and its own sustaining conditions
even as it helps itself to the wealth of the community as a whole, treating the polis as if it were rulers' prosthetic stomach. Or put otherwise,
in Aristotle's analysis unjust regimes produce their own gravediggers;
thus, to attempt to preserve them is to at once effectively change their
character in fundamental ways.

There is, however, one apparent textual glitch in this reading of Aristotle,
focused on an apparent emphasis on political stability and on efforts to
relieve class tensions. Consider Aristotle's account of Solon's reforms in
the *Constitution of Athens*, reflecting on the consistency, consequences,
and principle of the reforms. Aristotle describes one of Solon's laws that
would have, in times of factional dispute, had all citizens choose a side
or lose their rights as citizens.[20] The sparse reason given is that this
would keep citizens from standing apathetically by when such factions
arose, opportunistically uncommitted until a decision was made. And
yet there is a strongly counter-intuitive sense to this particular piece of
legislation that seems at odds both with the general thrust of Solon's reforms as well as with Aristotle's ontological preference for stability, and
for a practical encouragement of the public use of deliberative reason to
find a middle way between sides. Plutarch calls the law 'peculiar and unexplained.' J.M. Moore in his detailed commentary sees it as 'surprising.'[21] And yet Aristotle apparently does not blink at the proposition,
presenting it as part of a package of reforms.[22]

Some explanation could be offered by the note that Aristotle makes
of the obscurity of some of Solon's laws, which other commentators
had apparently argued were deliberately intended 'to give the people
the power of decision.'[23] Aristotle calls this line of argument unlikely
and suggests that 'the obscurity arises rather from the impossibility of
including the best solution for every instance in a general provision.'[24]
In this sense, the indeterminate consequences of the law would, in
their indeterminacy, represent not a practical effort on Solon's part to

encourage political engagement so much as an inherent limit to legislation as such. The point is thus not to be found in the consequences of a law, but rather in the consistency of the ideas behind it. Thus, 'It is not right to judge his intentions from what happens now but by analogy with the rest of his provisions.'[25] How then is the law consistent with Solon's intents? One suggestion that could be made is that this particular law would reduce the influence of the most fervent elements of society (say, in this instance, those who were owed money in cancelled debts), arguably diminishing the polarizing and unsettling effects of factionalism by forcing more people to wade in; it would be as if factionalism were moderated precisely by encouraging all to take a side. Or, again broaching into pragmatic matters, it is worth noting that after Solon there would be not just the two classes at play in Athenian politics – democrats and oligarchs – but three parties: the parties of the Shore, the Plain, and the Uplands.[26] By legislating all to take a side, this could again likely diminish the influence of the most zealous partisans, who would naturally tend to support either the oligarchic party of the Plain, which promoted a reinstatement of debts and restoration of the political privileges of wealth, or the democratic party of the Uplands and its demagogue Peisitratus, who clamored for a more sweeping redistribution of property than Solon had provided. Far from polarizing Athenian politics, the law would add to the base of the party with the 'middle of the road policy.'[27] All surmising of the potential, practical consequences of reform aside, by making political idleness illegal, what Solon intended in essence was to make political engagement a matter of law rather than of economic interest.

The concern that informs the principle is that an insistence upon property as *the* public matter worthy of consideration would work to crowd out deeper deliberations on the public good, as inequality is inscribed in the constitution of oligarchies via the consolidation of wealth by law. One can point to an equal and opposite derogation of the political when radical democracies set out on retributive patterns of eviction and redistribution. If this unwilling exchange of power has any end for both sides it is in unlimited material acquisition, with money misunderstood as an end in itself rather than as the means that it truly is.

Reforming Oligarchies

Oligarchies are closed associations by nature. The category itself is essentially heterogeneous, with wealth, at least as it functions to distinguish membership in the governing elite, presented as a distinguishing characteristic, rather than as a certain package of goods needed by all in order to live well, which is how Aristotle presents wealth as a necessity for political life.[28] In the exergue to this chapter Hegel makes a similar reference to wealth as seen from the perspective of one alienated from the community, where wealth substitutes as a retreat from public life, a way of being a person short of the autonomy that an engaged political life offers. How does the notion that wealth is good make for virtue, and would it be a private virtue (like frugality) or a public one (like liberality)? How would material desire have its influence on public life?

There is a sense in which the moderns appreciate materiality more deeply than the ancients, as in the tendency among early modern thinkers – Machiavelli, Locke, Hobbes – to consider the material basis of life, or even life itself, as being of value. It may or may not be taken for an intrinsic value, depending on the thinker, but it is a value inasmuch as it adds to the general productivity of the species; that is its capacity to increase the well-being of human beings. The ancients insist rather that substance must point beyond the given human, corporeal condition and towards some higher good. The material dispensation of the moderns is directed rather towards the promise of the liberation of the human condition – most basically liberation of the appetites and freedom from fear of death – towards a self-determined fulfilment. And since that fulfilment is subject to appetites that are themselves conditioned by environment, genetics, the possibilities of a particular place and time, and so forth, the betterment of the human condition is judged in terms of general material progress.

The classical ontologies of Plato and Aristotle incline rather towards a more circumscribed conception of the emancipatory capacities of wealth. In an interesting example of the ameliorative and politically liberating dimensions of wealth redistribution, Aristotle proposes a redistributive tax that would ensure 'a permanent level of prosperity,' as well as having the rich provide for the fuller lives of the poor, effectively paying the demos to participate in political life and subsidizing every citizen's freedom from the necessity of toiling for mere existence.[29] Another specific recommendation Aristotle makes in Book 7 of the *Politics* is for the creation of a 'free market,'[30] where by 'free' he means free from articles of consumption and trade. This free market is intended as a public space for the free exchange of ideas and, as Aristotle suggests, as a place for older citizens to exercise together; today we might call it a community centre. The public realm in this sense is a gathering place for the multitude of citizens that make up the community, a forum for the expression of a plurality of opinions and interests and for the consolidation of agreement on the ends of a community's action. What distinguishes any one community from another is that the ends of public deliberations are relative to the specific regime within which they occur; hence the significance of a regimes-based approach, describing the structural modes of the various distributions of power, or the *politeia*; literally, who is the government, and who together constitute the political community?

With the nature of oligarchy being socially heterogeneous and hierarchically ordered, its constitution depends on a measure of deceit. Here we arrive at the more elusive aspect of oligarchy. For in the absence of other demonstrable virtues, the lie that must be told in order to sustain an oligarchy (as such) is that the virtue of the rich is precisely their wealth, which in its symbolic formation serves as a materialization of hidden qualities, in a kind of magical conflation of the power to conjure something into existence and the legitimacy to rule. The mythology of entrepreneurship is represented most famously in that example of Midas and his golden touch. In a sense, what this kind of magical productivity of riches accomplishes is to make the world gilded and yet valueless; made up to be valued beyond any real valuation; invested in by outward vestment alone.[31]

While oligarchic regimes have a clear outward basis for rule – i.e., those who are manifestly rich rule – what they lack is an intrinsic principle, in the sense that there is no reason why the possession of property in and of itself should legitimate rule by the rich. Certain half-hearted reasons can be found – along the lines that the qualities that won the riches could translate into political acumen, as in for example Ross Perot's bid for the American presidency on the basis that government could be managed like a corporation, or Alcibiades' insistence that his glorious displays of wealth would contribute to the overall glory of Athens.[32] The difference here owes to the kind of brash honesty unique to the ancients, but what is common is the difficulty that oligarchs have in tracing the outward dimensions of their wealth to some essential resource within themselves. So instead of locating the substance of the authority to rule in some quality in the person – whether that quality is said to be some kind of virtue, or knowledge, or divine dispensation – political rule is instead reduced to something that is routinely familiar and accessible to all, as money is common currency, or as household management is part of everyone's daily life. This reduction of political rule to a question of possessions leaves political legitimacy essentially unexplained; after all, if power is reducible to wealth, why then cross over that threshold from the private to the public? Why would the oligarch want to rule in the first place? Why not stay at home and enjoy one's private possessions within walls?

There is a persistent sense that money does not explain all that people do; contra Hobbes's claim that 'the value of a man is, as in all things, his price,' human beings are exceptional in that, as individuals and as groups, they are capable of holding themselves out towards all kinds of standards beyond the dictates of necessity and the compulsions of life. And it is thus that a person may, much as a community may also, be asked to give an account of themselves; when that person is a political authority they may be asked why they ought to rule. To this question a politically salient answer would have to go deeper than the mere conditions that enframe the holding of office – i.e., that I may happen to have free mornings, afternoons, and evenings and so be at liberty to do so – to some stated identity of the office and the person. So a general ought to have a knowledge and experience in matters pertaining to war; a judge ought to have a good knowledge of the law and be practised in its application; a forester should know about trees and be skilled in their management. What then has moneymaking to do with political leadership? Short of saying that all forms of expertise and practice are reducible to money, the exchange functions at a symbolic level – that is, money can be used to procure arms, bribe judges, or purchase woodlots, though significantly without making the owner of arms, briber of judges, or woodlot owner either a general, judge, or forester.

If the possession of means does not in and of itself provide adequate legitimacy to hold political office (this is not to say that property ownership may not serve as a necessary, as distinguished from a sufficient condition to establish political legitimacy), then the conflation of means and ends that characterizes oligarchic regimes depends upon a kind of secrecy. The oligarch cannot answer the question of why they ought to rule; they may have the means to do so, though not being themselves liberated from the insistence of those means they cannot propose an end that would distinguish and justify their tenure in office. So, with the consolidation of property within the ruling class serving as the dominant social priority, some sense of depth must be attributed to the wealth that distinguishes that class of citizens. The false sublimation of wealth into virtue is helped by the fact that it is inherently private to begin with, and this in-born secrecy contributes to the cultish character of oligarchic rule.

Because these essentially private and exclusive ends cannot be used to legitimize rule – that is, the people may ask of their rulers, Why is your wealth yours and not mine? – oligarchies depend on a measure of secrecy. Rule under oligarchy is inflected with the same quality of hidden-ness that pertains to the household properly considered, as in Arendt's poetic description of the *oikos* as 'some darker ground which must remain hidden if it is not to lose its depth in a very real non-subjective sense.'[33] If this sense of depth in the person is to be retained, then a person's substance, what the Greeks would call their *ousia*, cannot be held up in public as the basis of their authority. This sense of the non-subjective substance of a person, or what sustains them in their being, is a condition of possibility not only for the individual distinctiveness of the person, but also for a public realm composed of a plurality of such persons. Wealth out of place and held up as the basis of rule would undo both the value of the person and the possibility of political life. Thus Arendt insists that 'the only efficient way to guarantee the darkness of what needs to be hidden against the light of publicity is private property, a privately owned place to hide in.'[34]

If property is essentially apolitical in the sense that Arendt describes, borrowing as she does from Aristotle's distinction between household management and political rule, then just how does oligarchy actually rule, short of making slaves out of citizens? Being an unjust form of regime, like tyranny, oligarchies can be sustained by force, as Sparta punished its slave revolts, or as the brutal suppression of peasant movements kept a class of wealthy plantation owners and industrialists in power as in Nicaragua through the 1980s. Elements of a militarized society, dictatorial governance, and oligarchic interests can be mutually sustaining. Strict religious doctrine can also complement these modes of oppression, as in present-day Saudi Arabia. And yet oligarchies can also function less explicitly by promoting a certain mystique around the ruling class, as if their wealth provided a magical capacity to do for the community as a whole what they have done for themselves. That is to say that there is an aspect of fortune that pervades the prosperous reputation of oligarchs, and it is this sense of exceptionality that is promoted by the cabals, the secret clubs and hushed corridors of power, the cartels and wealthy cults cordoned off from public by the ruling rich. It is as if they say to the poor over whom they claim superiority: 'We have more than you, and more than you can ever know.' That is, the most radical form of oligarchy, most exactly true to the category as such, is the one that sees no need to account for its power. In the absence of political virtue rooted in regard for the common good, it is this secretive dimension of oligarchy that sustains an oligarchic class in power beyond the mere means of raw force, dictatorial privilege, and exclusive access to authority. This secretiveness about the terms of rule is thus put to work to make up for an inward reason that is otherwise lacking in this kind of regime.

Desire may be materially sublimated for the oligarch, for instance, into conspicuous consumption or charity.[35] This becomes a familiar trope among the ruling wealthy, who precisely because of their sense of self-distinction desire some irreducible virtue, whether in identity with the community, or some self-promoted cultural legacy, or a peace with god: something that would translate their eminence into terms at once understandable beyond the private limits of consumption (try to describe how good that wine really was, without referring to something else you have smelled, drunk, or eaten), and at the same time uplifted beyond the value of the common currency.

Of the possible sublimations of wealth, the identification of wealth with political power would also translate into the helpful capacity to inscribe the conditions of oligarchic distinctiveness, based on superfluous possession of wealth, into law and policy, thus attributing an air of respectable permanence to what is in actuality a flow medium. That is, in order to preserve power, an oligarch either can become a pious, liberal, community-bound aristocrat, thereby dismissing wealth as the substance of their virtue, or they could pretend to be so. Every counter-oligarchic revolt is in some sense coloured by this question of whether the rich are really virtuous. In this volume Newell notes the indignation of the Athenian oligarchs at the democratic claim that the many together have greater capacity and right to rule than the few, however gifted those few may be.[36] And yet the oligarchs' sworn oath that the virtue of the demos 'is far from clear, by God!' is as easily turned back upon the oath givers. What gives the oligarchs' oath its specific influence is that they can swear it together, a small mob being more suited to successful conspiracy than a large gathering would be.

Conclusion: The Oligarch's Mask

For a look at the secretiveness of oligarchic rule I would like to conclude by way of illustration in touching on the cult of personality that attended the public life of the most famous of the Athenian oligarchs: Alcibiades. We are fortunate to have an abundant source of suggestive biography in Plutarch's *Life of Alcibiades*, which is perhaps as reliable an authority on matters of rumour bred in secret as one could hope for.

Plutarch tells the story of a visit Alcibiades tried to make to Pericles, who was apparently thinking about how he would give an account of his policies before the people and was too busy to entertain the young guest. Wondering why the statesman would prefer the people's consideration to his own company, Alcibiades is said to have remarked as he went away, 'Would it not be better if he considered how to avoid presenting accounts to the people at all?'[37]

In this ancient sound bite the oligarchic sense of legitimacy is presented with just the kind of brutal honesty that makes Alcibiades such a fascinating figure, being at once transparent and suggestive.

One particularly remarkable feature of Alcibiades is that his famousness and the public honours given to him are difficult to trace to any specific word or deed of especial worth. There are the Olympic victories that he trumpets (and Nicias scoffs at) in Thucydides' *History*, but these were wins purchased at the expense of teams of horses and fancy chariots, hardly measures of fitness or skill on his own part. We have flashes of eloquence, birds let loose at public meetings, rumours of vandalism, some kind of profanity against the Eleusinian Mysteries perhaps, as well as the supposed plotting of an oligarchic coup, but even these alleged crimes have a thin quality to them. What did the man really do? He led the Athenians on their Sicilian expedition, though he only joined the armada for a short time before being called back to Athens, taking a side trip to Sparta on the way to court. The Spartans saw little concrete service from the man either, who fed them lies that served mainly to keep them overly suspicious of their enemies,[38] hardly bold moves of leadership, and not seeming to rise above common self-interestedness.

Alcibiades' notorious name is like a darkened veil cast over the life of a public layabout: a man of both substance and no substance. What remains then of his substance, his *ousia*, after his uncle's money is spent on hounds and horses, purple capes, and choruses, is the merest and yet still vital intimation that there is something behind the veil. Like a babushka doll, the thin shells of which stack neatly together, emptying out inwards into a solid figurine inside, what, one wonders, subsists at the core of such a self-interested public persona? What is

his substance? Alcibiades makes a similar complaint against his
beloved Socrates – that there was no really getting to know the man –
and perhaps in this there is a parallel between the openness of philosophic discourse and the hollowness of oligarchy as a form of rule.[39]

The difference between the two is that a philosopher stands or falls by
the capacity to give a critical account of himself, whereas an oligarch cannot afford to do just this. For if he does so he risks exposing that his substance is exchangeable, being currency always for something else that is
considered to be of value. Thus, what the oligarch claims to possess, but
does not – making him unconscious – philosophy holds out towards as
something essentially needful and the basis of self-knowledge – that is to
ask what is truly of substance, both in itself, and in a person. These two
essential questions then lead to the political question, pertaining to the
distribution of powers and responsibilities within a regime, namely,
what is owed to others?

NOTES

1 G.W.F. Hegel, *Phenomenology of Spirit*, trans. J.B. Baillie (New York: Harper,
   1967), 523.
2 Aristotle, *Politics*, trans. E. Barker (Oxford: Oxford University Press, 1958),
   1337a27.
3 There is, of course, debate on this point of an ontological identity in the ancients. Heidegger's account of Aristotle's treatment of the question of Being
   in the *Physics* relates the things that are by *physis* and the things that are by
   techne to an underlying field of movedness, of coming into and out of being.
   Consider: 'On the Essence and Concept of Phusis in Aristotle's *Physics* B, 1'
   (1939), in *Pathmarks*, ed. and trans. William McNeil (Cambridge: Cambridge
   University Press, 1998). Heidegger's historicizing mode of interpretation is
   carried out in a similarly creatively critical manner where he treats Plato's
   image of education in the cave as a passage punctuated by turnings, which
   are conceived as moments of eidetic instability, each one not so much enduring over time as existing as a coming into appearance, with the forms
   themselves being epiphenomenal to Being coming into presence, like
   the glinting of sunshine on rippled water. See 'Plato's Doctrine of Truth'
   (1931–2, 1940) in *Pathmarks*. In this pattern of interpretation, reading the
   thinker as a metaphor for an historical horizon, Heidegger translates apparently stable forms or ends into moments of critical movement – turnings in
   the history of Being. It is as if Heraclitus gets in the last ontological word,

and that is becoming. But however much Aristotle's *ousia* may seem to move as a final cause, or underlie change as a mysterious middle term between forms and formlessness, at the Being level of beings, for Aristotle it most definitely persists as a 'self-subsistent' phenomenon (Waterfield's translation of *ousia*). This sense of substance as self-subsistence translates directly into Aristotle's assessment of human conduct, with substantial persons being capable of sustaining themselves, and from there capable also of calling upon unchanging virtues that would inform action within a political reality that is indeed shot through with diversity and change. Their very lives, and the communities which are the products of many such lives taken together, would thus mediate that which changes and that which endures. Perhaps there is some reconciliation between these two ontologies, the one privileging changing appearances, the other emphasizing the reality of that which endures: in an intriguing passage from the *Physics* Aristotle insists that 'there must always be something underlying which is the coming-to-be thing' (190a13). In this insistence, *ousia* becomes an underlying element that changes in its distinguishing forms while persisting in its capacity to be changed this way or that. *Ousia* is the thing that changes and endures; it exists both in itself as a self-subsistent being and within its changes as a changing being. The term serves ontologically for Aristotle in much the same way that Heidegger intones *Being*, as that which comes to presence; though for the latter *Being* becomes a historical horizon of changing comportments towards what is real. I have relied heavily upon Robin Waterfield's translation of the *Physics* (Oxford University Press, 2008) along with the P.H. Wicksteed translation of the same (Loeb Classics Library, 1986).

4 The metaphorical sense implicit in this kind of reference to a person's substance, as in 'a man of substance' (*Lysias* 24.11; Henry George Lidell and Robert Scott, *A Greek-English Lexicon* [Oxford: Claredon Press, 1968] 1274–5.), is present also in the meanings of *ousia* given in the *Physics*, where Aristotle indicates that the substance of beings must be grasped by analogy [191a7]. The challenge for understanding in both instances is that *ousia* both participates in pure 'stuff' *and* is capable of being informed; or in ethical terms the substance of a person both depends on wealth *and* gives virtuous direction to those means of life.

5 Here I would put myself in the company of Bradshaw, whose reading of Arendt in this volume emphasizes an essential distinction between violent modes of hierarchical management and political rule between equals. A fascinating counterpoint to this pretty common-sense distinction is given in Newell's essay in this volume, where he argues that any such egalitarian priority is provisional and not given in the order of reason itself, which

would, if given free rein, incline rather in the direction of monarchical rule by a leader of superlative virtue. It appears that what keeps politics from such a realization, in his view, and in our time as in Aristotle's, is the usual messiness of politics, along with a particular, democratic aversion to giving up the public sphere to just one person.

6 *Politics*, 1252a2. I have relied on both Carnes Lord's accurate translation (Chicago: University of Chicago Press, 1984) and Ernest Barker's more heavily glossed interpretation (op. cit.).

7 See Hannah Arendt, *The Human Condition* (Chicago: University of Chicago Press, 1958), 23.

8 Proudhon writes that 'the motive behind revolutions is not so much the distress felt by the people at a given moment, as the prolongation of this distress, which tends to neutralize and extinguish the good.' Pierre-Joseph Proudhon, 'General Idea of the Revolution in the Nineteenth Century,' in *The Essential Works of Anarchism*, ed. Marshall S. Shatz (New York: Bantam, 1971), 84. For Proudhon what moves people to revolt is not some Hegelian spirit of history turned to necessity, but rather a gathering sense of progressive reforms in retreat, where such progress would otherwise be judged by 'a tendency towards comfort and virtue' (ibid.).

9 On the hopeless resentment that persists between those who are materially deprived and those whom Nietzsche calls 'inverse cripples,' those 'human beings who are nothing but a big eye or a big mouth or a big belly,' see 'On Redemption,' *Thus Spoke Zarathustra*, trans. Walter Kaufmann (New York: Modern Library, 1995), 138.

10 *Politics* 1301a37. It is interesting to note that Aristotle describes aristocrats, who would have an eminent claim to revolt if they were denied the privilege of sharing in the regime, as those least inclined to engage in factional conflict so as to claim what is by justice theirs.

11 Homer, *Iliad* 2.245.

12 Homer, *Iliad* 12.320–32.

13 *Republic* 372a.

14 *Republic* 372c.

15 The wildness inherent in a libidinal economy of desires delinked from natural ends is perhaps most clearly manifest in George Bataille's theory of economic surplus, *The Accursed Share*, trans. Robert Hurley (New York: Zone Books, 1988). There he argues that a general political economy must be concentrated on how surplus is sacrificed to symbolic value, with the terms of necessity in his view ultimately reduced to a cosmogonic cycling of creation and destruction, release and restraint, expenditure and accumulation. It is something like this mythic, netherworld version of order in

excess and of a literal bleeding off of a society's best that, we might suppose, Plato and Aristotle reacted so violently against in their idealized notions of relatively autonomous cities within walls, contra the imperiously acquisitive violence of their times. Thus, in what has become a familiar division, an uneasy mediation between the necessary and the good, or in more modern terms necessity and freedom, is deployed so as to settle societies otherwise characterized by bands of pirates alternately engaged in vicious raids and wild parties – just the kind of social disorder that Bataille seems to prefer. Elsewhere he writes (and I think this is representative of the general sense of purpose that he sees in wealth): 'For it is human to burn and consume oneself to the point of suicide at the baccarat table,' a sentiment with which Alcibiades might well have agreed. 'The Sorcerer's Apprentice,' in *George Bataille: Visions of Excess Selected Writings 1927–1939*, trans. Allan Stoekl (Minneapolis: University of Minnesota Press, 1985).

16 There are fifty-six references that treat the subject of oligarchy indexed in the Barker translation.

17 General discussions on the classification of regimes, of intertextualities between Plato's, Xenophon's, and Aristotle's *Politeia*, and works concerning the best and worst kinds of regimes are abundant, but few bring specific focus to the topic of oligarchy in classical political theory. Some exceptions can be pointed to. David Keyt's translation and commentary, *Aristotle: Politics, Books V and VI* (Clarendon Aristotle Series. Oxford: Clarendon Press, 1999), draws attention to the place of oligarchy in Athenian and Spartan politics through historical supplements to these central books of the *Politics*, where Aristotle sought to find a realistic way between ideal regimes and what constitutional possibilities were available at the time. Our collection's historical comparative approach towards classical concepts of oligarchy is employed similarly by C. Fred Alford in his essay 'The "Iron Law of Oligarchy" in the Athenian Polis ... and Today,' *Canadian Journal of Political Science / Revue Canadienne de Science Politique* 18, no. 2 (June 1985): 295–312. This apparent gap in classical scholarship is noted in J. Sikkenga's essay 'Plato's Examination of the Oligarchic Soul in Book VIII of the Republic,' *History of Political Thought* 23, no. 3 (2002): 377–400.

18 *Politics* 1314a30–b7.

19 *Constitution of Athens* XI.2.

20 *Constitution of Athens* VII.5.

21 J.M. Moore, *Aristotle and Xenophon on Democracy and Oligarchy* (Berkeley: University of California Press, 1975), 222.

22 *Constitution of Athens* IX.1.

23 *Constitution of Athens* IX.2.

24 Ibid.

25 Ibid.

26 *Constitution of Athens* XIII.4

27 Ibid.

28 *Politics* 1258a14–19.

29 *Politics* 1320a32–1320b4.

30 *Politics* 1331a30–41.

31 For a modern variant on the entrepreneur's ontological function as a creator of value see economist Joseph Schumpeter's theory of business cycles. Schumpeter is clear that what the entrepreneur does is two-fold: (1) to bring new values into being via innovation in either the ends or means of the organization/technical/systemic means of production; and (2) to act as the primary exogenous driving factor within the business cycle, a factor ultimately identified with technological development – hence time – in the production function. See Joseph Schumpeter, *The Theory of Economic Development: An Inquiry into Profits, Capital, Credit, Interest, and the Business Cycle*, trans. Redvers Opie (Oxford: Oxford University Press, 1934). It is interesting to note that within the discourse around economic development, even lapses in productivity are considered as increments in an overarching course of historical development. The lapses are by convention considered as periods of 'negative growth,' in what is a clear impasse and lapse of symbolic capacity within the progressivist, neoliberal faith. See Alpha C. Chiang, *Fundamental Methods of Mathematical Economics* (Singapore: McGraw-Hill, 1984), 280–1. For a re-evaluation of this underlying assumption in modern economics, see my *After the Last Man: Excurses to the Limits of the Technological System* (Lanham, MD: Lexington Books, 2008), 46–50.

32 Thucydides, *History of the Peloponnesian War*, trans. Martin Hammond (Oxford University Press, 2009), 6.16.

33 Arendt, *The Human Condition*, 71.

34 Ibid.

35 Drug lords in Mexico are great beneficiaries of private donations, beautifying churches and playgrounds and acting as patrons of the arts. They appear especially generous in their renditions of the traditional Mexican *corrido* ballads, sponsoring self-glamourizing *narco-corrido* songs that serve as folk agitprop to immortalize the criminal legends of drug-trafficking cartels, with their leaders singing their own praise as street-level heroes. Listen at http://www.cbc.ca/thecurrent/episode/2010/02/05/february-5–2010/ (accessed 25 May 2011).

36 Waller Newell, 'Oligarchy and *Oikonomia*: Aristotle's Ambivalent Assessment of Private Property,' in this volume. See especially note 6.

37 Plutarch, *Lives*, trans. Ian Scott-Kilvert (Middlesex: Penguin, 1960), 'Alcibiades' §7.

38 Plutarch, *Lives*, 'Alcibiades,' §14. Clearly the man was a skilled rhetorician and brilliant tactician, at least inasmuch as that rhetoric and those tactics allowed him to serve his own self-interest; yet questions remain as to what ends those means served, and if it is the self that is served, then what is the substance of that self? For to serve self-interest alone is to leave an empty signifier at the core of one's political purposes, with acumen in the manipulation of a shifting field of happenstance and perceptions unmatched by any justification of that measure of control.

   For instance, while Alcibiades' advice to the Spartans to fortify Decelea is noted by Thucydides as one of the reasons for the fall of Athens, his claim to being a clever turncoat hardly makes him a virtuous person; it would seem rather that a dim criminal would be preferred to a savvy one. Indeed, Alcibiades' encouragement that the Spartans cease their peace with Athens is shot through with duplicity, as when he comforts the Spartans that his playing along with the Athenian democracy was a matter of convenience, seeing as 'it was necessary in most things to conform to established conditions' (*History*, 6.89). What is really amazing about the man, revealing the void of purpose at the oligarch's core, is that he can characterize his words and deeds back in Athens as being 'more moderate than the licentious temper of the times' (ibid.) and then go on to justify his treason as the work of a 'true lover of his country' (6.93). If this presents an image of political virtue, it is one that, like much political rhetoric, is readily inverted, along the lines of a Heraclitean aphorism that good and bad are the same, or that our enemy's vices do double duty as our virtues.

39 See Socrates' reported response at *Symposium*, 219a.

10 Oligarchy and the Rule of Law

CRAIG COOPER

> It is agreed that there are three forms of government in the world, tyranny, oligarchy and democracy; tyrannies and oligarchies are governed by the temperaments of those in power, but democratic cities are governed by the established laws. You should be aware, men of Athens, that it is the laws that protect the persons of those living in a democracy and their system of government, but it is suspicion and armed guards which protect the affairs of tyrants and oligarchs. Oligarchs and those who operate any type of government based on inequality need to be on guard against those trying to overthrow their systems by the law of force; but you, who operate a government based on equality and the law, must be on guard against those whose speeches and styles of life are contrary to the laws.
> – Aeschines 1 *Against Timarchus*, 4–5[1]

According to Athenian democratic ideology, as expressed here and elsewhere, democracies are governed by the rule of law, which protects the persons of those living under democracy. Suspicion and armed forces govern the affairs of oppressive forms of government such as oligarchy and tyranny. But is this entirely true? Does the rule of law exist only in democracies and never under oligarchies, which by their very nature entrench systems of inequality? This is the question which I wish to explore from an ancient and modern perspective.

Aristotle, *Politieia*, and the Rule of Law

In the *Politics* Aristotle identifies four kinds of democracy and four kinds of oligarchy. In the first three forms of democracy the rule of law prevails, but in the fourth the multitude (*plêthos*) are sovereign and not the law.[2] This happens when decrees of the assembly are sovereign and not the law. Under this form of democracy, where the laws are not sovereign, demagogues arise and the people become a single composite monarch. A democracy of this kind is comparable to tyranny. In similar fashion the first three forms of oligarchy are governed by the law; only in the fourth which Aristotle labels a dynasty, where rule is hereditary, do magistrates govern and not the law. This form of oligarchy corresponds to tyranny and the tyrannical form of democracy. For Aristotle, then, what is important is not the form of government so much as the rule of law. Oligarchy and democracy are acceptable forms of government provided the laws are sovereign. Indeed for Aristotle the best form of government and the most stable is one that blends both oligarchic and democratic elements. Let us examine Aristotle's position more closely.

In the first form of democracy the stress is placed on equality (*malista kata to ison*), for the law dictates that equality involves neither the poor nor rich having any greater advantage than the other; neither is sovereign but both are treated alike. Since freedom and equality especially characterize democracy, then all share in the *politeia* equally.[3] Since the demos are the majority and resolutions by the majority are sovereign, this for Aristotle must by necessity constitute democracy. Though a property qualification is required for holding office, it is low and by necessity anyone who acquires the requisite amount, is entitled to share in office.[4] The next two forms of democracy, which Aristotle regards as *politeiai*, are simply variations on the first, with the right to share in office determined by citizenship alone.[5] At the end of his discussion of the fourth form of democracy Aristotle draws an interesting conclusion that seems to guide his taxonomy and explains why this particular form of democracy is not a *politeia*: 'For where the laws do not rule, there is no *politeia*; for the law must rule all things and the magistrates the particulars, and this we must judge a *politeia*. The consequence is that if democracy is one form of *politeia*, it is clear that such a constitution where all things are administered by decrees, is not a democracy in the proper sense, for in no way is it possible for a decree to be about the universal.'[6] By contrast, all other forms of democracy, where the law prevails and is sovereign, by Aristotle's taxonomy constitute *politeiai*. The same would also be true of oligarchies governed by the rule of law.[7]

When Aristotle describes the tyrannical nature of the fourth kind of democracy, he obviously has fifth-century Athens in mind; in the fifth century, as opposed to the fourth century, the demos was sovereign, decrees of the assembly became law, and politics was dominated by demagogues like Pericles and Cleon.[8] According to Aristotle, the 'apolitical' nature of this kind of democracy, in the sense that it is not a *politeia*, arises through influence of demagogues. In democratic *politeiai* under the rule of law demagogues cannot emerge since the best citizens dominate. Where laws are not sovereign, however, demagogues emerge since the demos acts as a monarch, for the many are sovereign not as individuals but collectively.

Aristotle goes on to note that this sort of demos seeks to act as a monarch by not being ruled by law, and becomes instead despotic and open to flatterers. Such a democracy is comparable to tyranny, since both exercise despotic control over the better classes. Decrees of the assembly resemble edicts of the tyrant and demagogues resemble flatterers who exercise great influence over the demos. In such a case, demagogues cause decrees to be sovereign and not the laws, because they refer all matters to the demos. Their importance stems from the fact that the people are sovereign over all things, while demagogues are sovereign over the opinion of the people. And when they bring charges against magistrates the demagogues assert the demos must judge the suits (*krinein*). The people gladly welcome the summons (*proklêsis*) so that all magistrates are put down (*katalusis*). Aristotle's language here is peppered with legal terms. The people are to judge; they receive the summons issued by the demagogues and the magistrates are convicted. Obviously Aristotle has in mind the Athenian *euthuna* system by which all magistrates were audited at the end of their term of office. The audit took place before an Athenian *dikastêrion* comprised of the demos, who themselves provided the auditors and prosecutors, elected from the assembly.[9] And indeed in the fifth century demagogues like Cleon exploited the system to attack magistrates and other political enemies. But there seems to be an apparent contradiction in Aristotle's line of reasoning. The sovereignty of the demos is reinforced by the rule of law at least from an Athenian perspective in that the *euthuna* was a legal requirement regulated by the courts.

The other forms of democracies that are characterized by the rule of law seem to promote the better classes and limit the scope of direct democracy. What seems to be at work in these other forms of democracy is Michels's 'iron law of oligarchy,' which maintains that in every kind of human organization, including democracies, that strive for certain ends, oligarchic tendencies develop, whereby a ruling elite controls matters.[10] Michels based his conclusions on an examination of the operation of twentieth-century political parties but argued that this oligarchic tendency was natural of all forms of government if they were to operate. If one compares Aristotle's discussion of how best to safeguard a democratic constitution, we see the same kind of oligarchic tendency at work. The measures he suggests are aimed at protecting the better classes and limiting the scope of the popular courts.[11] But if that were to happen, the rule of law could not exist at least as Athenians envisaged it. If, however, we accept Aristotle's taxonomy, Athenian democracy, which Aristotle clearly has in mind here and which resisted the inevitable march to oligarchy, is not a *politeia* at all.[12]

Let us step back and look for a moment at the defining features of democracy and oligarchy, both from Aristotle's perspective and the Athenian perspective. According to Aristotle, the starting point for any *politeia* is an agreed-upon notion of justice and proportionate equality (*to kat' analogian ison*). On the one hand, democracy emerges from the notion that those who are equal in any respect are equal absolutely and since they are all alike free, they are all equal absolutely. Oligarchy, on the other hand, is based on the supposition that those who are unequal in wealth are unequal absolutely.[13] Although Aristotle is not explicit, we presume notions of equality and inequality apply also to the application of justice and the rule of law. This much is made more explicit when Aristotle first discusses the defining principles (*opoi*) of democracy and oligarchy and what constitutes democratic and oligarchic justice.[14] There he notes that all claim some sort of justice for themselves, but only go so far and never speak of absolute justice in its entirety. So for instance it is thought that 'justice is equal' (*ison to dikaion*) and applies not to all but only to those who are equal. In a democracy that should mean everyone regardless of wealth or status. For others, 'inequality is just' (*to anison dikaion*) but not for everyone – only those who are unequal. Thus in an oligarchy justice only applies to certain segments of society. Clearly then notions of justice which are bound up in the application of law are defined in terms of equality and inequality. Aristotle reiterates the point when he sums up this part of his discussion: because both sides speak of justice up to a point, they believe they are speaking of justice absolutely; for the one side, namely the oligarchs, think that if they are unequal in some respects such as wealth, they are entirely unequal, and this we presume applies also to the application of justice. The other side, by contrast, thinks that if they are equal in some respects such as in freedom, they are entirely equal, and this equality must, we assume, express itself in terms of the administration of justice.

Elsewhere Aristotle notes that a defining principle and chief aim of any democratic *politeia* is freedom (*eleutheria*).[15] By freedom Aristotle is thinking of equality in terms of both political participation and justice. As he notes, 'one element of freedom is to rule and be ruled in term; for democratic justice entails equality (*to ison echein*) according to number and not worth, and if this is justice, the multitude must by necessity be sovereign and whatever is decided by the majority must be final and constitute justice, for they say each citizen must have an equal share [*ison echein*].' A second element of freedom is to live as one likes, since not to live as one likes is the life of a slave.[16] In his enumeration of features of a democratic form of government (election of officials from all, to rule and be ruled, use of the lot, etc.) Aristotle notes that judicial functions are exercised by all and judges are selected from all, and they decide either all matters or at least the most important matters, namely the *euthuna* (audit of magistrates), constitutional matters, and private contracts, which regulate how men can live as they like.[17] In Athens, these last three items were all regulated by law and by the popular courts (*dikastêria*) that administered the law.

If we accept Aristotle's argument that oligarchies are organized along opposite lines from that of democracies, then freedom and equal justice, which are the hallmarks of democracy, are never the aims of oligarchies. Democracies, we are told, are safeguarded by the large numbers of people (*poluanthrôpia*), which is the antithesis of justice by worth (*to dikaion to kata tên axian*), which characterizes oligarchy. Oligarchies, we are told, are safeguarded by good order (*upo tês eutaxias*).[18] Oligarchy thus sustains itself by administering justice unevenly and by emphasizing good order over equality and freedom.[19] Good order and unequal justice are what define oligarchy; equal justice and equal participation democracy. The latter might be messy and can lead at times, as it did in Athens, to a lack good government, and may explain why Aristotle advocates limiting legal suits and the scope of the popular courts and promoting the better classes over the masses.[20]

The Athenian Context and the Rule of Law

For political theorists like Aristotle, then, the differences between democracy and oligarchy lay in the distribution of justice, whether it was equal or unequal, the level of political participation, whether it was equal or unequal, and the presence of freedom or good order. To ensure the latter, oligarchies must by necessity limit the former and exclude certain segments of society from participation in both government and the administration of justice. Democracies, which promote freedom, equal participation, and equal justice, assume that respect for the rule of law that issues from those democratic values will lead to good government. From the Athenian perspective, two ideals underpinned Athenian democratic freedom and influenced the Athenian approach to law: *isonomia*, equality of law, and *isêgoria*, equality of speech. In democratic thinking law could be enforced and justice served only when there was an equality of speech. These ideals were reflected in the judicial process itself, much of which was given over to hearing speeches delivered by litigants. Each litigant was given an equal time to speak measured by a water clock under the supervision of one of the jurors; jurors swore an oath to vote according to the laws and decrees of the Athenian people and council, after hearing both sides.[21] Litigants themselves, particularly defendants, would remind the jurors that they had sworn to give an impartial hearing. The judicial process reflects to some extent the legislative process in Athens. In the fifth century, after listening to speeches in the assembly, Athenians voted on laws and decrees by which they would be governed. In the fourth century the process for creating new laws had changed, and not the assembly but a panel of *nomothetai* (law-givers) selected from sitting jurors, would vote on laws after hearing the arguments for and against changes.[22] Again equality of speech underscored the process. Laws in the courtroom were themselves persuasive evidence that needed to be supported by arguments to show their relevancy to the case. Jurors themselves were sometimes referred to by the litigants as *nomothetai* in deciding the case.[23] In a sense, jurors, when they voted in favour of a litigant, having been persuaded by his speech, created law. Prevalent throughout the Athenian notion of the administration of equal justice and its corollary, the rule of law, is unencumbered speech. But if we accept Aristotle's taxonomy, Athenian democracy, which claimed for itself alone the rule of law, was not a *politeia*.

Ironically *isonomia* seems to have been coined by Athenian elite to commemorate their struggle against the tyranny. The word appears in drinking songs (*skolia*) sung by the elite at symposia to celebrate and commemorate the assassination of Hipparchus, the brother of the tyrant Hippias: 'I will carry my sword in a myrtle branch, as

Harmodius and Aristogeiton did, when they killed the tyrant and made Athens *isonomos*.'[24] Equality in terms of political participation, which had long been the prerogative of the Athenian elite, had been denied under the tyrants. The terms *isonomia* and *isêgoria* were likely created to reassert those Aristocratic values.[25] We even see it reflected in the name Isagoras, a member of a leading Aristocratic family, who came to political prominence after the expulsion of the tyrant Hippias in 510. An intense political struggle ensued between Isagoras and Cleisthenes, another leading aristocrat, likely over the election to high office. Facing the prospect of political defeat, Cleisthenes responded by introducing a package of reforms that brought the demos into the political process.[26] He likely co-opted the terms that had previously been used by aristocrats to highlight their natural rights to rule to describe his reforms, which would ultimately empower the people politically and judicially. Certainly by the mid-fifth century they were terms regularly used to describe democracy.[27]

At the heart of Cleisthenes' reforms was the creation of ten new tribes into which all citizens were divided, with each tribe drawing citizens from different regions of the country. Aristotle's *Athenaion Politeia* notes that the intent behind the tribal reform was to mix up the people so more men could have a share of government.[28] The important aspect of these reforms was the creation of the deme as a political organization. A new representative council of 500 was created to which each tribe contributed 50 members, but the council members were elected from the demes of the tribe, the various villages and communities within a particular tribe. Each deme would provide a certain number of council members based on its population and size. Though the council of 500 was a representative body, it was not like representative bodies of modern oligarchic democracies that vote on legislation along party lines. The council of 500 prepared the agenda for the full assembly at which all citizens could attend; at the assembly citizens directly debated items put before them by the council, and could modify, reject, or refer them back to the council for further consideration.[29]

More importantly for our discussion is the role that the demes played in this democratic process. Each deme had its own active municipal life with an assembly (agora) where members met face to face to discuss local business, vote on citizenship of new members, and annually elect a demarch and treasurers to oversee the deme's business.[30] It was at the deme level that Athenians learned and exercised *isêgoria* in face-to-face meetings, which in time would translate into political power at the corporate level.[31] As Ober notes, 'the council of 500 allowed "local knowledge," gained through face-to-face interactions [at the deme], to be "networked" and thereby made available at the national level.'[32] Osborne sees the creation of a deme as a political revolution. They 'had no physical boundaries as such, but were communities whose members ... identified themselves as members of that community because that was where ... they felt at home.'[33] I have focused on the deme since it is at the community level that citizens can recapture *isêgoria*, which is essential for democratic life governed by the rule of law, and thereby resist the oligarchic tendencies of modern democracies. In fact citizens should be encouraged to recreate their own demes; if we take things a step further and see a deme as a community not necessarily tied to any geographical location, but as a place where members can identify with each other and openly debate issues, as indeed happened in the Athenian demes, then political revolution and change might even be possible in the twenty-first century. Space on the World Wide Web can become the virtual agora of the new demes of modern democracies.

By the mid-fifth century rule of law in Athens was embodied in the Athenian court system. The Athenians adopted the practice of selecting by lot 6,000 citizens to serve as dikasts or jurors for that year.[34] The process of assigning jurors to courts became increasingly sophisticated over time to prevent corruption and ensure an impartial hearing.[35] The selected jurors were required to swear an oath that they would vote according to the laws after giving each litigant an impartial hearing. As we noted above, speech played a crucial role in the judicial process and application of law. At the heart were citizen jurors who had sworn to give an impartial or equal hearing. If we return to our opening quotation, the context is a legal matter. Aeschines was prosecuting Timarchus for exercising his civic rights contrary to the law.[36] Oligarchy, he notes, is based on inequality and the law of force (literally 'law in hands'), the very antithesis of the rule of law, whereas democracy is based on equality and the law, and that equality is assured through active participation.[37] And here Aeschines is thinking of the role that the jurors play in upholding the rule of law. As Aeschines goes on to note, those 'who operate a government based on equality and the law (*tên isên kai ennomon politeian*) must be on guard against those whose speeches and styles of life are contrary to the laws.' Not only must they enact laws that are good and advantageous to the *politeia*, once they are enacted, they must obey them and punish those who disobey them if the polis is to flourish.[38] Aeschines makes essentially the same comments in the opening statement of his prosecution of Ctesiphon, who had been charged with proposing an illegal measure in the assembly:[39]

> You are well aware, men of Athens, that there are three kinds of constitution in the whole world, tyranny, oligarchy and democracy, and tyrannies and oligarchies are governed by the temperament of those in power, whereas democratic cities are governed by the established laws. None of you should fail to note, in fact everyone should be clear in his mind, that when he enters the courtroom to judge an indictment for illegality, he is about to give a verdict that day on his own right to free speech (*parrhêsia*) This is why the legislator made this the first clause in the jurors' oath 'I shall vote according to the laws.' He was well aware that when the laws are protected for the city, the democracy too is preserved.[40]

In the Timarchus passage, Aeschines equates equality and law, namely *isonomia*; here he equates it with freedom of speech. *Parrhêsia* was an extension of *isêgoria*.[41] It entailed not only equal opportunity to speak but speech that was frank and open and without fear of recrimination. As Saxonhouse notes, *parrhêsia* is speech that is egalitarian, rejects hierarchy, and reveals and uncovers the truth as one sees it.[42] This is in sharp contrast to speech expressed by the handlers of modern governments, which tends to be scripted in order to produce a pleasing sound bite that keeps the government's message on track. Such speech, which is not meant to be open and frank, limits debate and rarely reveals the truth. For Athenians this kind of speech characterizes life under tyranny and oligarchy, where there is no rule of law but only fear.[43] Aeschines appeals to the jurors to uphold the law by voting for conviction; their verdict will guarantee their own *parrhêsia*. Ironically, Aeschines' reference to the jurors' oath reminds the jurors that they are to vote according to the laws only after giving an impartial hearing to both litigants. The legal process itself must adhere to the principle of *isêgoria*.

Speech is an essential feature of the Athenian conception of the rule of law, so much so that it forms an important metaphor for describing the administration of justice. The jurors become the voice of the law. Often litigants would remind jurors that law is ineffective without them. Demosthenes, for instance, in his prosecution of Phaenippus, urges the jurors not to 'grant more than what is just to those who consider their own shamelessness stronger than the laws.'[44] Otherwise, they will cause many to mock the just provisions written in the laws. Rather, they must aid those, namely the prosecutors, who consider the voice of the laws as the jurors' voice and the appointed day in court for the benefit of the wronged and not of wrongdoers. The laws have no voice of their own; they are simply written provisions, which, however, are given voice by the jurors, assisted by the prosecution, who speak to the laws and to the jurors. This image of the voiceless and near lifeless laws is developed more fully by Demosthenes in his prosecution of Meidias. In his epilogue Demosthenes asks the jurors what is it that gives the jurors empanelled in numbers of 200 or 1,000 power (*ischuroi*) and binding authority (*kurioi*) in all the affairs of the city.[45] It is not by the strength of arms, by physical strength or youthful vigour, the very things on which oligarchs rely, but by the strength of the laws. But what, he asks, is the strength of the laws? 'If one of you is wronged and shouts out, will the laws run up and assist you? No. They are written texts and are unable to do this. So what is their power? You yourselves, if you secure them and make them binding (*kurious*) for the one in need. So then the laws are *ischuroi* through you and you through the laws.' Demosthenes continues. The jurors must assist the laws as much as one would assist himself if he were wrong, and they must consider wrongs done to the laws as common wrongs, that is, wrongs done to themselves, nor must liturgies, pity or any other *technê* be found by which one can transgress the laws and not pay the penalty. With these last words Demosthenes warns the jurors not be deceived by the defendant's rhetorical tricks; any rehearsal of his public service or pleas for pity, which were common rhetorical ploys, should not sway the jury and thus weaken the power of the laws to punish. Though speech can be abused and manipulated, it still remains the essential aspect of the rule of law and its application through the jurors.

Oligarchic Opposition

I have tried to suggest that the way to resist oligarchic tendencies inherent in modern democracies and other forms of modern governments is through freedom of speech that allows all members of society to voice their opinion. Equality of justice, the hallmark of democracy, depends on equality of speech. Not surprisingly, it is these very aspects that oligarchies try to discourage or limit. In 411 BCE, the

Athenian democracy was overthrown by an oligarchic coup that led
to the creation of the Four Hundred and to a significant narrowing of
the franchise. The coup came about rather innocently through a decree
of the assembly that led to the creation of a commission of thirty
men who were entrusted with the task of drafting a proposal for
Athens' safety and with searching out the traditional laws enacted by
Cleisthenes. One of the first acts of the commission was to suspend
constitutional safeguards, such as the indictments for illegal proposals
(*graphai paranomôn*), impeachments (*eisangeliai*), and summons (*proklêsis*), legal devices that gave the demos control over its magistrates
and constitution.[46] Aristotle's *Athenaion Politeia* indicates that these
measures were intended to allow free deliberation over matters laid
before the assembly, but clearly they were meant to stifle debate and
opposition, to muzzle *isêgoria*, particularly when it was accompanied
by threats of intimidation. If anyone imposed a fine,[47] issued a summons, or brought a case to court over these matters, he was subject to
summary arrest to the generals and would be handed over to the
Eleven for execution.[48] In his account of the coup, Thucydides notes
that the assembly was not held at the Pnyx, the usual meeting place,
but at Colonus outside the city walls, which may have added to the
whole atmosphere of intimidation and discouraged many Athenians
from attending.[49] Though Pisander made the motion that stripped
Athenians of their constitutional rights, Thucydides remarks that the
architect of the whole plan was Antiphon, whom he regarded as one
of the ablest Athenians of his time, with the most powerful intellect
and ability to express his thoughts. He was, however, held in suspicion by the masses for his cleverness and after the restoration of the
democracy was tried for setting up the oligarchy and condemned to
death. In Thucydides' estimation the speech delivered by Antiphon in
his defence was the best ever given.[50]

If we identify this Antiphon with the fifth-century sophist of the
same name, as some scholars do, we have an interesting convergence
between the pragmatic actions of an oligarch, who was prepared to
deny equal rights, and the theoretical musings of an intellectual.[51] In
particular I am thinking of Antiphon's *On Truth*, which I would argue
provides us with the theoretical framework as to why Antiphon, a
skilled speech writer and orator, who could have thrived under
democracy, chose instead to support oligarchy. The underlying
assumption is that justice cannot necessarily exist under a system of
government that encourages *isêgoria*. In the papyrus fragment 44 B1 to

B7 of his work *On Truth*, as part of his wider discussion of the differences between *phusis* and *nomos*, Antiphon underlines the weaknesses of the rule of law based on *isêgoria*.[52] Antiphon, defines justice (*dikaiosynê*) as not violating the rules (*nomima*) of the city in which one resides as a citizen. Such justice only advantages the citizen, if he agrees to consider the laws (*nomoi*) effective in the presence of witnesses. The requirements of nature, he argues, are effective without witnesses as they are necessary, natural, and not based on agreement. The requirements of the laws, by contrast, are additional, based on agreement and not on nature. Consequently, someone who violates the law can avoid punishment if he goes undetected by those who have agreed to uphold the law. He is only punished when he is noticed.[53]

Later in the fragment (B5), Antiphon lays out three scenarios where the laws do not necessarily provide assistance: 'those who defend themselves when attacked and do not themselves begin the action, and those who treat their parents well even when they have been badly treated by them, and those who let their opponent swear an oath when they have not sworn one themselves.' In Athens assault was an offence that could be prosecuted in a number of ways, by a private suit for violence, a private suit for battery, or a public suit for *hubris*. Mistreatment of parents was an indictable offence in Athens which could result in the loss of citizen rights. Oath challenges were an important form of evidence in the judicial process. Antiphon continues:

> One would find many of the things I have mentioned hostile to nature; and involve more pain when less is possible and less pleasure when more is possible, and ill treatment that could be avoided. Thus if the laws provided some assistance for those engaged in such behaviour, and some penalty for those who did not but did the opposite, (B6) then the towrope of the laws would not be without benefit. But in fact it is apparent that justice (*to dikaion*) derived from the law (*ek nomou*) is not sufficient to assist those engaged in such things. First it permits the victim to suffer and the agent to act, and, at the time did not try to prevent the victim from suffering or the agent from acting, and when it is applied to punishment, it does not favour the victim over the agent; for he must persuade the punishers that he suffered, or else be able to obtain justice by deception. But these means are also available to the agent (if he chooses) to deny ... (B7) ... the defendant has as long for his defense as the plaintiff for his accusation, and there is an equivalent opportunity for the victim and for the agent.

There are a number of weaknesses that Antiphon points out. First laws are of use only when witnesses are present; an individual can commit a crime with impunity, if he goes unnoticed, and is only punished if he is noticed by those in agreement (to accept these laws). And even if the crime is witnessed, there are problems with the laws. According to Antiphon, justice based on laws is not sufficient, first because it cannot prevent the crime from being committed in the first place – that is to say, the law is powerless in and of itself – and secondly, because it does not favour one litigant over the other; the effectiveness of the laws in defending the victim depends entirely on persuasion and its corollary, deception, which are equally available to the criminal should he choose to deny the charge. Both defendant and plaintiff have an equal opportunity to persuade those who enforce the law, the 'punishers' in Antiphon's words, which in the Athenian judicial system were the *dikastai* or jurors. In Antiphon's estimation *isêgoria*, which Athenians regarded as foundational for the rule of law, is not sufficient to ensure justice. Nowhere does Antiphon suggest that *nomos* is bad in and of itself, but he is critical of certain instances of *nomos* that are not advantageous to society, in particular aspects of popular justice.[54] Indeed Antiphon later (44C) concludes that trying cases, giving verdicts, holding arbitration hearings, all aspects of the Athenian judicial system, are not just, as they help some people but harm others.[55] Not surprisingly, under the oligarchic coup of 411, which Antiphon masterminded, aspects of the legal system that ensured *isêgoria* were restricted, and perhaps with justification, as they do not lead to good order, after which all oligarchies strive.

Conclusion

We have tried to suggest that oligarchies and democracies with oligarchic tendencies try to restrict and limit freedom of speech. And these limitations have a direct impact on the rule of law. In a modern context, this point could not be more vividly illustrated than a television clip aired in October 2009 on the CBC that showed a number of Uyghurs, who were allegedly involved in the uprising in Xinjang province in July 2009, standing in silence as the court read out their sentences. What we know is that none of the trials were publicly announced and lasted less than a day. In one related trial nineteen 'men were convicted of "endangering state security" and sentenced following an eight-hour trial on October 21 in the Yili (Ghulja) Kazakh

Prefecture Branch of the XUAR Supreme Court.'[56] Good order, which is the aim of the oligarch, was upheld, but rule of law subverted. What was striking was the silence of the accused, which is a visual metaphor of oligarchy that seeks order over justice, whereas speech serves as a metaphor of the rule of law under democracy. The silence of the accused underscores the judicial process. Initially Uyghur prosecutors were assigned to these cases but were removed by Chinese authorities out of fear of bias. But as the leader of the Uyghur democracy movement, Rebiya Kadeer, states: 'Uyghurs in East Turkestan are frequently seen as untrustworthy outsiders, and are given no real voice in legal and judicial affairs.' The voice is silenced. Soon after the uprising began, the use of Twitter and Facebook, two forms of social media that allow freedom of speech under oligarchy, were limited.

But we can turn closer to home to see the same kind of behaviour by democratically elected governments. On 30 December 2009, the prime minister of Canada, for a second time in as many years, prorogued Parliament. Many suspect that the suspension of Parliament was directly related to the Afghan detainee issue, over which the government was coming under increasing scrutiny by the parliamentary committee investigating detainee abuse.[57] In the weeks leading up to prorogation the government stonewalled, reluctant to release information, and when it did, the documents were heavily redacted, effectively muzzling free speech.[58] Government ministers claimed that Canadian law (Canada Evidence Act) granted them the legal authority to release highly censored and redacted documents.[59] Critics think otherwise, and legal opinions might even suggest that the government was acting illegally and flaunting the rule of law.[60] Whether these legal opinions are right is not important to our discussion; what is important is the persistent ideological connection we see between speech, democracy, and the rule of law.

Prorogation effectively shut down the committee's work and silenced debate. The prime minister claimed that prorogation allowed the government to 'recalibrate' for the upcoming spring budget, but few, it seems, accepted his explanation and instead saw the move as cynical and undemocratic. A backlash resulted that no one could have predicted. A non-partisan Facebook site was created: Canadians Against Proroguing Parliament, which over 200,000 Canadians joined.[61] A new deme was created where citizens could meet in their virtual agora to debate and openly express their opinions. In a sense *parrhêsia* and *isêgoria* were restored. Prorogation galvanized Canadians; rallies across the country followed on 23 January. Although their success may be questioned, since attendance at the various rallies was by no means overwhelming, political debate in the end could not be silenced. The Facebook site in fact became a forum (to use the Roman term) for discussion of a wider range of political issues. If there is one lesson that we can learn from ancient Athens, it is that the demos is not easily silenced. The oligarchic coups of 411 and again of 404 were only short-lived. In each case democracy was quickly restored and with it equality of speech and the rule of law.

NOTES

1 All references from Aeschines come from C.D Adams, trans., *The Speeches of Aeschines* (Cambridge, MA: Harvard University Press, 1919). Translations, however, are my own.

2 Aristotle, *Politics* 1291b31–1292b10; 1292b23–1293a 3. All citations of the *Politics* come from H. Rackham, trans., *Aristotle XXI Politics* (Cambridge, MA: Harvard University Press, 1932). Again translations are my own.

3 The term *politeia* has a range of meanings from government to constitution, and given that range I have decided not to translate the word. For Aristotle it seems only certain forms of governments can be true *politeiai*, constitutional forms of government, and thus I use *politeia* (and its plural) in the sense of constitution or constitutional government; for Aristotle democracies and oligarchies can be 'constitutional' and thus constitute *politeiai*, if the rule of law is present.

4 *Politics* 1291a31–41.

5 In the second form of democracy office is open to 'all citizens who are not liable to an audit (*anupeuthunoi*).' How this differs from the third form of democracy where 'all share offices if only they are a citizen' is not clear. *Anupeuthunoi* should mean 'not subject to an audit or *euthuna*.' In Athens all magistrates were subject to an audit at the end of their term in office. Before the citizen could take up his office he had to undergo a *dokimasia* or scrutiny to determine whether he was a citizen and what kind of citizen.

6 *Politics* 1291b31–1292a38.

7 On Aristotle's theory of oligarchy see Peter Simpson's 'A Corruption of Oligarchs' in this volume.

8 In the fifth century, the procedure to create new a law was by simple decree of the assembly; in the fourth century the Athenians adopted a new procedure known as *nomothesia*. The process was still initiated in the assembly in

that any new law or proposed amendments to an existing law had to be introduced in the assembly first. If the assembly voted in favour of the change, it was passed to a board of *nomothetai*, who were made up of sitting jurors; they voted on the proposal after hearing arguments both in favour and against the proposed change. Only if the *nomothetai* voted in favour was a new law adopted or an existing law amended. As well, the Athenians adopted a new law that recognized the distinction between a law and a decree (Andocides 1, *On the Mysteries*, 67). On the process see Douglas Mac-Dowell, *The Law in Classical Athens* (Ithaca, NY: Cornell University Press, 1978), 48–9; Mogens Herman Hansen, *The Athenian Democracy in the Age of Demosthenes* (Cambridge, MA: Basil Blackwell, 1991), 167–74. On the question of whether Athens' democracy evolved from sovereignty of the demos to sovereignty of the law, see M. Ostwald, *From Popular Sovereignty to the Sovereignty of the Law* (Berkeley and Los Angeles: University of California Press, 1986), and Hansen, *Athenian Democracy*, 150–60.

9 On the *euthuna* see Aristotle, *Athenaion Politeia* (hereafter *AP*) 48.4–5, 54.2. in M. Chambers, ed., *Aristoteles Athenaion Politeia* (Leipzig: BSB B.G Teubner Verlagsgesellschaft, 1986); MacDowell, *The Law in Classical Athens*, 170–2, and A.R.W. Harrison, *The Law of Athens*, vol. 2: *Procedure* (Oxford: Oxford University Press, 1971); new edition, Foreword and Bibliography by D.M. MacDowell (Indianapolis, Indiana: Hackett, 1998), 28–31, 208–11.

10 Robert Michels, *A Sociological Study of the Oligarchical Tendencies of Modern Democracy*, trans. Eden and Cedar Paul (Glencoe, IL, 1915; reprinted New York: The Free Press, 1962), 50–1, 85–91, 333–56. Cf. Josiah Ober, *Mass and Elite in Democratic Athens* (Princeton, NJ: Princeton University Press, 1989), 15–16.

11 *Politics* 1319b33–1320b16.

12 This is the premise of Ober's book that Athenian democracy attained a level of social stability between rich and poor without institutionalizing elite leadership. See his concluding remarks in *Mass and Elite*, 333–9.

13 *Politics* 1301a26–37.

14 *Politics* 1280a8–25.

15 *Politics* 1317a40–1317b2.

16 *Politics* 1317b11–13.

17 *Politics* 1317b17–30.

18 *Politics* 1320b18–1321a5.

19 Cf. *Politics* 1321b5–7.

20 See *Politics* 1319b33–1320b16.

21 On the jurors' oath see Demosthenes 20.118; 23.96; 24. 149–51; 39.40; 57.63; cf. Harrison, *The Law of Athens*, 48, and MacDowell, *The Law in Classical*

Athens, 44. The jurors swore to vote according to the laws and decrees of the Athenian people and the *boulê*, and in a matter not covered by the law according to most just opinion, without favour or enmity, on the matter at hand after listening to both sides, and without being bribed.

22 On the *nomothesia* see note 8.

23 Lysias 14 *Against Alcibiades I*, 4.

24 Athenaeus, *Deipnosophistae* 695 ab, in Charles Burton Gulick, trans., *Athenaeus The Deipnosophists Books 14.653b-15* (Cambridge, MA: Harvard University Press, 1941).

25 Kurt Raaflaub, 'Equalitites and Inequalities in Athenian Democracy,' in *Demokratia: A Conversation on Democracies, Ancient and Modern*, ed. Josiah Ober and Charles Hedrick (Princeton: Princeton University Press, 1996), 144.

26 Herodotus, *Histories*, 5.66.2, speaks of Cleisthenes making the demos members of his *hetaireia* and (5.69.2), associating the demos, which had formerly been utterly despised, with his side. *AP* 20.1 similarly tells us that Cleisthenes, who was getting the worst of it in the *heteireiai*, enlisted the demos by handing the *politeia* over to the masses. See Josiah Ober, ' "I Besieged That Man": Democracy's Revolutionary Start,' in *Origins of Democracy in Ancient Greece*, ed. Kurt Raaflaub, Josiah Ober, and Robert Wallace (Berkeley, Los Angeles, and London: University of California Press, 2007), 83–104, for a discussion of these two passages and his arguments that democracy was the result of a spontaneous popular uprising. Ober believes that democracy was not discovered or invented but arose in response to an ideological shift.

27 Herodotus, *Histories*, 3.80.6: *isonomia*; 5.78: *isêgoria*. In the later passage Herodotus directly connects the term with the establishment of Athenian democracy.

28 *AP* 22.1. Herodotus (6.131) notes that Cleisthenes was the one who established Athens' tribes and democracy. Likewise, Aristotle (*Politics*, 1275 b36, 1319 b22) connects the creation of the tribes with increasing democratic power.

29 The council of 500 also had important administrative functions in that it ensured that all acts of the assembly were carried out and oversaw all boards of magistrates responsible for implementing decrees of the assembly.

30 Only those Athenian males enrolled in a deme at age eighteen, who had been democratically scrutinized by their fellow demesmen, were citizens and eligible to exercise citizen rights. For the process of enrolment see P. Brook Manville, *The Origins of Citizenship in Ancient Athens* (Princeton,

NJ: Princeton University Press, 1990), 7–9. Macdowell, *The Law in Classical Athens*, 69.

31 Robin Osborne, *Greece in the Making 1200–479 BC* (London and New York: Routledge, 1996), 296–9. For a detailed examination of the demes see Robin Osborne, *Demos: The Discovery of Classical Attica* (Cambridge: Cambridge University Press, 1985), and David Whitehead, *The Demes of Attica* (Princeton: Princeton University Press, 1986).

32 Ober, 'Revolutionary Start,' 98.

33 Osborne, *Greece in the Making*, 296.

34 I use the words dikasts and jurors interchangeably, though the Athenian dikast acted both as judge and juror.

35 Initially dikasts were assigned by lot to a particular court, such as the archon's court, in which they would serve for the entire year. In the early fourth century the system was reformed and the 6,000 dikasts were assigned by lot to particular jury panels for the year (perhaps of 600), and each day the courts sat jury panels were assigned randomly by lot to courts. In the 370s the system was refined even further and individual jurors, not whole jury panels, were assigned randomly by lot each day to a court, making it impossible to corrupt jurors, who would not know until they were assigned that day which court they served on or even whether they were selected to serve. See *AP* 63–6; cf. Macdowell, *The Law in Classical Athens*, 35–40.

36 Certain immoral behaviours, such as the mistreatment of parents, cowardice, or male prostitution, debarred a citizen from addressing the assembly. See Aeschines 1.26–7. Timarchus was accused of male prostitution.

37 As Aeschines implies, inherent in any democracy is an implicit respect for the law that issues from a sense of equality under the law. See for instance Pericles' funeral oration: Thucydides, *History of the Peloponnesian War*, 2.37.1. For translation see Rex Warner, *Thucydides: The History of the Peloponnesian War. Revised Edition* (Penguin Classics, 1972).

38 Aeschines 1.6.

39 In 336 BCE Ctesiphon had proposed a golden crown for Demosthenes for his war efforts after the battle of Chaeronea (338). In 337 Demosthenes had been chosen to serve on the board of wall builders to strengthen Athens' fortifications; he supplemented state funds with his own money. Aschines had charged Ctesiphon with making an illegal proposal on the technical grounds that the crown had been proposed for a magistrate (namely Demosthenes) who had not yet submitted his audit and the award was announced in the theatre. The case came to court in 330.

40 Aeschines 3.6.

41 Arlene W. Saxonhouse, *Free Speech and Democracy in Ancient Athens* (Cambridge: Cambridge University Press, 2006), 94.

42 Ibid., 87

43 See ibid., 89, who quotes Aeschylus's *Persians* 584–94: under Xerxes the tongue is bridled out of fear; his overthrow means that the common tongue is uncurbed and can prate of freedom.

44 Demosthenes 42, *Against Phaenippus*, 15: 'But, men of the jury, you should not grant more than what is just (*tou dikaiou*) to those who consider their own shamelessness stronger (*ischuroteran*) than the laws. If you do, you will cause many to laugh at the just provisions written in the laws. No; you should help those you regard the voice of the laws your voice, and that this day, appointed for coming into court, exists for those who have been wronged, not for those who have wronged.' For text see A.T. Murray, trans., *Demosthenes V* (Cambridge, MA: Harvard University Press, 1939).

45 Demosthenes 21, *Against Meidias*, 223: 'For in fact, if you should wish to consider and investigate by whatever means those who at any given time are jurors have power (*ischuroi*) and authority (*kurioi*) over all the affairs of the city, whether the city convenes two hundred or a thousand or any other number, you would find that it is not because you alone of all other citizens are drawn up under arms, or because you have the best bodies and the greatest strength (*malista ischuein*) or are the most youthful in age or any such thing, but because you have power in the laws (*tois nomois ischuein*). And what is the power of laws? Is it, if any of you are wronged and shout out, they will come running to your aid? No. They are written documents and they cannot do this. So what is their power? You, if you secure them and make them authoritative (*kyrious*) on each occasion for the one who asks. So the laws have power (*ischuroi*) through you and you through the laws. You must therefore aid them in the same way one would aid himself if he is wronged. And consider wrongs against the laws as common wrong, regardless who is caught, and neither liturgies, nor pity, nor any individual man, nor any skill (*technê*), nor any other thing has been discovered, through which means someone who has transgressed the laws will fail to be punished.' For text see J.H. Vince, trans., *Demosthenes III* (Cambridge, MA: Harvard University Press, 1935).

46 *AP* 29.2–4; see also Thucydides 8.67–8; on the oligarchic coup of 411 and the rule of the Four Hundred, see Donald Kagan, *The Fall of the Athenian Empire* (Ithaca, NY, and London: Cornell University Press, 1987), 131–86. On the discrepancies between *AP* and Thucydides see Peter Rhodes, A *Commentary on the Aristotelian* Athenaion Politeia (Oxford: Oxford University Press, 1981), 362–9.

47 Likely this was targeted at the *pyrtaneis*, the presidents of the council of 500 who presided over meetings of the assembly.

48 *AP* (29.4) refers to two summary procedures, *endeixis* and *apagôgê*, which were forms of citizen arrest used against common criminals like thieves. *Endeixis* involved pointing out the criminal to the magistrate, who would make the arrest, and *apagôgê* involved the citizen hauling the criminal off to the magistrate. The usual magistrates to receive such citizen arrest were the Eleven who oversaw the state prison.

49 Thucydides 8.67.2–3.

50 Thucydides 8.68.1–2.

51 For arguments in favour of a single Antiphon, see Michael Gagarin, *Antiphon the Athenian: Oratory, Law and Justice in the Age of the Sophists* (Austin: University of Texas Press, 2002), 37–62.

52 For a full text and translation see ibid., Appendix A, whose translation I follow; for a commentary see ibid., 61–80, and Carroll Moulton, 'Antiphon the Sophist, On Truth,' *American Philological Association* 103 (1972): 329–66.

53 Antiphon, *On Truth* B1–B2: 'Justice (*dikaiosynê*) is not violating the rules (*nomima*) of the city in which one is a citizen. Thus a person would best use justice to his own advantage if he considered laws (*nomoi*) important when witnesses are present but the requirements of nature (*phusis*) important in the absence of witnesses. For the requirements of the laws are supplemental, but the requirements of nature are necessary; and the requirements of the laws are by agreement and not natural, whereas the requirements of nature are natural and not by agreement. (B2) Thus someone who violates the laws avoids shame and punishment if those who have joined in agreement do not notice him, but not if they do. But if someone tries to violate one of the inherent requirements of nature, which is impossible, the harm he suffers is no less if he is seen by no one, and no greater if all see him; for he is harmed not in people's opinion (*doxa*) but in truth.'

54 Gagarin, *Antiphon*, 70, 73.

55 In 44C Antiphon continues his discussion of justice by arguing that testifying truthfully for another, though it is customarily considered just, in fact is not as it violates another principle, namely that it is just not to wrong another, if one is not wronged himself. It is possible that Antiphon went on to propose a system based on a larger idea of justice; cf. Gagarin, *Antiphon*, 78. In any case throughout his discussion there is the implication that the laws can be improved upon to be more advantageous.

56 For details of this and other trials see Uyghur Human Rights Project, http://www.uhrp.org/articles/3159/1/China-replaces-quotbiasedquot-Uyghur-judicial-personnel-according-to-report-/index.html; cf. CASCFEN

(Central Asian and Southern Caucasian Freedom of Expression Network), http://www.cascfen.net/?p=1051.

57 See the CBC and the *Globe and Mail* for some background details: http://www.cbc.ca/canada/story/2009/11/18/diplomat-afghan-detainees.html; http://www.cbc.ca/news/background/afghanistan/detainees.html; http://www.theglobeandmail.com/news/national/article743285.ece.

58 For sample articles on that issue see: http://www.cbc.ca/canada/story/2009/11/24/mulroney-colvin-detainee-committee.html; http://alethonews.wordpress.com/2009/12/02/canada-redactions-hamper-afghan-detainee-probe/http://www2.canada.com/topics/news/story.html?id=2295600 http://www.ottawacitizen.com/Business/Detainee+documents+heavily+censored/2296568/story.html

59 See http://www.canadaeast.com/news/article/886853; http://alethonews.blogspot.com/2009/12/canada-redactions-hamper-afghan.html.

60 For legal opinions see http://noprorogue.whyweprotest.net/showthread.php?t=112.

61 http://www.facebook.com/group.php?gid=260348091419; see the *Maclean's* article 'Will the Prorogation of Parliament Set Off a Populist Revolt?' for this political phenomenon: http://www2.macleans.ca/2010/01/25/the-people-speak/.

Contributors

Laurie M. Johnson Bagby is Professor of Political Science at Kansas State University. She received her PhD in political science from Northern Illinois University. Her specialty is political philosophy, with research emphases in Thucydides, Hobbes, and classical liberal political thought. She is author of *Thomas Hobbes: Turning Point for Honor* (Lexington Books, 2009), *Hobbes's Leviathan* (Continuum International Publishing, 2007), *Political Thought: A Guide to the Classics* (Wadsworth/International Thompson, 2002), and *Thucydides, Hobbes and the Interpretation of Realism* (Northern Illinois University Press, 1993). Her latest book is *Locke, Rousseau, and the Enlightenment's Answer to Honor* (forthcoming).

Leah Bradshaw teaches in the Political Science Department at Brock University. Much of her work has been preoccupied with the break between ancient and modern political thought and practice, building upon the concerns laid out by Hannah Arendt. She has written a book on Hannah Arendt as well as many articles and book chapters on interpreting the tradition of political thought. Recent research and teaching have been on the themes of cosmopolitanism and citizenship, as well as the origins of the understanding of the self in the eighteenth century. She has contributed essays to two previously published books by David Tabachnick and Toivo Koivukoski: *Confronting Tyranny* (Rowman Littlefield, 2005) and *Enduring Empire* (University of Toronto Press, 2009).

Craig Cooper is Professor of Classics and currently Dean of Arts and Science at Nipissing University. His research interests cover Athenian law, the Attic orators, ancient Greek rhetoric, and Greek historiography and biography. His most recent work, *Epigraphy and the Greek Historian*, was published by University of Toronto Press in 2008.

Geoffrey Kellow is Assistant Professor of Humanities in Carleton University's College of the Humanities, specializing in the history of ideas. In his current research, Kellow is particularly interested in the philosophical and intellectual origins of liberal capitalism and most especially the philosophy of Adam Smith. He has also conducted related research on liberalism, liberal education, and the role of the philosophy of Cicero in Smith's *The Wealth of Nations*.

Toivo Koivukoski is Associate Professor of Political Science at Nipissing University. His first monograph, *After the Last Man: Excurses to the Limits of the Technological System* (Lexington Books, 2008) explores Hegel's 'end of history' thesis and the available, alternative ways of conceiving progress in an integrated environment characterized more by iterative feedback loops than linear developments. He is presently working on a book project on the so-called 'wise barbarian,' Anacharsis, towards understanding the cultural specificity of notions of barbarism and the possibility of seeing the other in the self.

Jeremy S. Neill is an ethicist, political philosopher, and philosophical historian. He completed his PhD in philosophy in 2009 and has taught at Saint Louis University and the University of Notre Dame. Currently he is an Assistant Professor in the Philosophy Department at Houston Baptist University. Among the journals in which his work has appeared are the *Review of Metaphysics*, *Faith and Philosophy*, *Political Theology*, and *Philosophy and Social Criticism*. He is currently working on several issues at the interface of ethics and political philosophy: ideal theory, morals legislation, and the various definitions of democracy.

Waller R. Newell is Professor of Political Science and Philosophy at Carleton University. His books include *Ruling Passion: The Erotics of Statecraft in Platonic Political Philosophy; What Is a Man? 3000 Years of Wisdom on the Art of Manly Virtue; The Code of Man: Love, Courage, Pride, Family, Country;* and *The Soul of a Leader: Character, Conviction and Ten Lessons in Political Greatness.* He has been a Fellow of the Woodrow Wilson International Center for Scholars, the National Humanities Center, and the Institute for United States Studies at the University of

London, and has held fellowships from the National Endowment for the Humanities and the Social Sciences and Humanities Research Council of Canada. He is currently writing a book on the differences between ancient and modern tyranny.

Jeffrey Sikkenga is Associate Professor of political science at Ashland University in Ashland, Ohio, and an adjunct fellow of the John M. Ashbrook Center for Public Affairs. He also has been a senior fellow in the Program on Constitutionalism and Democracy at the University of Virginia. He has published in journals such as *Political Theory, History of Political Thought, Journal of Politics, Journal of Markets and Morality,* and *Religion and Liberty.* He co-edited *History of American Political Thought,* edited *Transforming American Welfare,* and co-wrote *The Free Person and the Free Economy.*

Peter Simpson is Professor of Philosophy and Classics at the City University of New York. He was born and educated in the UK but has lived in the United States for over twenty years and is a naturalized US citizen. His main interests are ancient philosophy (especially Aristotle) and moral and political philosophy. He has written books on Aristotle's *Politics,* on moral philosophy, and on Karol Wojtyła, in addition to numerous articles on philosophical topics more generally (for details, see www.aristotelophile.com). He is currently working on translations and explanations of Aristotle's *Magna Moralia* and *Eudemian Ethics.*

Steven C. Skultety received his PhD in philosophy from Northwestern University and is an Assistant Professor of Philosophy at the University of Mississippi. He is co-editor of *Aristotle's Politics: Critical Essays* (2005) and is currently working on a book about the role of conflict in Aristotle's political thought.

David Edward Tabachnick is Associate Professor of Political Science at Nipissing University and a former Fulbright University Research Chair. He has published articles on Heidegger, technology, and Aristotle. He has co-edited three books (with Toivo Koivukoski), including *Confronting Tyranny: Ancient Lessons for Global Politics* (Rowman and Littlefield, 2006) and *Globalization, Technology and Philosophy* (SUNY, 2004). His monograph *The Great Reversal: How We Let Technology Take Control of the Planet* is forthcoming from University of Toronto Press.

Index